# Right Here, Right Now: The BUFFALO Anthology

Edited by Jody K. Biehl

Photograph by Nancy J. Parisi

First edition 2016

ISBN: 978-0-9977742-6-9

Belt Publishing
1667 E. 40th Street #1G1
Cleveland, Ohio 44120
www.beltmag.com

Book design and cover illustration by Julian Montague

# Table of Contents

## Neighborhood Stories

# Neighborhood Stories (continued)

# Food, Art, Books & Music

# Home & Belonging

# Art & Photography

Additional images are credited where they appear.

# Introduction

## Jody K. Biehl

This is the book I wish existed when I moved to Buffalo.

It's a book for long-time residents who want to spend a few minutes or an afternoon thinking about their city. It's for those who've moved away but still feel nostalgic when they get a whiff of Cheerios or see a towering elm or watch the Bills fumble in the end zone.

Buffalo, for all its messiness, is magnetic.

This book doesn't list the coolest places to stay, where to get the best Thai food, or which restaurants serve breakfast at 2:00 a.m.

It's more personal than that.

It's an inside-out portrait of the city told by those of us who call or once called this beloved, abused patch of earth by the lake home. Our youngest author is fifteen; our oldest is ninety-one. Some of us have just arrived. Several have never left.

This book touches on the meaning of home, how to find it, and how tightly roots can hold. It's about snowstorms and dogs, big trees, mean nuns, kind neighbors, and ones who deflate children's basketballs. It's about old houses and older hatreds. The wicked creativity of our art, food, and music burns in these pages, but so does the racism that singes our dreams.

This book will help us think about where Buffalo is today, where it's been, and where it's going next. It's packed with love for Buffalo—and with worries. We love Buffalo's new energy, but we worry about gentrification and inequality, about bad water, bad sports teams, and bad planning. We laugh with comedian Mark Russell as he recalls beer deliveries to Jesuit priests in the 1940s and with David J. Hill as he goes to his first meat raffle in 2013. Jeff Miers takes us on a raucous romp through Buffalo music's boozy underbelly and leaves us hoping Buffalo's scrappy weirdness endures. The book doesn't offer answers or recipes for Buffalo's future. It tells stories. Through vignettes, it scrapes at our frozen surface and offers glimpses of the warm interiors we too rarely share.

We've put together an original, kaleidoscopic view of the city, which includes reflections and images by more than sixty writers and artists. Some —like CNN anchor Wolf Blitzer, Goo Goo Dolls bass player Robby Takac, Buffalo Philharmonic Orchestra conductor JoAnn Falletta, and legendary Bills coach Marv Levy, are well-known, but few of us, I think, know how Falletta, who shares a poem for this anthology, feels when she's alone at

Kleinhans Music Hall, or what Levy was thinking as that fateful kick drifted right and the Bills lost their first Super Bowl.

Some of the authors take us into uncomfortable places we often don't acknowledge in ourselves or in our community. Sara Ali, whose family is Muslim, writes about the torment she faced in her predominantly white elementary school after the 9/11 attacks. Jeff Klein flips back the decades to Hertel Avenue of the 1960s and the bullying he endured as the only Jewish boy on his block. Henry Louis Taylor, Jr. laments the racism he believes has laced city planning for decades and insists that the renaissance sweeping Buffalo is leaving out African Americans and other minorities. He wants a better way.

We've given the book the title "Right Here, Right Now," which, as Bills fans of a certain era remember, was part of the rallying cry Coach Levy used to motivate his players. "Where else would you rather be than right here, right now?" he asked them, emphasizing the magnitude of the moment.

So, too, we ask you, our readers, to appreciate this moment in Buffalo. The city buzzes with newness. Yet, the shiny promise sits atop layers of history, good and bad, some of which our authors bring alive in these pages.

I wish I could have had this anthology when I was considering moving to Buffalo in 2007. I scoured the internet and found guidebooks and history books and cookbooks and plenty about architecture, grain elevators, and snowstorms. But none of it helped me get a sense of what living here was like or how longtime residents viewed their hometown. It didn't explain that everyone in Buffalo is connected by no more than four degrees of separation.

I remember my awe the first time I drove through the Parkside neighborhood and saw the magnificent homes, the towering trees—and then two giraffes poking their heads from behind a leafy wall. Giraffes?

I lived here five years before I understood how arduously Buffalonians love this city, and that the real "lake effect" has only a little to do with the snow that piles up every winter. The real lake effect is what happens inside heated homes and around fireplaces. It's when your neighbor tromps through the snow to bring you soup or cupcakes or to shovel out your front door. It's your kids popping out of bed at 5:00 a.m. to check the snow-day-predictor apps they've installed on your phone and then sledding to each others' houses to build igloos. It's the beers and steaming mugs shared with neighbors when you can't see past your front porch. The lake effect starts when there is just enough fear to make us open up and nothing left to do but talk. It's humorously and subtly portrayed in Jon Penfold's "Surprise."

Over generations, the lake effect has helped establish an invisible bond among Buffalonians, a can-do sense of neighborliness that, I think, both draws people in and hauls deserters back—even if it's only via memories. This anthology is packed with those—Ronald Wendling's recollections of Mrs. G's pies and how his North Park neighbors filled in for his drunken father, Lynette D'Amico's grappling to understand her Italian immigrant mother's connection to a home D'Amico never knew. TV writer and producer Pat Obermeier just returned to Buffalo and hopes she'll find the wildness she remembers, while *Washington Post* media columnist and longtime *Buffalo News* editor Margaret Sullivan grapples with her new standing as a Buffalo ex-pat.

History books gush about Frederick Law Olmsted's magnificent plans for Buffalo and the stupidity that destroyed pieces of that vision. In the pages of this anthology, those choices come alive, not as academic lessons but as memories of lives lived. In her essay—the opening piece of the anthology— the novelist Lauren Belfer reminds us of the power of Buffalo's enchanted trees to ignite the imagination and hints at the physical and psychological destruction that followed the loss of the Humboldt Parkway.

Great cities have secrets. Paris, Rome, Istanbul, Berlin, New York, Washington, D.C., San Francisco, Los Angeles. They evoke mystery, a sense that they are hiding something or that wonderful things are happening around the corner or happened last week or a century ago right where you are standing. I've lived in and reported from these places, and people often seem surprised to learn that I'm now happy living in Buffalo. Some people express pity or assume there must be a family connection—which there isn't—or some crisis that forces me to stay.

I just smile.

They don't know Buffalo's secret.

Buffalo's secret is that it's secretly great. Not for everyone, of course, and not across racial divides, and sometimes, literally, as many authors point out, not east of Main Street. But it has those beautiful old Olmsted bones. Now, our trees are returning, as is our waterfront, and many of our historic homes and institutions are intact or being refurbished. Filmmakers are starting to notice the uniqueness of our architecture and our landscape and are increasingly using Buffalo as a backdrop. Eighty-five percent of us live within a ten minute walk of a park. Our food and music scenes are electric, and we're still a nurturing and affordable home for artists.

It's a fine place to be, right here, right now.

Open up the book. Stay a while.

# Our City, Then & Now

# Finding Inspiration in Frederick Law Olmsted's City

## Lauren Belfer

This is my first memory of Buffalo:

I'm sitting in the backseat of my parents' car, and we're driving home from a Sunday afternoon visit with my grandparents. It's summer, and the car windows are open. We turn onto Humboldt Parkway. . . 200 feet wide, six rows of trees across, almost two miles long. The trees meet in an arch high above me, and sunlight flickers through the dense canopy of leaves. The breeze touches my bare arms. The aroma of fresh cut grass fills the air, along with a sudden silence, except for children's laughter. For those two miles, I inhabit a place of enchantment. Humboldt Parkway sparks my imagination and becomes a realm of fairy tales.

Years later, I reflected upon that childhood moment of enchantment. I was researching and writing *City of Light*, my novel about Buffalo in its glory days in 1901, when it was one of the most prosperous cities in America, its port among the most bustling in the world. I began to think about the spiritual, emotional, and inventive power of Buffalo's landscape. "If Frederick Law Olmsted had been a painter," school head Louisa Barrett muses at the beginning of Chapter III in the novel, "Buffalo would have been his canvas. Beginning in 1868, he created in the city a vast system of parks linked by forested roadways wider than the boulevards of Paris. ... Each time I stepped out of the school, I entered Olmsted's vision as if I were walking into his mind, surrendering to the eloquent unity of every avenue."

Olmsted's plan for Buffalo encompassed the entire city. He and his firm designed not simply Delaware Park but also South Park, Cazenovia Park, Days Park, and what is now called Martin Luther King, Jr. Park, to list only several; Lincoln Parkway and McKinley Parkway are among many others. I name them, just briefly, because much of this history is now forgotten.

Almost every day of my childhood, I traversed the city's residential boulevards, lined with their rows of mature elm trees, some branches meeting in a sun-dappled roof above me while others swept down to touch the grass. In the summer, I rode my bike along the shaded paths of Delaware Park. Pausing to catch my breath, I gazed across the park lake at the Albright-Knox Art Gallery rising in the distance. For my piano lessons, I went to Olmsted's Parkside neighborhood, with its idyllic, curving streets. I babysat for a family that lived on Olmsted's Richmond Avenue, near his Symphony Circle. During my high school years at the Buffalo Seminary, I felt comforted by the sylvan retreat that was Bidwell Parkway. I watched the shifting of the light through the day. I imagined the possibilities of my future. I made up stories about people far different from me, stories set within this landscape where nature and city intermingled.

The trees of my youth were cut down, of course. Dutch elm disease destroyed most of them. Misguided city planning (I could use other words for this civic crime, but I'll leave it at that) killed the rest, in the form of the Kensington Expressway, which took the place of Humboldt Parkway. Paradoxically, and adding to the tragedy, Humboldt Parkway was planted with tulip and linden trees, which would have survived the scourge of Dutch elm disease. I remember years when the Delaware Park lake, originally called Mirror Lake, but now known as Hoyt Lake, was filled with rotting garbage and even a half-sunken car.

Then the citizens of Buffalo organized to rescue their legacy of history and natural beauty. Olmsted's parkways were replanted where they could be. Hoyt Lake became crystalline in the sunlight, although it remains polluted. In 1995, Buffalo's Garden Walk began to transform block after block across the city.

Today, on a visit to Buffalo, I decide to walk from my family's home to Delaware Park. When I turn onto Chapin Parkway, its half-dozen rows of trees beckon. The raking sunlight of late afternoon is yellow and brilliant, the shadows precise. Although these relatively young trees don't yet meet in an arch above my head, light shimmers within them. The breeze tosses their luxurious canopy of leaves and creates a roar that blocks out the sounds of traffic. I walk, as Louisa Barrett says in *City of Light*, along "a radiant, ceremonial path into a forest," and so into Frederick Law Olmsted's still-living vision of Buffalo. My imagination takes flight.

This, to me, is *home*.

Lauren Belfer is the bestselling author of three critically acclaimed novels, *City of Light*, *A Fierce Radiance*, and *And After the Fire*, which came out in 2016. She grew up in Buffalo, diagonally across the street from Delaware Park. She graduated from Public School #64 and the Buffalo Seminary. After college, she moved to New York City, where she lives today.

# A City Spoke

## Greg Shemkovitz

It's been nearly two decades since I left Western New York, and all I ever hear from friends back home is how it has changed. Dilapidated buildings have been renovated into condos and hubs of entrepreneurial innovation. Folks are moving back into the city proper. People are drawn to the region now, after years of seeing the population dwindle. There's culture and art and—well, the Bills and Sabres still struggle, but that's part of the city's charm. It's getting better, they tell me. And I believe it—not because I never thought it would happen, but because when I wanted nothing more than to get out, I learned just how much potential the city was hiding beneath its rough exterior.

I grew up in West Seneca, just another white kid, barely aware of his heritage—Polish, Italian, Irish, whatever. Didn't matter. Everybody I knew was born somewhere nearby in the Southtowns and was just as Polish or Italian or Irish, which is to say not really at all, considering how many generations removed we were from our ancestral motherlands, our last names the only trace of heritage—O'-this, *Mc*-that, something-*elli* or whatever-*ski*.

In 2001, on summer break from college, I took a job carrying the mail. A *casual carrier*, they called me. I delivered the mail around suburban West Seneca, cutting across lawns to the dull murmur of distant mowers, swatting the noses of yappy little dogs, and going about my day without seeing another soul, save for the occasional dog walker or retiree camped on a front porch and waiting for a Publishers Clearing House envelope.

Then one day I was transferred to the West Side, the Grant-Ferry neighborhood, north of downtown. *The city*. I had been up that way enough times, but not so far west of Elmwood, where all the artsy kids and college students hung out. What I knew of the city was simple: nobody lived there. Not permanently, anyway. White flight, they called it back in the 1950s, when those with the luxury to leave ran like hell. And the term made sense when you looked at Williamsville or Orchard Park, the well-off towns farther out. Buffalo was a place that folks left behind.

I'd felt that way since I was a kid. Somebody, maybe a neighbor or a teacher in middle school, said it to me once, and maybe it was the truth, a fact as cold and hard as the winter. They said the population of Buffalo had been nearly sliced in half since the turn of the century. The city was dying. They probably even told me to run while I could. Maybe it was my father who said it, and who showed me a map, pointing out how the city was planned like a wheel, its streets stretched like spokes away from the axle of the city center. They may not have all been evacuation routes, but as a child, I got the sense that the wheel of Buffalo was not unlike a carnival ride that spins and spins, its force hurling you outward and away. And so I grew up with the idea that Buffalo, by design, pushed people out.

But there I was, plunged deeper into the city than I had ever been. Before dawn, on my way to the post office on Grant Street for my first shift, I drove along Niagara Street, with its rundown buildings and its storefronts with the cages rolled down. I kept thinking about how I would be out there in a few hours, walking those streets, and I wondered what sort of world it would become when the sun came up. After all, nobody could possibly live down here, I thought. To a kid like me, this was the backdrop to crime and who knows what.

In the sorting case, the route is nothing but a series of numbers, short sequences that take you down one side of the block and back up the other. I would be running relay boxes now, a job unique to city carriers. No hiding in a truck. I might have to go a few blocks on one side of the street, hit a relay box, and start down another street, only to work my way back to the other side of that original street where I began. *Who knew what I would run into along the way?* That's the thought my brain kept taunting me with while I tossed mail that morning, shoving envelopes into slots marked by colors and numbers, no different from the sorting cases back in West Seneca.

Then I hit the street with my satchel, and right away I felt just how unfamiliar a territory this was. No more clearly numbered cookie-cutter homes. No manicured lawns. No predictable, familiar neighbors.

Just follow the mail, I thought. Pay attention to the numbers.

I started down a sun-bleached block of single-family homes along West Ferry, working my way over to the smaller mill homes along Boyd Street. The closer I was to Grant Street, the denser the blocks became, until I reached an apartment building with cluster boxes, then two blocks of small businesses, a dollar store, a bodega, and finally a school. It was like every delivery was new. A box here, a door slot there, a cluster box, a business that took its mail at the counter, another door slot. By the time the sun was out, the streets were alive. Not like the desolate suburbs, where the only sign of life might be a dog barking. This was something different altogether.

People were out and about, and not just to set the sprinkler in place. Folks were walking around and interacting. Take it from a white kid from the suburbs who once wanted nothing more than to get a driver's license so he could get to what he thought to be the epicenter of culture—the mall. Watching a man in slippers walk from his apartment building with a laundry basket to a Laundromat down the block, all the while greeting people he knew along the way, was about as foreign as baklava.

And so, on that first day, I kept my suburban head down, followed the letters in my hand and the flats against my forearm, and got through the route without incident, thank goodness.

Over the next few weeks, I did the route in this fashion, head down with a casual nod or a "mornin'" when necessary. Much to my chagrin, people kept greeting me as I passed by. And a funny thing happens when humanity keeps extending kindness: you begin to actually notice that humanity.

Soon, I found myself paying attention to the names on the mail. Different names. And not just different from the ones I knew on the other side of the city. These were names I never would have associated with the Buffalo I had grown up around. These names were Eastern European and Middle Eastern and Asian and Latin American. And as the days went by, I began to pay attention to the people who would wave to me, who would nod in a welcoming way, like the Burmese family who owned a small market that smelled like lemons, or the Lebanese lady who served me my first taste of shawarma.

At the end of each shift, I returned to my home in West Seneca, and each evening I began to notice something new—or new to me, at least—about my hometown.

There was a Russian family who ran an ice cream place in a strip mall near my house and a Vietnamese couple who took over the corner store near my elementary school, a school now closed and abandoned. The Vietnamese family lived above the store. They'd been there for years. I just never noticed or thought about them. I had kept my head down for so much of my life to that point. I had my friends and my family. I had paid so little attention to life outside of my immediate circle that I didn't even notice the foundation there. The city was waiting to be reborn. Maybe it had already begun, albeit slowly.

One Sunday evening, later that summer, I stood along my tree-lined suburban street, a leaf blower whirring somewhere in the distance, an ice cream truck's jingle delightfully chiming not far away. There was a young girl riding a bicycle along the sidewalk across from me, looking down in frustration at her wobbly rear wheel. The girl stopped and knelt beside her bike. I crossed the street to help her. I lifted the bike by its seat and gave the wheel a spin until it stopped against the brake pad where the rim had bent. When I looked at her again, she seemed curious but overwhelmed. I glanced past her at the row of homes along our quiet street. I knew her family well. Her mother used to babysit me when I was younger. She had moved away for a while, gone to school, gotten married, and bought a house on our street to be near her family again.

The girl asked if the wheel was ruined. I laughed and said that it would be fine, that all she had to do was tighten the spokes, that each spoke pulled the wheel into alignment by drawing the rim closer to the axle. I waited for the girl's face to soften with relief, the way I imagine my face had each day on my route. Because her wheel was just like the city—far from ruined.

**Greg Shemkovitz** grew up in West Seneca, where he attended West Seneca Senior High School and later worked for a South Buffalo car dealership that became the backdrop for his debut novel, *Lot Boy*, published through Sunnyoutside Press, a small publisher also in Buffalo. He now lives in North Carolina, but his writing lingers in the Rust Belt. His work has appeared in the *Journal of Compressed Creative Arts*, *Prick of the Spindle*, *Foundling Review*, *Ghost City Review*, and elsewhere.

# Where is Buffalo?

## Luke Hammill

Philadelphia is on the East Coast. Seattle is on the West Coast. Atlanta is in the South.

Where is Buffalo?

It's in New York. But it's on Lake Erie. It's in the Rust Belt. But the closest major city is a cosmopolitan, international center of commerce—and it's in Canada.

Is Buffalo in the Northeast? The Midwest?

It belongs to New York State, but it's definitely not East Coast, as many people assume. (Most people I've met while living in Portland, Oregon, are surprised to learn Buffalo isn't the sixth borough of New York City.)

Buffalonians call sugary, carbonated drinks "pop," as they do in Minnesota. But Buffalo's music scene is highly influenced by Phish-inspired jam bands, akin to Vermont. Buffalonians lack the accent and swagger of East Coasters, but they retain the underlying grit and street knowledge.

This question, about where Buffalo is, has always obsessed me. It shouldn't matter. But it does—there is value in identity, and we Buffalonians have always projected one: friendly and earnest like Midwesterners, but tough and smart like East Coasters. Lovable losers like Chicago Cubs fans. The scrappy, underdogish stepsister to New York City and Boston.

So what are we?

The Erie Canal may be obsolete, but its legacy is not. Buffalo made its name as the great gateway between the Northeast and the Midwest. Sailors ate and drank at the Swannie House on their passage between two distinct regions of America.

Labels matter. The geography nerd in me has always been fascinated by Istanbul, because it is both a European and an Asian city. I only recently realized Buffalo is similar. Our iconic 1925 Liberty Building has two statues at the top. One looks east. One looks west.

New York State is reliably Democratic. Western New York—a more accurate term, I explain to outsiders, than the meaningless "upstate"—isn't. Like Ohio, Western New York likes to change its mind. We're up for grabs. Six years before Donald Trump hijacked the national Republican party, Buffalo's own Carl Paladino did the same at the state level by running for governor against Andrew Cuomo. (He was crushed like the Bills in Super Bowl XXVII.)

If he lived today, Buffalo's most famous mayor, Democrat Jimmy Griffin, might well be one of Trump's voters.

Western New York is far enough inland to resist the groupthink of coastal, liberal elites. But it is also largely composed of Catholics and immigrants, and it's relatively short on wealth and so-called White Anglo-Saxon Protestants. The result is a political patchwork. And that's interesting.

Buffalo is relatively populist, but not aggressively so. Bernie Sanders resonated in post-industrial Western New York, fueled by laid-off white steelworkers who understood his message. But the region voted according to the coastal, prevailing wisdom, for Hillary Clinton—barely.

When I moved to New York City in 2012, and then Portland a year later, it was like watching someone's head explode in real time when I explained that Buffalo is three hours from Cleveland and Pittsburgh, two from Toronto, four from Detroit, and nearly seven from New York City. You could see them trying to envision the impossible map in their minds.

It always gives me a sort of buzz.

So where is Buffalo? The Rust Belt? The Great Lakes? The Northeast? The Midwest?

It's all of the above, and more, too.

**Luke Hammill** grew up in West Seneca and attended Orchard Park High School, where he was sports editor at the *Voice*. He graduated from the University at Buffalo and served as managing editor for the school's independent student newspaper, the *Spectrum*. He then moved on to the Columbia University Graduate School of Journalism. He completed reporting internships at the *New York Times* and the *Buffalo News* before taking a job at the *Oregonian* in Portland in 2013.

# Keeping It Real: Slices of a New Buffalo

## Elizabeth Licata

There is talk of renaissance across America's urban landscape. Young people want to live in cities, and older people want to move back. Dense urban streetscapes are in; suburban cul-de-sacs are out. It's a good time to be editing a city/regional magazine, as I do. But journalists can't be just boosters. They have to ask themselves: how much of this is reality and how much hype?

Buffalo's reality may not rise to the level of a renaissance. It's something else—a reinvention. As a smallish city of around 300,000, Buffalo is growing down into its new identity, learning to accept itself and improve what it has. Here are three of the clearest examples, with the perspective of a quarter-century.

## I.

### 1991: Dignified Obscurity

In a reuse of former classroom space, the galleries of the Burchfield Penney Art Center are still where they were when the museum was founded in 1966: the second floor of Rockwell Hall, on the Buffalo State College campus. The floors are politely carpeted; the windows are covered by temporary walls. There is little indication from outside that the museum exists. It's fine. It's the way it is. Across Elmwood Avenue, the Albright-Knox Art Gallery has been exhibiting the same limited selection from its astonishing modern and contemporary collection for decades. It's fine. It's the way it is.

### 2016: Art as Destination

Now Buffalo has the beginnings of a museum row, with the 2008 addition of the new Burchfield Penney, an 84,000-square-foot contemporary structure by the architects Gwathmey Siegel. The silvery-gray façade is striking, but, more important, its existence indicates that Buffalo is finally taking seriously not only the legacy of Charles Burchfield, but also the presence of a vibrant local art scene. Other art organizations are raising their profiles in similar ways, including Hallwalls Contemporary Arts Center. It's now ensconced at Babeville, a historic restoration of a church by Ani DiFranco's

Righteous Babe Records. Meanwhile, the 154-year-old Albright-Knox has been rejuvenating itself through a series of mixups and mashups of the collection and borrowed works. And an expansion is in the works.

## II.

### 1991: Rubble and Parking Lots

Though many plans have arisen and gently subsided, Buffalo appears to have given up on its waterfront. The Buffalo River is polluted seemingly beyond hope, and access to what was once the terminus of the Erie Canal, once the bustling nexus of Buffalo's nineteenth-century economy, is long gone. Virtually no recreation or commerce can be found on the inner or the outer harbors.

### 2016: Canalside!

Where once was wasteland, now ice rinks in winter and boardwalks in summer attract kayakers, paddle-boarders, ice bikers, skaters, and strollers enjoying local brews, artisanal coffee, music, and craft markets. A children's museum is under construction. Waterway remediation continues. *Travel & Leisure* magazine ranks Buffalo atop its "favorite cities," with Canalside as one of the reasons.

## III.

### 1991: Poster Child for Urban Blight

Walking Buffalo's downtown means passing block after block dominated by empty buildings, many of them built by distinguished architects, but empty all the same. Some, like Louise Blanchard Bethune's Lafayette Hotel, are barely surviving as single room occupancy housing and taverns while their roofs and plaster crumble. The 100 block of Genesee Street and the 800 block of Main Street are among the worst examples of once-thriving commercial streetscapes now with just two or three occupied storefronts at best.

### 2016: Restored, Renovated, Revived

From the Webb, on Pearl Street, to the Granite Works, at Main and Virginia, buildings that were once discussed only in Housing Court, if at all, have been purchased by developers and transformed into loft apartments, wine bars, flower shops, boutique hotels, and restaurants. Empty-nesters and young professionals have decided to move downtown. Historic tax credits have helped create their new living spaces.

There are new ways to live, play, and enjoy art in Western New York—and the old ways are still available, maybe even improved. That doesn't mean Buffalo's longtime burdens of poverty, crime, and economic stagnation have been mitigated to any significant degree. It's still a typical postindustrial city that has lost much of its economic excitement.

The difference now is that many people who have always lived here, who have just moved here, or who are planning to relocate here feel that Buffalo's positives outweigh the negatives. There is finally a critical mass of what makes living in a city desirable, and it's enough to create a higher percentage of millennial population growth in Buffalo than in Los Angeles or New York (according to 2000–2012 census data).

As a city/regional publication, *Buffalo Spree* documents these incremental steps. It doesn't focus on the drugs, the gangs, the blocks of empty houses. Every city has those. Not every city has a waterfront district whose original stone paving has been uncovered, a spectacular train station that might finally be redeveloped, or a grain-elevator complex that hosts movies and concerts. These are the stories that help Buffalonians make decisions about how they want to live and what they want to do. These are the stories that help them create their own realities in Buffalo.

**Elizabeth Licata** is editor-in-chief of *Buffalo Spree* (buffalospree.com), an art writer and curator, and a garden writer who blogs at gardenrant.com. A graduate of DeSales High School and the University at Buffalo, Licata lives and gardens in Buffalo's historic Allentown neighborhood.

# Latte City or Just City: Will Blacks Rise or Be Forgotten in the New Buffalo?

## Henry Louis Taylor, Jr.

In black neighborhoods scattered across Buffalo's East Side, residents must be wondering what all this *Buffalo Happy Talk* is about. Buffalo is not a happy city for most of them. It never has been. When black folks look around Buffalo, they see the city being recreated for whites: college-educated millennials, the creative classes, refined, middle-aged urbanites, and retired suburbanites.

As a black historian and urban planner, looking through a glass darkly, I can see Buffalo rising. Yet, I can't help but wonder, for whom the city ascends? If you visit Buffalo's so-called hot spots, Harbor Center, the waterfront, Allentown, the Elmwood Strip, Chippewa Street, and the Theatre District, you will see mostly hipster, latte-drinking whites. When you visit those neighborhoods where housing prices are rising and where swank rental apartments are found, you will find the same, hipster, latte drinking whites living there. Even in upscale apartments, like the Bethune and Elk Terminal lofts, which are located in the black community, you will find latte drinkers.

Yeah. I hear the rhetoric. The new buzzwords are equity, inclusiveness, and diversity. For example, the Greater Buffalo's regional plan, "One Region Forward," says "Woven throughout the planning framework are two critical issues that define where we've been and where we want to go—our relationship to our fresh water resources and our desire to grow our economy in a way that is *more equitable* [emphasis added] and locally rooted."

*Yet, I am troubled.*

I can't stop thinking about that old African proverb, "What a person does speaks so loudly that I cannot hear what they say."

I believe that Black Buffalo will be marginalized in the rising city, just as it was in the shrinking city and in the prosperous industrial city. The plight of Black Buffalo has never been important to Buffalo's leaders. At every stage in the city's history, black neighborhood development has been an afterthought in city building. Buffalo and its Erie County suburbs were never meant to nurture and provide a healthy place for blacks or Latinos to live.

In the 1930s, when Buffalo leaders imagined a new metropolis—a combined city and suburbs—it was designed as a place for white, higher-paid workers and the professional classes. The most desirable housing and neighborhoods in the city and suburbs were reserved for them. These places enabled whites to obtain the highest paying jobs, the most desirable recreational areas, and the best education, health care, and police services. In their fancy, segregated neighborhoods, whites lived longer, healthier, and happier lives than their black, Latino, and immigrant cohorts. My friend Carl Nightingale, the University at Buffalo historian, says this segregated world was the consequence of political action, not economic realities or simple racial hatred.

*Don't get caught up in this race hatred thing.*

This was mostly about white privilege; it was about whites using the neighborhood edge to get the economic and higher standard of living edge. This was about whites being given an advantage over blacks, which was rooted in the economic organization of the city. Whites did not get this socioeconomic edge by accident or simple merit. They had help. City leaders consciously and deliberately designed an urban metropolis anchored by mass homeownership, race-based suburbanization, and neighborhoods stratified by housing cost and type. Whites were empowered to use guaranteed Federal Housing Administration (FHA) loans to purchase homes in the suburbs or along the city's leafy West Side parkways and avenues.

Blacks, meanwhile, rented in the grimy East Side. To keep them there, Buffalo's leaders used urban planning, zoning laws, building codes, subdivision regulations, and eminent domain. They forced blacks to live in houses situated in the shadows of factories, railroads, and commercial establishments. These were the worst places to live in Buffalo and Erie County. The racist FHA gave money to whites, but denied blacks access to home-buying dollars. And when blacks did manage to get mortgages, the location of their neighborhoods caused housing values to fall rather than to rise. For them, homeownership produced debt, not wealth. African Americans were stuck in place.

*Whites and blacks experienced the metropolitan city differently.*

The 1950s and 1960s were the most dynamic period in metro Buffalo's history. Whites and blacks experienced it differently. Thousands of whites moved to the suburbs, where they found the *American Dream*. Blacks, on the other hand, found the *American Nightmare*. As thousands of black newcomers poured into Buffalo City, the urban bulldozer roared through their neighborhoods, destroying homes, playgrounds, churches, shops, stores, and fraternal organizations in its wake.

Black neighborhoods were collateral damage in the remaking of Buffalo and Erie County. Remaking the city and suburbs meant that black neighborhoods had to be knocked down to make way for downtown expansion, institutional development, interstate highway connectors, and wider roads. These "unbuilding" activities merged with plant closings and outmigration to hit the East Side with sledgehammer force. This urban disfiguring process left the East Side with miles of vacant lots and empty structures; it's a physical setting, so scarred and foreboding that Robert M. Silverman, University at Buffalo urban planner, called it *Zombieland*. Today, the most distressed and blighted properties in Erie County are found in this part of Buffalo.

*The mutilation of the East Side is not benign.*

It robs people of the value of their homes. An East Side homeowner said to me, "Dr. Taylor, the house next door to me is empty, with a tree growing through the roof. It is worth $16,000. My house is in good condition, and I have big investments in it; and it is only worth $18,000. I don't get it. I'm still going to put in another $20,000 in my house, even though I know I will never recoup it. So, I am making this investment in my family and my children." This is how housing market dynamics operate on the mutilated East Side.

*Cities don't grow like weeds.*

The city's shape and form are the result of political decisions, not the invisible hand of economic determinism. Yesterday, Buffalo was built for white higher-paid workers, professionals, and business elites. Today, the city is being built for the white *creative classes*, or the *latte group*, as I call them. This is a broad group of whites, including folks in the arts, educators, researchers, doctors, and other professionals. To make them happy, urban leaders are refashioning the city with hipster neighborhoods, recreational areas, and public spaces where the latte group can conversate, bike, jog, workout, attend outdoor concerts, and congregate in restaurants, bars, and coffee shops. The *latte group* bathes itself in liberalism and issues a clarion call for diversity and social justice, while simultaneously condemning the black and Latino masses to a blighted and disfigured *urban dystopia*.

The hardcore reality is that Buffalo's *latte city*, when stripped of its fanciful colorblind mask, is nothing more than a *neo-liberal white city*—a place where millennials and the creative class claim the most hedonic houses and neighborhoods for themselves, where they live longer, healthier, happier, and more prosperous lives than Buffalonians of color, who are forced to live in the most undesirable and unhealthiest neighborhoods in the metropolis.

*Black Buffalo is invisible.*

Black Buffalo is Ralph Ellison's *Invisible Man*. Whites see blacks, but not really. Whites hear blacks, but not really. In preparation for a presentation at a recent forum on blight in New York State, I read numerous reports and newspaper articles on blight in metropolitan Buffalo, and the terms black and African American were rarely, if ever, mentioned. For example, even though blight concentration is synonymous with the East Side black community, *Blueprint Buffalo*, an action plan for reclaiming vacant land said, "At the beginning of the 21st century, Buffalo has an unprecedented opportunity to identify, assemble, and reclaim vacant parcels for start-up businesses, new families, artists, entrepreneurs, and major commercial partners to join in the region's renaissance." Most of that vacant land is on the East Side, but there was not a word about black neighborhood development. There was not a word about urban leaders uniting with the black masses to transform and change the East Side.

Not a single word.

In the "One Region Forward" report on housing and neighborhood strategies, the challenges facing the black community are barely discussed, except in a veiled language that suggests "...for areas where disinvestment has left few of the assets, anchors and actors that are needed to power successful neighborhood revitalization... the time for conventional neighborhood development might be decades away." The authors never use the terms "black" or "East Side," but any person knowledgeable of Buffalo understands their code, and knows they are talking about the East Side black community.

My point is city leaders know about the challenges facing Black Buffalo, but they constantly feign ignorance and surprise. But they know. More than two decades ago, I teamed up with a group of scholars to produce the most comprehensive study of Black Buffalo ever undertaken. This blueprint for change, written by a team of scholars from the University at Buffalo, Buffalo State College, and Fordham University, along with support from the Buffalo Urban League and the City of Buffalo Common Council, was never implemented. Later, my center conducted an investigation of the health status of Black Buffalo, funded by Kaleida Health and the Black Leadership Forum. The study was celebrated and then put on a shelf.

In 2000, I led a team that outlined a strategy for the redevelopment of the Fruit Belt community and demonstrated how tax increment financing could fund the plan. The study was funded by the City of Buffalo's Office of Strategic Planning. City and medical campus leaders praised the report, ignored its findings, and then launched their own redevelopment strategy, which displaced 65 percent of the Fruit Belt's population.

Yes, Buffalo is rising and happy talk abounds; simultaneously, thousands of blacks are being displaced from their traditional neighborhoods along Main Street. They are being pushed out of every neighborhood of opportunity in the city. But no one seems to care or notice. Black Buffalo is *invisible*. Black needs, hopes, and desires are systemically ignored; promises are made, but never kept.

*Yeah. I know some white person in Amherst is saying, "But, Mayor Byron Brown is black. I don't get it."*

Let's be clear. Black faces in high places don't mean a thing if they have the same agenda as white faces in high places. From a city building perspective, the sad reality is there is no difference between Byron Brown, who's been in office for the past ten years, and Jimmy Griffin, who was mayor from 1978–1993.

Yeah, yeah. I know the mayor does hire more blacks and he makes better speeches than his predecessors, but his approach to city building still marginalizes and deems black neighborhood development unimportant.

It pains me to say this, but the mayor is fiddling while blacks are being displaced from neighborhood after neighborhood in Buffalo. He is fiddling while underdeveloped neighborhoods are spewing undesirable outcomes in housing, education, employment, and health. He is fiddling. The mayor knows about black suffering and pain, but the solutions to these nasty problems do not fit into the economic growth model he celebrates.

So black neighborhood development is chronically placed on the backburner. Yes, black faces in high places can support *systemic structural racism.*

*But we, the people, have a choice. We have a right to the city.*

*Don't get me wrong. The white latte group moving back to Buffalo is a good thing.* I get that; but the choice we face is not between the white hedonic latte city and blacks living in blighted, disfigured, and slum-like neighborhoods. *That's where the mayor gets it wrong.* The real choice, my friends, is between the hedonic latte city and the just city.

Hear me, Buffalo.

Our city does not belong to those powerful faces in high places; it does not belong to the developers, the bankers, and all those folks profiting off the *latte city.* We have a right to this city. The masses of black, brown, yellow, red, and white faces have a right to build the just city. We can make that choice. The future is "uncreated." It is not some type of pre-ordained, futuristic place, which is immutable and fixed. *No!* The future is "uncreated," and we have a right to build the just city, a good place, where we find liberation and the higher freedoms.

Buffalo! The time has come for us to answer Rabbi Hillel's question, "If not us, who? And if not now, when?"

**Henry Louis Taylor, Jr.** is a full professor in the Department of Urban and Regional Planning at the University at Buffalo, and director of the university's Center for Urban Studies. He received his Ph.D. in history from the University at Buffalo. Taylor has authored or edited five books, and written more than 120 articles, essays, and technical reports on planning and neighborhood development. He has received numerous awards for his research and neighborhood planning activities, including the 2016 Excellence in University–Community Engagement Award. Taylor lives on Buffalo's West Side.

The ovens shut down at the Wonder Bread plant, 313 Fougeron Street, in 2004, resulting in the layoff of 150 workers. The five-story, 134,000-square-foot-factory was built in 1914. East Side residents today still remember buying bread and Twinkies—still warm—at the ground-story shop. As dozens of Belt Line buildings elsewhere are reclaimed for loft apartments, office space, and breweries and distilleries, this building remains vacant.

Photographs by David Torke.

The Northland Corridor Redevelopment Project, a 50-acre redevelopment project announced by Mayor Byron Brown in 2014, will center on a $55 million rehabilitation of the former Niagara Machine & Tool Works, 683 Northland Avenue. The 247,000-square-foot plant, built in 1910, once churned out stamping presses and press brakes for sheet metal. It will soon be the location of an advanced manufacturing training center and incubation space for manufacturers. The project represents the most ambitious bet to date on resurrecting an industrial job base on the East Side.

# Pedaling through the Snow

## Simon Husted

A sky swirling in lake-effect snow; roads, sidewalks, and buildings obscured by white drifts; people dressed like burglars. In Buffalo, that is the reality most winter mornings.

Most Buffalonians have driven through such weather. Brent Patterson pedals through it.

In the winter of 2014–15, the assistant professor of design at Buffalo State College biked five miles to campus on all but ten mornings, despite snowfall eighteen inches above average. On those ten other days, Patterson, who now lives in the Parkside neighborhood, took public transit or got a ride from a co-worker.

Commutes like Patterson's may become more familiar in Buffalo, which is becoming one of the nation's fastest-growing bike-commuting cities.

Patterson, his wife, Stacy Bisker, and their four children are steering away from the traditional habits of a car-reliant household. They began about five years ago, when one of their sons was diagnosed with Guillain-Barre syndrome, an autoimmune disease. To save money, the family slowly began using bicycles and public transit to go grocery shopping, to appointments, and even to haul home their Christmas tree.

"There's this weird thing that happens when you start driving less and loving it," said Bisker, a stay-at-home mother and a native of Troy, Ohio. "You do it more. You get to know your community better, and you start realizing what you have outside your own front door instead of driving to the suburbs or driving to the mall."

She and Patterson, who are in their late thirties, started the switch while living in Huntington, West Virginia, which gets a fraction of Buffalo's snowfall and is warmer in the winter. The family arrived in Buffalo in August 2013 because Buffalo has a center of excellence for treating Guillain-Barre.

Patterson and Bisker each own a cargo bike equipped with either studded tires, which dig into ice for traction or an electric assist. Their three oldest children, ranging in age from eight to thirteen, each have a bike. The couple have shared their family's story in local newspapers, in the magazines *Kiplinger's Personal Finance* and *Bicycle Times* and in their own short documentary, "Comfortable."

The couple is part of a national trend.

Between 2000 and 2013, the number of Americans using bikes to commute to work increased 63 percent, with some cities, including Buffalo, recording far higher gains, according to figures from the National Household Transportation Survey. The increase has been especially apparent in Rust Belt cities, said Bill Nesper, director of the Bicycle Friendly America program at the League of American Bicyclists.

He said cities like Buffalo, Pittsburgh, Detroit, and Cleveland can accommodate bicyclists easily because much of their infrastructure and dense street grids date from a time before cars became a dominant force in urban design. Buffalo also has a flat, lakefront topography, wide thoroughfares, and a vast grid of calm side streets for carless commuters.

The League reviews applications by communities, businesses, and universities that want to call themselves "bicycle-friendly." Buffalo, Cleveland, and Pittsburgh are ranked as bronze, the fourth rung of a four-level ladder, but there are high hopes that Buffalo will move up as the cities get re-ranked every four years.

Although more than 260 other communities have bronze ratings, more than half of the communities that apply to be in the Bicycle Friendly America database don't even make it to bronze, Nesper said.

Nesper, a Washington, D.C. resident whose father is a Buffalo native, visited Buffalo in August 2015 to look over the city's bike-infrastructure advances.

"I think Buffalo can be a great bicycle-friendly city and a great leader for other cities," Nesper said. "If I can say Buffalo is doing this, I think it comes across stronger than pointing at cities like Boulder, Colorado."

Buffalo makes a better test case than smaller, more economically and socially homogenous outposts like Boulder because its problems are reflected in a lot of small and large legacy cities: a hollowing out of core neighborhoods for suburbs, an expansion of highways and thoroughfares to accommodate motorists rather than cyclists and pedestrians, and a pattern of demolishing structures in favor of parking lots and garages. A car-friendly city needs space for motorists to cheaply store their cars, and downtown Buffalo provides plenty of options. A 2008 study commissioned by the city showed that the downtown core had 5,200 more parking spaces than needed during peak hours.

But cities are backpedaling from a car-centric pattern as a growing urban demographic forgoes the motor-vehicle lifestyle in favor of walking, transit, and biking. That's good for legacy cities, especially Buffalo, because backpedaling here doesn't mean reinventing the wheel, but restoring the place as it was originally built.

But it also means Buffalo needs to catch up to other cities and add facilities to accommodate bicycle traffic on streets.

There are three ways of doing that. The first and least glamorous option is painting shared-arrow signs along one or more lanes of car traffic. It usually ends up being nothing more than an awareness-building exercise. The second option is adding dedicated lanes for cyclists at the shoulders of the street—typically costing nothing more than a new paint job and up to one car lane. The last and most glamorous option is the protected bike lane. Space for cars gets sacrificed, but it is the model that most successfully motivates newcomers to bike.

Over the last few years, bike advocates and city officials have been working on a plan that within ten years would create a network of 300 new miles of bike lanes, shared-arrow lanes, and trails (for cyclists and pedestrians). City officials released the complete master plan on May 6, 2016. In addition to mapping out new bike routes, the plan calls for the city to spend $2,775,578 on eleven high-priority "catalyst projects."

Some of the proposed projects and routes have already been completed. One is a $1.7 million four-mile rail-to-trail path that leads bikers and pedestrians between a LaSalle Metro Rail station and pockets of neighborhood streets in North Buffalo and its adjacent suburbs.

In 2015, the city completed a street makeover that has spurred investment in new office and retail space, recreation amenities, and housing along the Buffalo River. The $12 million Ohio Street project added lights, green space, and a twelve-foot-wide paved path for pedestrians and cyclists. The one-and-a-half-mile stretch doesn't just offer a safe passage between downtown and the attractions along the Outer Harbor. It is also an example of an old, underused street finding new life using what urban planners and road engineers call a "road diet."

Buffalo has been putting its streets on such so-called diets since 2008, when it became the first city in the state to pass a complete streets policy, said Justin Booth, the founder of Go Bike Buffalo and the city's leading advocate for urban biking. Many such diets involve no more than taking one or two car lanes for bike lanes following resurfacing projects. Of course, accommodating car traffic hasn't been as troublesome as in cities with rapidly growing populations.

But in 2015, the U.S. Census Bureau said Erie County gained population for the first time since the 1960s, fueled by an influx of international immigrants, including refugees.

At the end of 2016, the city expects ninety miles of bike lanes, shared-arrow lanes, and trails for cyclists and pedestrians. In addition to growing that figure beyond 300, the city has proposed increasing the number of public bike racks from 400 to 600, said Booth. Booth's goal is to reach 150 miles of bike paths by 2018, when the city is up for a new rating by the American League of Bicyclists.

"I can't give you a set timeline when that will happen, but we're going

Photograph by Julian Montague

to be very aggressive on reaching that goal as fast as possible," Public Works Commissioner Steve Stepniak said. At the very least, the city is committed to adding ten miles of new bike lanes each year—a conservative commitment, he acknowledged.

Road engineers aren't usually seen as advocates for cutting back one or two car lanes to make room for bicyclists, but Booth said the city's public works department has become a major ally for the biking community.

Infrastructure, however, is only one part of building a bicycle-friendly city. A cultural shift in the way non-bicyclists think about getting around town is also crucial.

Buffalo is home to mass biking events like the summer-long Slow Roll, the special annual bike route celebrating the winter solstice, and the Sky-Ride, during which the elevated portion of Route 5 above the Buffalo River is closed for a bicycles-only scenic commute in the spring.

In 2015, Go Bike Buffalo expanded its Slow Roll from monthly to weekly, with routes stretching all over the city. The group counted 16,390 riders on the twenty-four routes.

From 2012 to 2014, bicyclists accounted for about 1.4 percent of Buffalo's commuting population. That's shy of Pittsburgh's 1.9 percent, but far from Portland's 6.3 percent, the highest rate in the nation.

Nevertheless, Buffalo's biking population is well above some cities rated higher on the "bicycle-friendly" scale, like Long Beach, Anchorage and New York City. In fact, more than half of the nation's largest seventy cities don't even break 1 percent, according to an analysis by the League of American Bicyclists.

"We are the seventh-fastest-growing bicycling city in the country," said Booth, whose goal is to see Buffalo's bicycle-commuter rate increase to 3.2 percent by 2017. "Every time we add more bicycle lanes, we see more people out there riding. That is significant, and that is a trend we are seeing nationally."

That doesn't mean everyone needs to display the same level of commitment as the Bisker-Patterson family.

"It is important for us to consider not just being a city that is bicycle-friendly, but making sure we're pedestrian-friendly and transit-friendly as well," Booth said. "There's going to be some days where people are going to say, 'I am not going to bike today.'"

Patterson, the professor, bicyclist, artist, West Virginia native, and father of four, knows that feeling. He eventually convinced his wife, reluctantly, that owning a minivan might be necessary for emergencies. Even so, Bisker and Patterson still drive only once or twice every week.

He now likes to call their lifestyle "car-lite."

**Simon Husted**, twenty-five, studies urban planning and development in Cleveland State University's graduate program. A graduate of West Seneca East Senior High and Kent State University, he previously was a reporter for the *News-Herald*, in Ohio. Most of his family lives in West Seneca and South Buffalo, where he was raised.

# Recover the Radials

## Christina Lincoln

*"If you think it best to let a few people through the practice of thoughtlessness, selfishness or improvidence, destroy your turf..."*
    –Frederick Law Olmsted

Buffalo is going through a renaissance of sorts—a revival of old industrial spaces and the lighting of grain elevators, with a gentrifying, hipster-infested West Side leading the way. But missing out on that wealth and spirit is a struggling East Side, with high poverty and blocks gutted of buildings and businesses, desperate for a break. Separating the two hemispheres is a festering, open wound, infected with cars and noise and oozing exhaust. It cuts through what used to be a part of Frederick Law Olmsted's legacy, Humboldt Parkway, the removal of which would forever alter travel and amputate the lifeblood of the east side of the city.

Welcome to the Kensington Expressway.

Humboldt Parkway opened in 1874, nearly a decade after Olmsted started planning Buffalo's park and parkway system. The Humboldt was the grandest parkway of them all, hosting six rows of trees along the entire 1.8-mile median, a forest within the city, where families picnicked and children played, enjoying the peaceful air and sedate setting.

But by 1953, public transportation officials warned that something had to be done about traffic. "As the city has grown and as the automobile use has increased, this system of streets and highways has become congested to a point where relief must be provided," they wrote. Property values were decreasing, officials explained, because of all of the congestion at rush hour. The Kensington, or the "33," nicknamed for its state route number, would raise property values and increase business along major commuter routes—especially Main and Genesee streets, since it would cut the congestion.

More than 70,000 cars a day traveled to the eastern suburbs and the northeastern portions of the city—the region had seen a 40 percent increase in traffic between 1946 and 1952 alone. It could take nearly an hour to get the eight miles from downtown to the airport on a normal city street. That was apparently unacceptable.

And the best place to put the new highway was through an Olmsted parkway.

Construction on the Kensington started in 1961 with the slaying of hundreds of Humboldt trees. Heartbroken parkway residents pleaded with public officials to no avail. The $42.8 million project displaced 570 homes and sixty-five businesses. In 1955, there were almost 5,400 businesses along the affected commercial routes of Bailey Avenue, Broadway, Fillmore Avenue, Genesee Street, Jefferson Street, Kensington Avenue, and Main Street.

Just four years after construction, that number shrank to 4,700.

Genesee and Broadway had already seen high vacancy rates. They were among the original radial streets laid out by Joseph Ellicott in 1805. Emanating from the downtown traffic circle at Niagara Square, the radials allowed commuters to reach the eastern suburbs and passed through neighborhoods—and past their businesses—along the way.

But the traffic that once served those businesses was now redirected to the highway instead.

The state transportation department in 1953 promised that the Kensington would relieve traffic, boost East Side property values, and invite new development along the area's arterial streets. But those same streets have been gutted. Litter-strewn fields have replaced the urban streetscape of the radials, a victim of the vile highway that stripped the traffic from these commercial corridors. A 2015 directory showed that only 2,140 businesses remain. Main Street, Broadway, and Genesee Street suffered the worst losses.

Of course, the hardship can't solely be attributed to the creation of the Kensington—urban renewal eviscerated lower downtown as well. Entire neighborhoods were razed, the commercial districts plundered along Main and West Genesee. The amount of loss to the city's architectural fabric and residents' psyche is impossible to compute. Livelihoods ceased to exist and residents eventually turned their backs on the concrete that replaced their parks, their properties worth nothing.

Architect Robert Coles literally turned his back on the highway when he designed the front of his house to face the rear of his property.

Today, a trip along Genesee to the airport takes less than twenty minutes along a desolate four-lane city street where vacant lots are prolific and neighborhood business has struggled for decades. The Restore Our Community Coalition has fought valiantly for a cap on the highway, complete with grass and trees and the feel of the former parkway. The price tag is steep to recreate something that never should have been sacrificed in the first place. It likely would increase the property values of the beautiful homes fronting the park, but as long as the Kensington below still exists, it would do little to revive the lost transit corridors. It would still allow traffic to bypass critical urban neighborhoods.

The Kensington has been bleeding the surrounding businesses and neighborhoods for decades, all because of the need to get to the suburbs as quickly as possible. No one working in City Hall today is responsible. There is no blame to be placed—just steps to be taken to right a wrong.

Although such a move would be unpopular to many commuters, closing the Kensington forever would force people to wind through Buffalo's deadened radials, adding five minutes to the trip, but benefitting the community.

**Christina Lincoln** has a master's in urban planning, design, and development from Cleveland State University. She has worked extensively with issues in community development and historic preservation in Cleveland and in Buffalo and believes that the strength of our cities directly impacts that city's entire region. She's in love with Buffalo and strongly believes in the East Side. She lives in the Hamlin Park neighborhood.

# Buffalo Grows Up

## John Kordrupel

Buffalo buzzes today in a way it didn't six years ago when I came home from a year in Boston. My family, friends, and colleagues now gush about the city.

Six years ago, this was the reality: until local sponsors came up with funding at the last minute, the annual New Year's Eve ball almost didn't drop; Buffalo's waterfront remained largely vacant; and the long-awaited Bass Pro project had evaporated after a decade of political posturing. Disappointment, failure, even shame ruled. For years, we as Buffalonians had believed promises, but project after project never materialized and so we became an understandably pessimistic bunch.

But now, the region's collective attitude is shifting.

The valuable Lake Erie waterfront has awakened. The Buffalo medical corridor has (mostly) appeared after a decade of incremental yet steady development. I recently took a stroll through the Buffalo Niagara Medical Campus and for a moment I felt as though I was back in Boston. The University at Buffalo's relocated medical school is rising atop the Allen/Hospital Metro station. Solar City—despite recent questions about financing—is planning to make Buffalo a mecca of clean energy. Bak USA has put Buffalo on the map as one of the few companies currently manufacturing tablets on American soil. For the first time in many decades, seeing a crane on Buffalo's horizon doesn't lead to heart failure.

Young people, both singles and couples, are coming to the city to live, work, and/or raise a family. Suburbanites and Canadians have stopped seeing Buffalo as merely a Saturday night destination for a hockey game or a place to guzzle beer and chicken wings.

Many of us never gave up hope for Buffalo. I had always wished for more, for better. I had always known Buffalo was capable of greatness.

Yet, despite its recent successes, Buffalo remains one of the most segregated and poverty-stricken cities in the country. I see this regularly in my job as Youth Services Planning Coordinator with the Erie County Youth Bureau, a position I've held for almost four years. The Youth Bureau and its advisory board make funding recommendations for approximately seventy-five agencies annually that offer after-school programming, mentoring, and services to Erie County's kids. We provide help for runaways, and homeless, pregnant, and drug-addicted youth. It is a difficult, but gratifying job that forces me to confront political and social challenges and to test my personal boundaries.

My office is located at the Secure Youth Detention Facility on East Ferry Street. It's the place where youth await trial or placement after an alleged crime. A percentage of these youth do turn their lives around, but unfortunately, many return a second, third, or even fourth time, and many are not able to find a way of escaping the environment they face every day.

It's a hard place to come to every day. It can be upsetting to see so many young people in jumpsuits walking single-file with their hands behind their backs.

But this is the slow, incremental work that I believe our city needs—along with the kayaks at Canalside, the rock climbing at Silo City and the solar panels and tablets—if we are to find that greatness.

Some youths don't mind detention because it gives them more structure and safety and meals than their families are able to offer. From academic help to conflict resolution and creative art to break dancing lessons and pregnancy prevention education, agencies across the city are working to empower these struggling young people, about 1,500 of whom become homeless every year and about 200 of whom have children while registered in Buffalo Public Schools.

This work is not glamorous. It is nice to be able to point to the high-profile successes, like Dr. Daniel Alexander, who grew up impoverished and relied on a local after-school program for help. In March 2016, he donated $1 million to help renovate Seneca-Babcock Community Association in his old South Buffalo neighborhood.

But more often, this work feels thankless. The progress made with a teen on Monday may vanish the next day when the teen picks a fight with a once best friend because of a girl. The same is true of work being done with new immigrants and refugees. These families and their children—about 10,000 since 2003—are helping Buffalo and other Rust Belt cities grow and they are bringing new ideas, new restaurants, and new markets to our area.

In the past few years, the largest groups of refugees in Buffalo came from Burma, Bhutan, and Somalia. Many of these families arrive with no English skills and Buffalo schools—already troubled—have struggled to provide the needed assistance and translation for students and parents. Groups like Peace of the City, Helping Everyone Achieve Livelihood (HEAL) International, Habitat For Humanity-Buffalo, and Jericho Road Ministries are vital in the work of assimilating and teaching these youths.

Every summer, Peace of the City, which provides mentoring and literacy help for at-risk children, puts on a Shakespearean play. The kids choose the play, audition, and then practice and perform. It's called "Shakespeare Comes to (716)." It's an astonishing example of a by youth, for youth program that empowers, teaches, and helps integrate kids through literature and poetry. Many of the youth who take part in the program are first-generation children of immigrants and refugees and others are at-risk teens who might otherwise be on the streets or in gangs. Peace of the City also boasts two youth-run businesses, one in which kids design and sell jewelry and the other in which these same young people create soaps and body washes. It also has a literacy club and a homework club.

Anything to keep the kids engaged and out of trouble.

The struggles that some of our at-risk teens face are, frankly, terrifying. One fifteen-year-old watched her mother being kidnapped and then raped by her mother's boyfriend. She required years of help and services. That sort of help doesn't happen overnight and it doesn't make headlines. But it is monumental and life changing. And it's happening every day in Buffalo. At first, the girl couldn't tell her story to staff without breaking down in tears. Now, she is proud of the strong relationship she shares with her mother and she is thriving in school and after school.

The most dangerous time for youths is after school, specifically 3:00 p.m. to 9:00 p.m. That's when the most youth-related crimes, drug and alcohol abuse, and unsafe sex occur. This is why after-school providers are so important, and why the providers are everyday heroes. Their work goes unnoticed most every day, and yet they are literally validating and saving lives on a daily basis.

Newcomers to the city—in this case immigrants and refugees—have fled their native countries to avoid imprisonment, poverty, violence, racism, and even disease. Their experiences in Buffalo should be the opposite. That's what Habitat for Humanity-Buffalo does by helping immigrant families acquire and build homes through sweat equity. It's also what Jericho Road Ministries does by providing warm meals and after-school programs that provide both academic enrichment and supervised recreation.

Helping Everyone Achieve Livelihood, or HEAL International, was founded by refugees, for refugees in 2009 and works to help integrate new arrivals by offering language and business classes. It also offers discussions on conflict resolution, female empowerment, and religious education.

I see this amazing work being done on a firsthand basis. Every day, I see a level of collaboration among agencies and people as well as a civic pride that I don't recall having witnessed in my adult life.

Last fall, the Erie County Youth Bureau planned and executed the first-annual Community Forum, where over fifty youth-serving agencies shared ideas and collaborated. Beyond Erie County, organizations such as the Mobile Safety-Net Team, the University at Buffalo's Regional Institute, and Say Yes to Education Buffalo have been working to ensure youth and families have access to fresh fruits and vegetables, clean drinking water, and affordable transportation.

People all around me are proud to be associated with Buffalo. It has always been a badge of honor; it is just now that outsiders are coming to realize the wonderful assets of our home. My hope in the years to come is not that Buffalo attracts as many Fortune 500 companies as possible, or that it have the hippest coffeehouses, breweries, and loft apartments; all of these things are nice by-products and are fun to write about and critique, and of course spend money on. Rather, my primary hope is that Buffalo becomes a model of sustainability—economically, environmentally, and socially.

When I was a child, the only place to go for fun was the Main Place Mall. As a college student, the most popular thing to do was visit the Chippewa Street bars and restaurants. My children, on the other hand, will have kayaks on the waterfront, a children's museum, bike lanes, and public art. When they grow up, they will have access to world-class, multi-cultural restaurants, bars, and cultural institutions. They will have friends from other countries and—I hope—other parts of the city.

For this to happen, Buffalo must continue to be a welcoming city for refugees and immigrants, but also for its native citizens, especially those populations that have traditionally been marginalized. My dream is that someday, racial and economic barriers will be torn down and replaced by a culture of tolerance and justice. I hope the new Buffalo will be known nationally and internationally both as the "City of No Illusions" and as the "City of Good Neighbors" that most of us would like to believe it always secretly was.

Then and only then will Buffalo have lived up to its full potential as the world-class city that it has always been destined to be.

**John Kordrupel** is employed by the Erie County Youth Bureau, where he works to ensure that the youth of Western New York have access to after-school, mentoring, and job-readiness programs. He received a bachelor's of science in law & government from Hilbert College and a master's in urban planning from the University at Buffalo. John is interested in the ways people interact with both their built and natural environments. He lives in Lancaster, but has previously lived in Parkside and on the West Side.

The all-refugee soccer team at International Prep-Grover Cleveland High School have been Buffalo city champions since 2013. The teens came to Buffalo with their families after war and persecution in their native lands of Somalia, Congo, Burma, Iraq and elsewhere, forced them to flee. They perfected the resilience, speed and quirky creativity that made them champions in the sandlots of refugee camps and in their home countries.

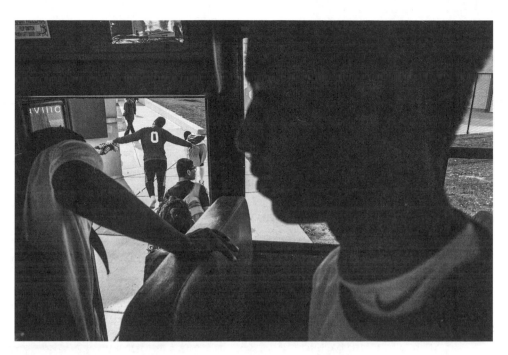

"What you learn from losing is to win the next game," said Yasir Alhadeethi, team co-captain, who is from Al Anbar province in Iraq. He is pictured as Number 0 in the photo on the upper right.

Photographed by Brendan Bannon, 2015.

# The Language of America: Stories of Buffalo's Immigrant Press

## Tyler Bagwell

I met Rubens Mukunzi at 2:00 p.m. on the Fourth of July, 2015. He was sitting at a wrought-iron table on the sidewalk in front of a café at 765 Elmwood Avenue. Rubens, a Rwandan journalist, had worked as a radio broadcaster in Kigali and also ran *L'Oasis Gazette*, an education-focused newspaper that printed stories in French and Swahili.

I'd moved to Buffalo the month before. It'd mark the third time I'd make the move. The first time I was five years old. I'd moved from Fort Leavenworth, Kansas, to an apartment in Amherst where I lived for a year with my mother and sister while our father was stationed in South Korea. We moved several more times and when I was eleven my family moved from Fort Shafter, Hawaii, back to Buffalo. At nineteen, I left for Chicago. After six years there, the timing seemed right to move back to the place that had been the closest thing to a hometown I'd ever known.

About a week earlier I'd responded to a Craigslist ad titled "Different positions in Karibu newspaper (art/media/design)." The Craigslist ad said nothing of the focus of the paper.

After I responded to the ad, I saw an advertisement in the *Public*, an alternative weekly, for *Karibu News*, calling it a "new voice for Buffalo's rapidly growing immigrant population." It said stories would be printed in Arabic, Burmese, English, and other languages. I was intrigued.

That same week, *Artvoice*, another alternative weekly, carried the story "Welcome = Karibu," which focused on Rubens and his ambitions to start a free immigrant newspaper. The author, Buck Quigley, wrote: "His true vocation seems to remain the one he took to as a teenager, when, undaunted by any obstacle he produced his first newspaper—handwritten. Based on his experiences here as an immigrant, meeting others who find themselves in a foreign culture, he is pursuing a new dream of starting a free publication called Karibu Community Newspaper. Karibu translates to "welcome" in Swahili."

The idea of a newspaper printed in multiple languages and alphabets fascinated me, as did the typographic challenges that came along with it. It seemed like something that had the potential to serve as a Rosetta Stone or Myazedi Inscription that bound and informed people across different language groups. I sent another email and Rubens asked me to meet him at the café.

Rubens had arrived in Buffalo two years ago, speaking no English, and had struggled to find a way to pursue journalism in America. He knew a lot of other immigrants and refugees who were also struggling to figure out this new land and culture. His vision, he told me, was to inform immigrants about Buffalo, but also to inform the native-born Buffalonians about the immigrant population. A large portion of new arrivals—10,000 came in the past ten years—didn't speak English, so he reasoned a portion of the paper shouldn't either.

Rubens saved his own money to start the paper and got loans from the Westminster Economic Development Initiative. He hired me at that first meeting and told me he hoped to have the first issue out in two weeks. I asked him who else he had working for him. He said no one. No writers, editors, photographers, or advertisers.

Still, Monday morning, we were printing business cards.

I had signed on to do layout, but also needed to be a reporter. I had worked on school-run newspapers and magazines, but writing is not something I thought I was good at.

Looking for stories, Rubens took me first to the shop of Louise Sano, a Rwandan woman who had started selling African fashions as part of the West Side Bazaar, a business incubator on Grant Street, and now owned and operated two stores around Grant and Lafayette. When we entered the store, she was behind the counter talking to Joseph Shi Shi, a Congolese leather craftsmen. They were speaking in either Swahili or French, I can't remember which, but it's also possible it was both. Rubens introduced me and they all switched to English.

As we talked, Sano suggested we interview Nancy Fuentes, a woman who did alterations at Sano's dress shop on the other side of Lafayette Avenue. Fuentes taught free sewing lessons and gave away sewing machines donated by her clients and others to students who completed her course. Her students ranged from Buffalo State fashion students to refugees.

The next week, I watched Fuentes teach and I chatted with her student, Lory Pollina, a middle-aged artist and musician who, like me, had just returned to Buffalo after years away. Pollina had taken on sewing because he wanted to design his own pants out of patterned fabric.

They both asked if I knew Joseph Shi Shi. Then Fuentes launched into her story of how she and Shi Shi met. "He came in here and he saw the little slippers that I make, my baby booties, and he told me how to improve them," she said as she showed me the stitching on a pair of boots. "I was making suede booties and he told me how to improve them, then we became friends."

The conversation quickly turned from sewing to Buffalo's recovery and the role of immigrants in it. Pollina noted that he and Fuentes both grew up the children of Italian immigrants on the West Side. "We grew up in the Italian community, and my family, although both parents spoke Italian, they never spoke it around us because they wanted us to seem American and fit in and all because there was great prejudice in the 1940s and 1950s. If you were an Italian immigrant they'd treat you horribly. So it all white washed everything and I can't speak Italian."

The first Italian to settle in Buffalo is probably Luigi Chiesa, who in the 1850's sold rat traps and bird cages on the corner of Elm and Batavia (now Broadway). The Italian language newspaper, *Il Corriere Italiano*, appeared a while after in 1898 and was joined by the Socialist Italian language paper, *La Fiacolla*, in 1909.

*Il Corriere Italiano* folded in 1950. In *People of Our City and County*, Stephen Gredel says, "The Italians had an ear for music and sound that made it possible for them to learn English quickly," leading to the end of the Italian-language newspaper in Buffalo.

The Italians weren't the first group to start a newspaper in their native language. In an 1855 issue of the *Commercial Advertiser,* a Buffalo-based English-language paper, the German population was described as "as little American as the duchy of Hesse Cassel; their population speaks a foreign language, reads foreign papers, isolates itself from the American element."

George Zahm, a printer from Zweibrücken, Germany, started the first German-language newspaper in Buffalo in 1837, just twenty-six years after any paper of any language was birthed in the city (The Salisbury Brothers' 1811 *Buffalo Gazette* was the first.). In the inaugural issue of *Der Weltberger* December 2, 1837, Zahm wrote:

"The number of German people in Buffalo has increased significantly in the past four or five years. The commercial and political situation of this city is of such great importance to the Germans living here that people have felt the urgent need for a newspaper in the German language for a long time. Its goal is to inform the German people of this country's politics and to communicate the most important American and European events. Indeed, informing the reader is its prime motive, therefore it will join no particular political party; rather it will attempt to remain independent and non-partisan in order to sustain the fundamental principles necessary to the preservation of the Constitution. In important political issues the platforms of both political parties will be communicated in order to put the reader in the position to form his own opinion. The newspaper will provide a definitive voice against the persecution of immigrant Europeans and it will make these people aware of their rights guaranteed by constitution and law."

When Zahm died in 1844 at age forty-five, after being crushed by a liberty pole being raised in Cheektowaga, his funeral procession was the largest to ever move through Buffalo. His wife took on the paper until

1853, when it merged with another German language paper, *Der Buffalo Demokrat*. At one point, there were six German newspapers operating in Buffalo concurrently. *Der Demokrat, Freie Presse, Volksfreund, Täglicher Republikaner, Tägliche Tribüne,* and *Volksblatt.*

Anti-German sentiment following World War I combined with the assimilation of Germans and the disuse of the German language led to the demise of the German newspapers. "Atrocity stories soon made all things German unpopular. The German-American Bank became Liberty Bank, and the German Language newspapers faded away," wrote A. Gordon Bennett in a 1974 pamphlet published by the Buffalo and Erie County Historical Society.

Since 1837 Buffalo has had numerous publications in German, Polish, Italian, Spanish, and at least one newspaper in French; each shared threads of the same story. Each paper came to an end due to assimilation and a loss of the language among succeeding generations.

One of the last of the Polish language papers, *Dziennik Dla Wsystkich*, also known as *Polish Everybody's Daily*, ended its forty-nine-year run in 1957. After it, came the *Am-Pol Eagle*, a weekly newspaper begun in 1960 for the Polish-American community and published primarily in English.

The 1950s brought the final editions of many of the German, Italian, and Polish language papers, but an influx of migrant farm workers brought a new population of about 1,500 Puerto Ricans to the area by 1953 and a need for news in Spanish.

*La Tilma,* a "four-page offset publication, in newspaper style, carrying news, articles on health, family life and on the Catholic faith" began in June 1955, according to a 1956 article from the *Union and Echo.*

Today, Buffalo has two Spanish language newspapers, *Ultima Hora* founded in 1987 and *Panorama Hispano News* begun in 1992.

After the interview with Fuentes and Pollina, I went to Sweet_ness 7, a café on Grant and Lafayette streets, to research the history of immigrants in Buffalo and the publications that catered to them. In the process, I came across "One Hundred Facts that Every New Citizen of Buffalo Should Know," a handbook for new citizens published by the city's Civic Education Association in 1917. Number twenty-five reads:

"More than 75,000 foreign born persons in Buffalo have learned to speak and understand the language. It is possible to get a working knowledge of the Language of America in one winter's study. The language of America can be learned easily by listening carefully whenever it is spoken, by watching the signs on stores, the posters, and street cars, and by purchasing every night an American newspaper. The person who asks the most questions learns the most."

I saved the page and went from there to meet Rubens who was working on painting what would become *Karibu News'* first office in Riverside. I showed him fact number twenty-five. We noted how much it reflected his vision. Still, we agreed, as important as it is for immigrants to learn "the language of America," it is equally important for Americans to embrace the diversity immigrants bring and encourage immigrants to maintain their culture and language. All of the other papers were so successful at helping immigrants assimilate, they put themselves out of business and the culture and languages died.

*Karibu News* is a new sort of paper. *Karibu News* publishes foreign-language stories side by side with their English translations. It also encourages immigrants to hold on to and celebrate their own language and culture.

The first sample edition came out July 22, 2015. We didn't quite make Rubens' wish for two weeks after our initial meeting. But we were close. We delivered the first edition, which carried stories in English, Burmese, and Arabic, on August 5.

Since then, *Karibu News* has published in Karen, Spanish, French, Swahili, Vietnamese, Somali, German, and Chinese. We continue to learn from the successes and failures of Buffalo's former foreign papers and are proud to carry on their legacy.

**Tyler Bagwell** is the creative director at *Karibu News*. He graduated with a degree in graphic arts from Robert Morris University in Chicago. He grew up an Army brat.

# Flashpoints

# Tampa Stadium, January 27, 1991

## Marv Levy

The ball rose, twirling end over end into the balmy Florida night sky. Forty-seven yards away from where it had been launched, the goalposts beckoned. An eerie silence descended on the packed stadium as the eyes of more than 70,000 people followed the solitary missile on its lonely journey. Elsewhere, in front of television sets throughout the world, millions of enthralled viewers joined in the vigil. Standing just outside the perimeter of the playing field, I too, mouth agape, gazed transfixed as the ball's flight reached its apex and then continued hurtling toward the uprights' outstretched arms.

The seven-month odyssey we had begun on a hot, humid July day at our training camp in Fredonia, New York, was split seconds away from its culmination. The New York Giants were leading our Buffalo Bills 20-19.

At stake? The Super Bowl championship!

Just a minute and twenty-six seconds earlier—it had seemed like ages ago—we had taken possession of the football on our own fifteen-yard line with a minute and thirty seconds remaining to be played in the game. We would have this one final opportunity to achieve the most coveted of all football triumphs.

We went to work.

No huddle. Jim Kelly to Andre Reed; a screen pass to Thurman Thomas; and then Thurman again, this time on a draw play. Another completion to Andre. The clock kept running. Spike the ball. Kill the clock. Now it was Jim to James Lofton, who caught the pass inches inside the left sideline stripe. Quickly, James stepped out of bounds at the Giants' twenty-nine-yard line. There were four seconds left to play.

I sent our field goal team out onto the field.

Snap! Hold! Kick! The ball leapt into the sky and soared toward the beseeching arms of the goalposts. Closer and closer it came. And then—it fluttered on by, a scant two feet outside of the right upright.

The game was over. The Giants were Super Bowl champions.

Imagine their jubilation. Imagine our desolation.

When you are a coach in the National Football League, there always comes one specific moment on game day when you are going to experience one of two intense emotions. Either a wave of ethereal serenity will wash over you, or—at the other end of the spectrum—you will become the victim of a despair so gripping that you can feel it physically. It is when you have lost the game, of course, that the latter sensation takes hold, and if that loss represents your outcome in the Super Bowl, the impact of what you are feeling is multiplied by infinity.

It starts with a throbbing in your temples; then you feel it creeping tightly up the back of your neck. You sense a weakening in all your joints and an invisible constriction clutching at your throat. You feel it in the shallowness of your breathing and in the absence of your appetite. There is a knot in your gut and a clenching of your jaws, which numbs your molars. You feel the heat behind your eyes, and you become aware of an unpleasant taste in your mouth.

Most of all you feel the energy from that despicable frustration flowing from your torso down your arms into your balled-up fists while your psyche screams at you to pound those fists against any inanimate object in the area.

Every coach knows when that exact moment is going to come.

Surprisingly, it does not occur as the final gun sounds and the certainty of victory or defeat has been determined. The game may have ended, but there are still many tasks that need immediate attention.

In leaving the field, a coach must be gracious in victory and able to maintain his dignity in defeat. In the locker room, there are tired, bruised, and often injured players. They, along with the assistant coaches and everyone else who had been so immersed in that week's effort, need a head coach who is in charge and who can provide a sense of perspective. Very soon after the game the coach will meet with the media. His words and his demeanor will come under close scrutiny.

In talking with the media, it is essential that the coach be honest and forthcoming, but he must also be keenly aware of the impact his words will have on his players, on the organization, and on the members of his staff. Most of all, he must remain in control even in those instances when he feels and wishes to convey anger. The time to allow his emotions to take over has not yet arrived.

It is only when he returns very late at night to the lonely quiet of his bedroom or hotel room that the coach realizes there is nothing more to be done until the following day when he begins preparations for the next game.

(WHAT NEXT GAME? WE JUST LOST THE SUPERBOWL, DAMN IT!)

That's when it really hit me.

I spent most of that tormented night trying to refrain, sometimes unsuccessfully, from kicking away my blankets and from pummeling my mattress. In the darkness I winced as I listened to an occasional sob from my dear wife, Frannie. She had dried the tears from the cheeks of our daughter,

Kimberly, just before we finally returned to our room that night, and now it was Frannie's turn to weep.

A few hours earlier I had been in a stadium rocking with noise, music, fireworks, and fanfare. I had stood along the sideline when Whitney Houston sang the most beautiful and stirring rendition of "The Star-Spangled Banner" I had ever heard. The spirit of patriotism that permeated our nation, then in the throes of the Gulf War, showed in the faces of the capacity crowd and of the players and coaches near me as fighter planes from the United States Air Force roared low over the stadium during the pregame ceremonies.

I recalled the pride that had welled up inside of me as our Buffalo-Bills, AFC champions, were introduced to the welcoming accompaniment of thunderous cheers just prior to the kickoff. The excitement, the adrenaline rush, and, yes, the confidence I felt while having to make 200 or more split-second decisions during the course of the game had been exhilarating and consuming.

Now, just a few hours later, I lay there in the darkness, disconsolate. As I tossed about, occasionally grunting in anger, I kept replaying the game in my mind, but it always came out the same. We had lost.

At about 5:00 a.m. I was exhausted, but still awake, when some words, in the form of a question, invaded my consciousness. I sat up in bed, startled, and then, whimsically, I gave voice to those words by whispering their challenge into the quiet of the night: "What are you going to do about it?"

My mind was racing now, and faster than any damn internet hookup ever it went directly back to a day I hadn't thought about for more than forty-seven years. It was December 13, 1943, and I was riding on a troop train full of recent enlistees heading from Chicago to Greensboro, North Carolina, where we were to begin basic training as members of the Army Air Corps. Just before I departed from Union Station in Chicago, my mother had given me a slim volume of English poetry, and as the train chugged southward, I opened the book and began to read.

As farmland slipped by outside my window, I became engrossed in the pages in front of me. There was one poem I reread several times because its message fascinated me. In its entirety it was composed of just four simple, poignant lines. An unknown English writer had composed it in tribute to some sixteenth-century Scottish warrior.

I did not recall having read those lines again since that forgotten day during World War II, but as I sat in bed and as this tortured night neared its end, the words sprang at me again, pristine and clear:
"Fight on, my men," Sir Andrew said.
"A little I'm hurt but not yet slain. I'll just lie down and bleed awhile,
And then I'll rise and fight again."

I repeated the question to myself, "What are you going to do about it?" This time, however, I spoke it firmly and resolutely because I now knew exactly what I was going to do (Thank you, Sir Andrew! Thank you, Mother dear!), and I'd begin first thing in the morning. I glanced over at Frannie, finally sleeping peacefully. Less than sixty seconds later I was, too.

After all, I had to be fresh for tomorrow.

I settled into my seat for the airplane trip back to Buffalo on the morning after we had played in Super Bowl XXV. The airline had provided a stack of newspapers for us at the entry door. No one picked one up. As they came on to our charter flight, our players were more subdued than I could ever recall having seen them. They were somber, but they came aboard—coats, ties, clean shirts, clean-shaven, their heads held high. There was no "angry with someone else" attitude about any of them. Quietly they filed back to their seats.

In just a few hours we would be back home in the midwinter cold of upstate New York, and our players were all carrying mittens. No one needed regular gloves, I would learn, because no one would be pointing fingers.

Once the plane was airborne, I made my way back down the aisle, something I did, win or lose, on the journey home after every road game. I didn't say much, and neither did any of the players. It wasn't the time for that, and we all knew it. I could feel their pain, and they could feel mine, too. Most of the players looked up as I came by, and when they did, we would exchange a reassuring glimmer of a smile.

However, as I continued moving toward the back of the airplane, I became aware that it wasn't the faint smiles tugging at the comers of their mouths that struck me. It was the look in their eyes. What I saw reflected was not defeat. I saw resolve. And do you know what? That's what I had expected. How could I not have been proud to coach men such as these?

I had expressed that exact sentiment to our team as soon as I could after the game the night before.

When I had returned to the locker room after congratulating the Giants' coach, Bill Parcells, most of them were sitting on the stools in front of their lockers gazing vacantly at a far wall or at the floor. You could hear the fan as it whirred overhead, but not much else. The only other sound was an occasional ripping of tape as a few of them absentmindedly pulled the wrappings from their wrists.

I knew they didn't want to listen to some long-winded speech at that grieving moment. There are occasions when a coach's words—and even his eloquence—are meaningful to his players. This was not one of those times.

Any lengthy oration by me now would be nothing more than irritating noise. Yet I knew that to refrain from all communication would have been a gesture that they could rightly interpret as a display of anger and disdain toward them. No feelings were further from my heart than those. And so I spoke, briefly and sincerely.

"There is not a loser in this room," I said.

I told them I was proud of them and proud to be their coach.

I injected no pep talk rhetoric, nor were my words tinged with remorse. I told them that I'd reserve making any further remarks until the next day after we had returned to Buffalo, where we would hold our final team meeting at our stadium complex in Orchard Park.

That was it for our team as a group, but there was still one player with whom I wanted to visit personally. He was our place kicker, Scott Norwood. Scott was a quiet, somewhat introspective person. He was conscientious, dependable, and respected by his teammates and coaches. On several occasions during our march to the AFC championship, Scott had delivered the game-winning kick in the game's final moments. There would also be contests in the following season when Scott's last-minute heroics would once again propel our Bills to a crucial victory.

His outward appearance now as he sat with his teammates in the almost silent locker room didn't seem much different from any of theirs, but I could only imagine the torment he felt inside. I found a stool, pulled it over, and sat down next to Scott. While I was searching my mind, seeking the right words to say, some other stalwarts did it for me.

Linebacker Darryl Talley and defensive back Nate Odomes stopped by, and Darryl spoke.

"Hey, Scott, if Nate and I had tackled their receiver on that third and fourteen during their touchdown drive, it wouldn't have come down to one last kick."

Nate nodded his assent.

Then our great wide receiver, Andre Reed, drifted over.

"You know, Scott," he said, "if I'd have hung on to that pass on their fifteen-yard-line in the first half, we probably would have come away with seven points instead of three."

Defensive lineman Jeff Wright also approached Scott.

"Doggone it, Scott, when Bruce Smith sacked Hostetler in the end zone and forced him to fumble, we could have had a touchdown instead of just a safety if I'd been able to recover it."

They kept on coming. Carlton Bailey, Pete Metzelaars, Kirby Jackson, Cornelius Bennett, Kent Hull, Frank Reich, Mark Kelso, Kenny Davis, Steve Tasker, Jim Kelly, Shane Conlan, Dwight Drane, Keith McKeller, Mark Pike, and others. Each with his own mea culpa. I knew by that time that Scott didn't need a "me too" from his coach. I patted him on the shoulder, and as I walked away, I couldn't tell whether that film of moisture I saw was in his eyes or in mine.

When our plane arrived at Greater Buffalo International Airport, we boarded the team buses expecting to go directly to Rich Stadium. Instead, we headed toward City Hall in downtown Buffalo. Why, I wondered. We had lost. We had let our fans down! What was there to celebrate?

In the next hour or so we found out.

The buses parked behind City Hall, and we were shepherded in through the back entrance. Then we proceeded down the long, quiet hallways to the foot of a winding stairway at the front of the building. We ascended several floors and emerged onto a spacious, old stone balcony that overlooked historic Niagara Square. Assembled below in the biting January cold and snow were 30,000 Buffalo Bills fans.

How long had they been waiting? I didn't know; and they didn't care. As our party moved out onto the balcony, a tumultuous welcome erupted from the assembled throng. They sustained the clamor. On and on it reverberated.

When finally the noise began to subside, several of the fans started a chant. Quickly, others joined in. Soon, they were bellowing in unison, "We want Scott! We want Scott! We want Scott!"

The crescendo mounted, and at last Scott Norwood, urged forward by several nudges from his teammates, stepped forth to speak. His voice was cracking, but he spoke for us all when he said, "I know I've never felt more loved than right now. We will be back. You can count on it, and we are dedicating next season to the fans of Buffalo."

Scott Norwood, a shy young man, less than twenty-four hours removed from his greatest professional disappointment, had given voice to the passion that would drive the Bills players and our fans in the seasons to come.

We learned a great deal about those Bills fans on that day and in the weeks that followed. Their support, their healthy ardor, and their warm-heartedness were always there to uplift our team whenever we needed it most. The resilience and admirable qualities of character that were to mark our Bills teams were inspired in great measure by the people of Buffalo. There are no fans anywhere like Bills fans. Their loyalty and their hardiness are unparalleled. We are so proud to have represented them on the field of play.

Excerpted from *Where Else Would You Rather Be?*, Marv Levy, 2004.

**Marv Levy,** ninety-one, was the most successful coach in Buffalo Bills history. Under him, the Bills won four AFC championships (1990-1993) and became the only team in NFL history to go to four straight Super Bowls (1991-1994). He was named NFL Coach of the Year in 1988 and 1995. In 2001, Levy was inducted into the Pro Football Hall of Fame. Before his coaching career, he served in the US Army Air Corps in World War II, got a bachelor's degree from Coe College and master's degree from Harvard University. After forty-seven years of coaching, he retired in 1997 at the age of seventy-two. He is tied with George Halas of the Chicago Bears as the oldest coach in NFL history. In his retirement, he has published three books: *Where Else Would You Rather Be?* (memoir), *Between the Lies* (novel), and *It's Time for a Rhyme* (poetry). While he coached the Bills, he and his wife Fran lived at the Briarwood Country Club in Hamburg. They currently live in Chicago.

# Surprise!

## Jon Penfold

I remember it was a Thursday because we were waiting for a new episode of *The Office* to air. I was playing *John Madden Football* on the Xbox with my housemate Jeff, who spent so much time in front of the television that I often wondered if he ever slept. We were listening to the Killers on the stereo, while Damian, one of my best friends from high school, and whose parents owned the North Buffalo house we occupied—thankfully charging us next to nothing for rent—sat at the computer station, surfing the Internet. That's just what we did, most every day, three unemployed guys in our twenties—out of college but not yet settled in careers—eager for any form of technological stimulus to occupy our time, to cure the boredom of our in-between lives.

"Touchdown!" As the cartoonish Buffalo Bills player did his own pre-programmed end zone dance on the giant screen in front of us, I threw my arms in the air and did a short celebration of my own.

"Oh, sit down. This game is obviously rigged." According to Jeff everything was rigged.

"It's snowing!" Damian, who was always optimistic and incapable of telling a lie, was staring out the window in disbelief.

"That's impossible," Jeff declared without looking away from the TV. "It's only the first week of October. It's too early for snow."

It was actually the second week of October, but when you're perpetually unemployed, it can be difficult to care about the date.

"No," I said, dropping my controller and walking to the window. "He's right. It is snowing."

"So what?" Jeff unenthusiastically replied. "It's Buffalo. It snows. Big deal. Are we going to finish this game or not?"

"All right." I sat back down and grabbed the controller. Jeff was right—it was just snow. It's not like we had never seen snow before. But then the noise started: *Creak! Crack! Crash! Crunch!*

"The branches are falling," Damian alerted us.

Again, I dropped my controller and hurried to the window.

Again, Jeff unenthusiastically bellowed, "So what? We're in the middle of a videogame for Christ's sake."

This time I ignored him and stared hypnotized at the streetlamp, its yellow glow illuminating endless flakes of snow, some the size of half-dollars, some even larger, as they fell fast from the black void above. Sure, we had all seen snow before, but not snow like this, never this early in the season.

"Come on!" Now Jeff's voice was becoming louder, more perturbed. "We need to finish this game before the show starts."

And that's when everything, suddenly and all at once, fell dark and quiet.

There were no more street lamps. No more Madden-glow from the television. No more pop-up ads on the PC. No more Killers crooning "*'Cause I'm Mr. Brightside...*" No more ceiling lights. No more dim table lamps. No more fan blowing out of the heating duct. No more flat buzz from the refrigerator.

Our inside world was dark and silent, which allowed us for the first time that night to comprehend what was happening to the outside world: *Creak! Crack! Crash! Crunch! Creak! Crack! Crash! Crunch! Creak! Crack! Crash! Crunch!*

And then the sirens started: *EEEOOOEEEOOOEEEOOO...*

"*The Office* starts in twenty minutes," Jeff stated with annoyance. "They'd better have the electricity back on by then."

But they didn't.

And we sat there in the dark, listening to a combined symphony of man mixed with nature: *Creak! Crack! Crash! Crunch! EEEOOOEEEOOOEEEOOO...Creak! Crack! Crash! Crunch! EEEOOOEEEOOOEEEOOO...*Until, after an hour or so, the "Creak! Crack! Crash! Crunch!" came to a halt—there were no more branches left to fall—and we were left only with the haunting sound of humanity in its most desperate time of need: *EEEOOOEEEOOOEEEOOO...*

It was intense. Exciting. Unnerving. It was like something out of a movie.

"Screw this," Jeff said. "I'm going to bed."

We all awoke the following morning expecting the electricity to be back on, because that's how it had always worked, our entire lives—the electricity would go out for a short while, no longer than a few hours, and then the good people at the utility company would fix the problem. *Voila: Electricity!*

But this time the problem was much bigger than anyone had ever experienced before. Much, much bigger. The electric outage wasn't contained to just our house, or just our street, or just our neighborhood for that matter. The power was out everywhere. The entire city had gone dark.

Of course, being the self-absorbed young Americans society had trained us to be, we had little concern for the rest of the city. We didn't consider the problems losing electricity could cause to such places that needed it the most, places like hospitals and nursing homes, or regular homes occupied by the elderly and handicapped.

Photograph by Julian Montague

After all, we had problems of our own to worry about. Problems like: *What are we going to do now?* No electricity meant: no television, or Xbox, or computer, or stereo, or smartphone (mostly because they didn't exist yet). We would eventually realize that we had larger predicaments—such as having no way to heat the house, refrigerate our food, or cook our meals—though at the time, we were really only concerned with dying from boredom.

First, we tried reading, but that didn't last very long. It's not that we despised reading or anything—in fact, I think we all read much more than the average American—it's just that there's a difference between reading for pleasure and reading because there's nothing else to do. Nobody wants to feel forced to do anything, even if it's something you usually enjoy.

Next, we decided to work on some art, but much like the reading experiment, it didn't last long. Finally, we settled on playing board games, but almost as soon as we started, we realized that in order to play games, we would need the one component that always made games more enjoyable—beer! Which meant that someone needed to venture outside.

Since Jeff rarely left the house even during normal conditions, it was up to Damian and me to brave the elements and make the half-mile trek to the grocery store, which we weren't sure would be open. We dug out our winter boots and jackets and hats and gloves and headed out the front door. There were about two feet of snow on the ground, heavy and wet, but that wasn't even close to being the worst of it. There were broken tree branches everywhere—in the middle of the street, in our neighbors' yards, on the roofs of their houses and cars. Other than our backyard, our property and vehicles had been spared, though the rest of our North Buffalo neighborhood looked as if an epic battle had taken place—a battle against Mother Nature, in which *she* clearly won.

Englewood Avenue hadn't been cleared yet, so we trudged through the snow to Kenmore Avenue, which, being a major thoroughfare, as well as having few trees, was one of the few roads in the vicinity that saw any automobile traffic. We were happy to find the Budwey's open, running on generators. We scoured the aisles before making our way to the checkout with a basket of food and two thirty-packs of Genesee Beer. But when I pulled out my bankcard to make our purchase, we were informed that the computers were down—cash only. Damian and I looked at each other, dug our hands into our pockets, and handed all the money we had between us to the cashier. As we walked home, carrying nothing but the two thirty-packs, slow-moving cars beeped their horns, their occupants flashing us smiles and giving us big thumbs up. This was Buffalo after all—nothing could keep us down!

We spent the rest of the afternoon, and most of the weekend, sitting around a table in our cold house, drinking beer and playing board games. When Jeff lost at Monopoly, he declared that the game was "obviously rigged!" And when I took Ukraine from Damian in Risk!, stating that "the Ukraine is weak!" Damian responded right on cue, pulling a line from an old *Seinfeld* episode. "The Ukraine is not weak!" he yelled with a semi-Slavic accent, pounding his fist on the table. It turned out that we didn't need a television to make us laugh, that we could create our own comedic scenes.

By the end of the weekend, the snow had all but melted, and the real cleanup began. We dragged the downed branches from the backyard to the front of our house and then helped our neighbors do the same.

Looking around the neighborhood, that's all I saw—neighbors helping neighbors, most everyone in a positive mood, happy to lend a hand. We did it, too. Amazingly, we discovered, there was an entire community of live people surrounding us. Many of them were at least as entertaining as our video games.

Sometimes it takes a natural disaster to bring a city together.

By Monday, the extent of the storm became clear. The *Buffalo News* reported that over 400,000 customers had lost power and 90 percent of the city's trees had been damaged, resulting in over six million cubic yards of debris, with a cleanup estimate of about $130 million. President George W. Bush had declared a state of emergency. Around a dozen deaths could be attributed to the storm. Suddenly, our lack of electricity seemed trivial.

Though the power wasn't back on, the streets were clear, allowing us to drive to our hometowns in Elma and Alden, which saw little to no damage from the storm. And each of us had family and friends who offered us places to stay—warm places with refrigeration and working ovens. But, a funny thing happened: we all chose to return to North Buffalo, to our house with no electricity.

We told everyone we didn't want to miss out on a once-in-a-generation event. Our parents had had the Blizzard of '77, and we had all heard their stories numerous times before. Finally, we had our own stories worth telling, about the time we survived the October Surprise.

Partly, though, we enjoyed the togetherness the storm produced. We didn't want to lose that magical bond.

We spent the remainder of the week drinking beer, playing games, grilling food, and drinking more beer. Plain and simple, we were having a good time. And then, on that Thursday, almost exactly a week later, down to the hour, the lights flickered back on, the television screen filled with colors, and the speakers from the stereo sang: "*'Cause I'm Mr. Brightside...*"

Damian looked at his watch. "*The Office* is on in an hour."

Jeff's eyes lit up. "I think we have time for a quick game of *Madden*."

I faked a smile. "Let's do it."

Things were back to normal, but it wouldn't be long before we all moved on with our lives. To nobody's surprise, Damian got a good job as an environmental engineer in Buffalo. To everyone's surprise, Jeff moved back to Alden to start a family.

And as for me, I got rid of everything I owned and rode my bicycle to the West Coast. Now, I'm not implying that the week we spent together during the storm motivated us to get our lives on track, but I do know that when I think back about the years I lived in Buffalo, it's that week without electricity that I remember most fondly.

I sometimes wish the power had never turned back on.

**Jon Penfold** is the author of *Where the Water Used to Fall,* a novel, and *The Road and the River: An American Adventure,* which tells the true story of his travels across the United States by bicycle and down the Mississippi River by canoe. His short stories have been featured in numerous anthologies. He grew up in Elma, attended Iroquois High School, and graduated with a degree in English from SUNY Potsdam. He currently resides in the Pacific Northwest.

# The Bells of Saint Ann's

## Brian Castner

The church is on the East Side of Buffalo, in my family's Old Neighborhood. The surrounding blocks, once filled with telescoping wooden houses that served as puppy mills for the city's European immigrants, are now mostly flattened and rotting, a scene of modern day postwar-like desolation. Whole housing tracts are weedy lots. Brick storefronts with boarded-up façades quietly implode, their roofs and upper stories succumbing to winter snow and time and forgetfulness. Only single homes occasionally poke out of the side streets, an addict's grin with barely two decent teeth worth saving per smile.

The church rises out of the wreckage and stands strong, unyielding since the moment the first limestone block was set in place 140 years ago. It is grey like the winter sky, the mortar joining each stone weeping dark black from every seam, and thrust so from the bedrock, the façade sheer and un-adorned, it remains a perfect reflection of those who built her by hand using the *kraftfull* skills honed in their daily secular labors.

In my family's mind, this Catholic church now is the Old Neighbor-hood. When I came home from the war in Iraq, where else would I go?

The eastern tower, the tallest tower, is the bell tower. A clever mechanical clock automatically strikes the bells with spring-loaded hammers, but they may be rung by hand as well. A winding marble staircase begins in the lower vestibule of the tower, then through a locked door quickly morphs into a zig-zag of wooden stairs. Those wooden stairs link platform to platform the full height of the tower, a crumbling vine within a timeless rock chimney. Climb that swaying scaffolding, ease through each trapdoor, and eventually you reach a platform with seven ropes. Bell ropes.

The size of the rope corresponds to the bell. Five thinner individual ropes lead to progressively larger bells. The two thickest ropes, however, form a loop, two ropes to the same bell, the largest bell, the biggest in the city, four tons of mountainous potential perched several stories above, a massive bell balanced on a rough-cut eighteen-inches-on-center beam of heartwood spanning the tallest tower.

That bell has a name. The bell's name is *Sancta Anna*.

When the six of us ring the bells, we start with the smallest rope and work our way up. A simple tug and a ring springs from above. A pull or two on the next larger ropes, and deeper tones imbue, a clong and a clang. A ring amongst the clong before the ring and then a clamor again. The bell-keeper and I each grab part of the thickest rope. He plants his feet wide and pulls down between his knees. I hop up on the clang and ring and grab the rope and use my weight to pull my side down until I am squatting too. We take turns using our weight to rock *Sancta Anna* to life, while her sisters ring and clang and ring. She hasn't made a sound yet, but a breeze is stirring. A downdraft of anticipation. The air is full of a sense of great movement just out of sight, a locomotive around the bend. The woman to my left turns her face upward and closes her eyes and her long hair blows off her forehead behind her. I ride the rope up and the bell-keeper rides the ringing rope down and the clonging air alights in the tower as I finally feel the massive clapper free itself from the side of the bell.

When *Sancta Anna* sounds, she strikes me blind and dumb. She says the first word of the universe. It feels like something solid in my mouth. The whole church vibrates in the harmonic. Dust falls in clouds of memory about our heads.

The bells call for the sick and shut-in. The bells call a neighborhood of the small and marginalized to itself.

The inside of the church is the exterior's multi-color photo negative, as illuminated as the face is bare. German stained glass, teacher of the illiterate, depicts the Apostle's Creed in turn around the nave. Frescos of lions and lambs, statues of gesturing saints, bright stars and deepest sky painted above. The fantastically carved wooden altar was so cunningly constructed, it contains only dowels and not a single nail or screw. And on one wall in the back, a list of names, the club of men who built and sustained the church over decades; the list of names begins with Albrecht and Meyer and Seitz and ends with Jones and Fisher and Smith.

The neighborhood comes early and late. They come in walk-up families and at bus times. They come black and white and immigrant, East African and native Polish. They come for three pieces of the free coffee cake afterward, fresh orange juice for their children. They come as they are, because they can afford to come no other way.

After the Gospel it is time to pray. I don't pray anymore, but I pray in this church, embarrassed with my head down and my pleas to myself. In the silence of my mind, I always pray for all my comrades in Afghanistan and Libya and Syria and East Africa and other battlegrounds where I never went.

I pray quietly, but not the rest of this congregation. They pray out loud, they are a prayerful people, respectful in patience for their turn, then vocal in plaintive need. The heavy woman in the wheelchair whose legs end in bandages. The half-grown man with a limp, victim of a disease long since cured. The wrinkled white woman who always prays for safe travel, in truth a plea that her distant family will travel home at all, will remember at all. And the elderly black man, as tall and thin as his impeccable pin-stripe suit, who nods and nods and nods with his eyes closed throughout.

The man who intones the first prayer, wearing his best shirt, his only shirt not stained by work at the industrial laundry six walking blocks away, with the daughter who left, and the other daughter whose misproportioned face shows she can never leave, who will pray for a cure to all that ails his family and took his wife, will not begin with a prayer for them. He will begin with a prayer for others.

"I'd like to pray for all of the soldiers currently in combat overseas," the poor man says, and I bury my face in my hands, and am grateful that the bell can speak for me, because my own amen would catch in my throat.

**Brian Castner** is a nonfiction writer and former Explosive Ordnance Disposal officer, and served two tours in Iraq, in 2005 and 2006. He is the author of *All the Ways We Kill and Die* (Arcade) and the war memoir *The Long Walk* (Doubleday), which was developed into an opera and named an Amazon Best Book of 2012. His writing has appeared in the *New York Times*, *VICE*, *Wired*, the *Los Angeles Review of Books,* and on *National Public Radio*. He is a graduate of Saint Joseph's Collegiate Institute and Marquette University, and lives with his wife and sons on Grand Island.

# It Couldn't Be Anywhere Else

## Perry S. Nicholas

You might have ignored me then.
I would have avoided the corners
where you hung out with teenage friends.
I'd have held back, waiting for you to age,

watching the counter at Woolworth's disappear,
hill at the foot of West Ferry grow less intimidating,
graffiti at the base of the rusty bridge fade away.
We were orphans dropped into the same scenes.

Raised nowhere near rich on its West Side
during different generations, presidents, wars,
we weren't conscious of time or location.
Age didn't matter and doesn't now.

Years later, I tracked you down to love you,
after the neighborhood changed color,
re-surfaced like clapboards on houses,
spaced so tight and close, a car's width apart.

This city makes everyone work hard
to draw closer and meet. In parallel lives,
we finally found each other on the fringes
of this tired place, surviving amongst strangers.

**Perry S. Nicholas** is an associate professor of English at Erie Community College, where he was awarded the 2008 SUNY Chancellor's Award for Scholarship and Creative Activities and the 2011 President's Award for Classroom Instruction. He received the SGA's Outstanding Teacher Award twice. He got his master's degree at the University at Buffalo and has published six books and one CD of poetry. He lives on the West Side.

View of City Hall from the partially-demolished Buffalo Memorial Auditorium, now the site of Canalside. February 2009. By Julian Montague

Buffalo Memorial Auditorium interior, February 2009. By Julian Montague

# Taking the Cake

## Maria Scrivani

Buffalo, late June 1967. I would turn thirteen that summer, but first my family was celebrating my sister's eighteenth birthday. I brought cake out to the policemen sitting on our front porch. They weren't exactly guests. They were posted there, in riot gear. It was the start of a long, hot summer of civil unrest.

We lived on the near East Side, practically on the corner of East Delavan and Jefferson, the main commercial thoroughfare of Buffalo's minority population. We were the last white family on our block, a middle-class enclave where well-tended flower beds rimmed front lawns. The lady next door had tall, technicolor tulips framing hers. We had roses in the back—planted by previous homeowners, these were hardy bushes that took the stage on cue every summer with blood-red and tender pink blooms, apparently oblivious to the abuse of nine rambunctious children playing outside every day, rain or shine. We also had a sturdy cherry tree which bore fruit annually, attracting birds and children. We all learned to climb its gnarly branches, some of us also learning how to break bones in falls. On our patchy front lawn, we had a standing army of dandelions, and I was nearly grown before I realized those pretty yellow starbursts were actually weeds. My parents were definitely not gardeners, though perhaps they might have been if they'd had the time.

On our street, deep-porched wood frame houses, painted in a rainbow of hues and some with great granite stones on the first story, held neighbors whose kids were our playmates. When my parents bought the house, in 1953, this was a mixed-race neighborhood. I didn't hear of "white flight" until I was grown up, but I could see immediately what it meant.

Racial tension had sparked race riots in many American cities in that heated season. Poverty, in all its manifestations, had fed resentment to overflow in the streets. We were under special protection because our house was next door to the Buffalo Gun Center, a tempting trove for looters. Across the street, at Jefferson and Main, was the Sears Roebuck, with a clientele and a labor force that crisscrossed racial lines. Seemed like everyone I knew shopped or worked there. At the top of its winding parking ramp, where we rode bikes and later, practiced our driving skills when the store was closed, we could see sharpshooters with weapons trained on Jefferson.

The rioters never made it to our corner. Rioters smashed car and store windows in the vicinity of William and Jefferson on that first wild afternoon, and the next day, they flipped cars and looters emptied stores. Some 400 police officers arrived. Three policemen and one firefighter were injured; dozens of residents were hurt, fourteen listed with gunshot wounds.

The police officers assigned to our home were sent on overnight duty when things looked bad, when it looked like the violence might spill all the way over to our more sedate middle-class neighborhood. I don't remember actually meeting the officers, just noting that they were young, maybe a decade older than I was. They looked formidable enough, though, in flak jackets and helmets, and of course wielding some scary weapons. On our street, the night was quiet, belying the inquietude of our minds and hearts.

On June 30, the great Jackie Robinson, acting as Governor Nelson Rockefeller's Special Assistant for Urban Affairs, came to Buffalo to meet with Mayor Frank F. Sedita. By July 1, the violence had subsided, and the city, which had been virtually shut down for five days, was getting back to normal.

Later that fall, Dr. Martin Luther King Jr. visited Buffalo, addressing the race riots in a speech at Kleinhans Music Hall. He did not condone such violence, but he called for a condemnation of its causes. "Disappointment breeds despair;" he said, according to a November 10 report in the *Courier-Express*, "despair leads to bitterness, and where there is bitterness an explosion will develop." He said "winters of delay" were "the causes of the summers of riots."

In a few months, his soaring rhetoric would be silenced.

Except for what was on TV and in the newspaper, I didn't see any rioting that summer. I felt the tension and the nearness of danger from a relatively safe front porch. I grew up quickly after that, and maybe our city and our country did, too, though don't Dr. King's words still resound today? Ferguson, New York City, Baltimore, Milwaukee, Charlotte, and on it goes, despair still leading to bitter explosions.

I remember one of the cops put down his assault rifle to take a slice of birthday cake—vanilla, with June strawberries in the frosting—from me. I think he smiled at me. I was white, too—I wasn't a threat. He took the cake, and I took the giant leap out of childhood, that coming-of-age summer.

**Maria Scrivani** is a former reporter for the *Buffalo News* and a contributing writer for *Buffalo Spree*. She is co-author of *Beautiful Buffalo: Preserving a City*, published by Canisius College Press in 2003, and wrote *Brighter Buffalo: Renewing a City*, published by Western New York Wares in 2009. Her latest book, a children's guide called *All About Buffalo*, was illustrated by Michael Morgulis and published in 2011. She is a graduate of Mount St. Joseph Academy and Canisius College. She resides in Buffalo's historic Delaware District.

# Run, Bucky, Run

## Justin Kern

Dad called with an update on the manhunt.

"Bucky's in the woods, near Peg's place. He's got people helping him. Peg hasn't seen him but her dogs are barking at night."

Peg was my uncle's second ex. Her dogs were prize-winning Chows. Bucky, or rather Ralph "Bucky" Phillips, was on the lam and had recently shot a cop who was trying to nab him. He had slipped out of a county jail in Alden, New York, after he carved a hole in a kitchen roof with a can-opener. Bucky's escape that spring of 2006 had heated up to a summer manhunt across Western New York. The sudden attention paid to this side of New York from the search made people giddy. Bucky's every nuance was news.

My Dad blurted at the guy seated next to him in The Duck Club. It was another uncle, his brother, just like Peg's ex.

"'Member to come home and sign in Thursday, big draw at the Fourth Ward Falcons. Let you know what I hear about Bucky."

"Bye, Dad."

Bucky had Western New York spellbound.

He went to jail on a questionable theft misdemeanor charge and left it on his own terms.

On the run for days, he came into it with a doltish cop and escaped in a shoot-out. As the cop nursed wounds and the state organized a mass search, Bucky vanished, from the law at least.

You didn't need the wanted poster to see who Bucky was. With trouble on his face and in his background, Bucky represented a sample of quite a few ne'er-do-wells, who lived in the rural ring outside of the city of Buffalo. Bucky had a ponytail fuller than the hair on the top of his head and the oily sheen of a guy you'd run into on a makeshift dirt bike track. And, as part of that half-backwoods resume, Bucky held a sliver of a connection to much of the population in a four-county radius. If he wasn't a relative, he had fixed your lawnmower or your friend's car or the truck of a friend who loaned it to someone who once made out with your younger sister.

Welcome back, Bucky. Lay low for a while, never mind those barking dogs. Did Bucky alarm Peg's prize-winning Chows? My father thinks he did.

I was a recent graduate of Buffalo State—the cheaper, urban counterpart to the University at Buffalo, whatever glory that held—and was in the last days of allowing my spare time to be bothered by a convenience store job on the West Side of the city. I planned breaks and shifts around the noon and five o'clock newscasts, where Bucky beat out Bills training camp for the lead. At work, I snuck newspapers into a cubby under the scanner to appear alert and ready to register commerce.

Eventually, New York's big, respected newspaper made its once-per-decade trek across the state to spotlight our misery. The last time was for the petty criminal who created a web of HIV infection. At that time, the *New York Times* reporter called everywhere south of Buffalo a "rustic outpost." In high school, most of my friends used the HIV panic as a chance to get out of school and stockpile condoms that came with the free tests. *Inside Edition* sent a crew. I had no reason to worry about sex or condoms yet at seventeen, though the tabloid spot would have been a perfect chance to use a fake name on TV. "Saul T. Nuts" was the plan.

For Bucky's escape, the frenzy of media from the outer regions was stumped by the hometown adoration. Bucky, like Buffalo, was the underdog. With Bucky, fugitive fears got reversed through local logic.

The initial conflict between Bucky and the cops was a matter of Man versus one of Our Men. That's how we saw it at first. While Bucky was loose, neighbors bragged over picked locks and absent walleye boats. People left sheds open. They collected the thank-you notes Bucky left behind after he heisted their cars for a ride and took their smokes and change and old coffee. Brownshirt deputies and navy blue troopers could poke through your friend's dad's Lumina, but he couldn't make him tear off his "Run, Bucky, Run!" bumper sticker or take off his "Where's Bucky?" T-shirt.

Stories spanned days that spanned weeks. Channel 7, birthplace of the fear-inducing "Do you know where your children are?" PSA at the start of the nightly news, fixated on Bucky's everywhereness. Any grandma in Arkwright who saw her garage motion light trigger could serve as an on-air witness to Bucky's omnipresent power.

Channel 4 based a whole segment on a diner near Peg's house that celebrated Bucky's renegade qualities with a sandwich less crafty than the man himself, but one that kind of spelled out his name: Bacon Under Cheese, Ketchup and Yellow (mustard). Other bar-restaurants followed form with specials sold only "to go" and breakfasts served "runny."

On the Seneca Reservation in southern Erie County, Bucky was spoken about as having mythological qualities. He was a shape-shifter, one woman, who looked about a million years old, told a reporter. Police helicopters couldn't spot him in the woods because Bucky became a maple tree, she explained. To turn up outside of the dragnet, Bucky had run until he grew legs like a fox, darting past cops to other counties and backyards.

Bucky had family roots that merged with those of local tribes. Those ties exponentially supported the potential for magic as well as cheap gas getaways and cop-free hideouts. Mystical abetting.

Sheriff's deputies pled with residents to comply with legal orders to call in this outlaw. Call in the pigs on a half-man/half-snow owl, motherfuckers? Are you out of your mind?

The next afternoon, Dad called with more savory hearsay.

"Bucky was at The Inn yesterday. Rod told me. They let him drink free. Left out the kitchen door. Yeah, Rod, the guy who did the steering column on your mom's Taurus. F'in' wild!"

He wouldn't normally have said "F'in'" when "fucking" would do. Bucky's pull had condensed swears into abbreviations. After Dad hung up, I called in sick to work and pretended I cared if I were fired. I spun the tales of Bucky to a stoner friend with a car. We drove an hour south to The Inn.

The Inn was the lone food-and-drink hole in a one-stoplight town, where bikers and their ol' ladies could be bikers and ol' ladies. To get there, we had to succeed through a bullish force of troopers and deputies on Route 20. Stopped once, we explained we were headed outside of the search territory to a friend's house in Jamestown. We welcomed the insight from the trooper that a maniac was on the loose. A ponytail, yes, we would watch for the maniac's ponytail.

A right turn after a tire yard and we pulled into the intersection that contained a corner store, two other closed corner stores, and The Inn. There was no stakeout at The Inn. In fact, it was deserted. We peered through the windows. No life, no police tape, no sign of my dad's buddy Rod. Happy hour, but The Inn was closed.

Of course he wouldn't come back the next day, dummy. If Bucky wanted beer and warm company like he found at The Inn, he'd find more of the same one town over at Skeeter's. It was a place you could bring in a hunting dog and be left alone. I imagine the same rules applied if you morphed into a hunting dog and wanted to be left alone with your Labatt's. We had already made the drive, so this excuse to stop into Skeeter's was as good as any.

We drove to Skeeter's, no uniforms or blockades in sight. We passed Peg's. I hadn't been to her house since she kicked my uncle out four years ago. She had waited for him when he went away for two years on a drug charge. When my uncle got out, he rewarded Peg's patience by running around with any mother or daughter he'd meet while painting houses. From the road, Peg's looked like the red-walled faraway farmhouse they make you focus on in an eye exam.

In the parking lot at Skeeter's, my friend and I smoked a one-hitter shaped like a highlighter. Inside, there was no Bucky in sight among the four local divorcees sitting at stools around the bar. The very energy Bucky seemed to create elsewhere was absent at Skeeter's.

A loud "'Sup!" by my friend fell flat. The bartender was handsome and had streaks of house paint dried to his arms and jeans. We ordered beers and asked him about Bucky. He chuckled and sighed.

I reasoned: "Bucky's a prisoner of peace! Like, uh … a castaway on Pitcairn, heard of but seldom seen again!"

We each drank one more under the occasional eye of the regulars. The dinnertime news came on with "Manhunt!" as the lead. One of the divorcees had previously loaded up the jukebox with Nazareth and Golden Earring so we were resigned to piece together updates through the newscast's pictures and misconstrued closed caption text. A barricade. Woods. Talking official. Talking cop. Thruway tolls. Pan across more woods. Incorrect captions spelled out warnings of a man named "Bulky."

"Now with … update from Santa John Fischer … Vance and the Action 4 Sports Team …"

We couldn't solve much with those resources and those townies. We drove home early, aware that the manhunt checkpoints would soon make way for DWI stops. No Bucky in our sights, though we played up a detailed review of every tree leaf and scruffy local for the entertainment of our friends back in Buffalo.

Within a few weeks, Bucky had embarrassed the cops enough to bump him past a religious cult leader on the FBI's "Ten Most Wanted" list. His family members and girlfriends were hauled in and out of police stations for questioning or priors, all with notice to the press. Whispers pulled apart like cobwebs to reveal leaping connections in conspiracy theories.

Of course all these cops can't find him—Bucky's in Canada! Either that or he's right under their noses, snuck back into jail or Brocton Shock. Behold Bucky, wizard of barroom pragmatism.

Then, another shootout. On a tip, two troopers entered the woods shy of Fredonia, the faux-genteel college village where last century's rumors kept the names Mark Twain and Abe Lincoln woven into its history. The troopers were ambushed by a circle of rifle blasts. One trooper died, another was hobbled, and claims abounded of Bucky's involvement.

That next week, the officer's death deflated the celebration around Bucky for all but a handful. August gave way to Bills season.

With no magic in September, Bucky was caught in the woods four towns away from Fredonia and minutes from his birthplace and The Inn. The police report bragged about Bucky's "defeated look." Dad called and he and his buddy Big Mikey blurted crumbs related to the capture—of a firewood splitting operation Bucky had run the entire time; of the joint of brick weed he'd swiped; of a busted jet ski found bobbing in Erie near a dock run by a guy named Rico; of a note about "splattered pig meat" that I thought everyone had already heard about.

It was a waste to be so sure.

*Ralph "Bucky" Phillips grew up around Chautauqua County and spent much of his adult life in and out of incarceration. In April 2006, he escaped from Erie County Jail and for the next five months eluded police capture but garnered countless citizen run-ins, sightings, and tall tales. During the manhunt, Phillips was involved in two shoot-outs with police, one which resulted in the death of State Trooper Joseph Longobardo, thirty-two. Bucky was captured without incident by Pennsylvania police on Sept. 8, 2006. He's presently serving a life sentence plus two forty-year sentences at a supermax prison in upstate New York, where he has reportedly attempted to escape just once.*

**Justin Kern** is a writer, nonprofit marketing manager and lifelong amateur musician. A native of Dunkirk, New York, he worked as a reporter for small city daily newspapers and has had other fiction and nonfiction works published by *Utne Reader, Forth, Milwaukee Record* and *Thinkerbeat*. He lives in Milwaukee with his wife and cats. No matter what year it is when you read this, he believes the Bills have a chance.

# Breathless

## Dennis Maloney

Hearing Creeley read
at Harvard circa `72
words flow
slow, deliberate,
with nervous energy and
significant hand gestures
sweeping air

Leaping from
chair to blackboard
uni-verse    re-vers-ible
one-turn    re-turn
all in a breath
and of breath

A sequence of numbers
for Robert Indiana
square / circle / triangle / star

Puffing a glowing cigarette
you pause between stanzas
to light one
from the other

And so on years
later in Buffalo
sharing poetry, beer
and conviviality

On the bye and bye
there are more
words to be said
but the body's
labored breath
that wants to keep
on breathing
leaves you breathless
that wants to keep
on breathing
leaves you breathless

Dennis Maloney is the editor and publisher of the widely respected White Pine Press in Buffalo. He is also a poet and translator. His works of translation include: *The Stones of Chile* by Pablo Neruda, *The Landscape of Castile* by Antonio Machado, *Between the Floating Mist: Poems of Ryokan*, and the *The Poet and the Sea* by Juan Ramon Jimenez.

A number of volumes of his own poetry have been published including *The Map Is Not the Territory: Poems & Translations* and *Just Enough*. His book *Listening to Tao Yuan Ming* was recently published by Glass Lyre Press. He grew up in South Buffalo and moved to the West Side later. He now divides his time between Buffalo and Big Sur, California.

# Wedding Day

## Elena Cala

"I know your house," neighborhood people say to me. "I used to play with the kids who lived there."

They remember the same details. Twelve or thirteen kids; the father was a "steel guy" from Pennsylvania; the girls were pretty. Not many recall the mother, the wife of the prolific steel man. I imagine she had plenty to do that kept her from the luxury of socializing with everyone who came by.

After several of these remembrances of the house and the people in it, I have come to understand that people of a certain age who grew up on the West Side of Buffalo in the 1960s and 70s at some point in their social rounds had stood on the porch, in the living room, or in the yard of the house on the corner of Vermont and Niagara, the house I'd just bought. They had come of age during a time of neighborhood schools and densely populated communities, a time when kids roamed the streets freely and safely in multitudes. It was a house where a dozen children grew up and that saw the heavy traffic of friends.

The house is not so busy now.

A red brick Victorian that faces the giant Connecticut Street Armory, it was my answer to a city residency requirement for a good job. It houses me, two dogs, and, occasionally, visiting daughters. No fighting for bathroom rights in the morning, no arguing at the table in this too-much-house for one person. If the walls could speak, they would probably say, "Where is everyone?"

The doorbell rang one Saturday afternoon as I was cranking pasta for a dinner party. Not expecting anyone, and not wanting to wash the flour and egg from my hands to handle a doorknob, I went to the window by the front porch and saw a profile in a dark suit.

"Jehovah's Witness," I said to the dogs, and made my way back to the kitchen.

The bell rang again.

"Persistent Jehovah's Witness," I said.

Looking through the window, I saw the man and, trailing from the porch down the walkway to the street, what looked like an entire wedding party outside a big rental bus at the curb. Sometimes the armory across the street is rented for receptions, but I couldn't imagine why all these people were here. So I wiped my hands on my apron and opened the door.

A handsome man with an Italian accent said, "Excuse me. My daughter is getting married today. My wife and I were married here thirty-five years ago, when her parents owned the house."

A pretty blond woman stepped beside him and said, "I'm his wife. My parents owned this house."

"You're a Shepard," I said.

"Yes! I'm Annie," she said. "Our daughter is getting married today and we wanted pictures on your porch for my mom. She's ninety-two. But we thought we'd better ask before you called the police." The Shepards last owned the house in the 2000s, three owners ago.

"Get in here," I said. Buffalo is known as the City of Good Neighbors. One doesn't need to know someone to invite them in unannounced—you only need to recognize their name.

Suddenly the house was full of people and happy noise: the bride and groom, their parents, the wedding party, the ring bearers and flower girl, the photographer and his assistant. We talked and laughed while pictures were taken on the porch, on the staircase, and in the front parlor, with bride and groom posing in front of the floor-to-ceiling mirror. These were not my people, but they belonged in the house based on history.

"Four more daughters," I said to Annie as the crowd left. "As long as I'm living here, you're welcome to do this again."

The interruption had come to feel like a sweet adventure. I was witness to a joyful milestone event that came out of the blue, a serendipitous first meeting to remember. I conceded when asked to pose with the group, but took my apron off first.

The photo acts as proof that this really happened, and I was there. The pop-up wedding party became the topic of that night's dinner party.

Annie visited about a month later. She thanked me again and brought espresso cups, pasta, flavored olive oil, and prints of the pictures. The photographer had done justice to the bridal party and house alike. The bride and groom looked beautiful on the curved staircase, as did the other daughters, lined up at the porch railing in their purple satin dresses.

Two of the pictures she showed me were taken in front of the parlor mirror. One, a color shot, was of the newlyweds on the day she first knocked on the door. The other, from thirty-five years earlier, was black and white and showed Annie Shepard wearing her wedding-day smile, encircled by her new husband's arms in front of the same mirror.

Because the house is large and imposing, visitors frequently ask me if I think I have ghosts. I answer that I believe the house itself has/is a spirit. They also ask why I would live in such a big house alone. My mother, at ninety, still has her big house, and a few times a year, some or all of us five siblings and our offspring fill it. Extra space makes sense at times like that.

Sometimes now, friends come by with guitars and we sing nights away under twelve-foot ceilings that throw our music back at us, surrounding us with good acoustic reverberation. At times like that, I think of the house as my unending season ticket to entertainment.

To my thinking, nothing stands long without absorbing the energy of those who touch it. That goes for houses, too. They absorb a bit of those who call them home. Of all the magnificent architectural backdrops in the City of Buffalo, the Shepards were called back here—to share their special day with what is now my house and to have it stand proud and majestic in the background of every photo.

The visit was so sublime that if I didn't have the photos and the espresso cups Annie left, I would think I had dreamed it.

**Elena Cala** is the former editor of *Buffalo Rising* and now works for the Buffalo Public Schools. She grew up in Jamestown and attended the University at Buffalo when it was still called the University of Buffalo. She graduated from Buffalo State College with degrees in art and journalism. She lives on the West Side.

Details from a continuous drawing of the East side of Main St. The whole accordian-folded drawing begins at Coe Place and travels south to North St. and the University at Buffalo Medical Campus.

Joan Linder, "Main Street," 2013, ink on paper, 6 x 324 inches.

83

# Power Lines

## Scott Reimann

My wife, Kelly, and I begin at the end of Jewett Parkway by turning our backs to the lush, expansive tracts of fairways, ball diamonds, and soccer fields that cover Frederick Law Olmsted's Delaware Park and take the Parkway's sidewalk past the zoo, heading east towards where Kelly recovered the best version of herself and where, perhaps, we as a city could find a better version of ourselves.

We walk into the drafts of speeding cars that turn our clothes into taut flags as we cross Parkside Avenue. Here, Jewett Parkway is lined with florid colonial and Tudor revivals. Other houses, eschewing elegance for muscularity, are made of brick. Some are neatly capped with warm, red, terra cotta tiles, others with Earl Grey slate. At more than two-and-a-half stories, with steeply-peaked roofs to discourage winter's snows from gaining purchase, these houses stick out their chins and puff out their chests.

The depth and scope of the trees, shrubs, and flowers could provide botanists with semesters of field experience. Towering swamp white and pin oaks, silver and sugar maples, beeches and blue spruces, Japanese maples, and ginkos compete with the architecture for our attention. We feel like we haven't left the park. The trees, unrestrained, grow to their full beauty and humble us with their majesty. Their thick, leafy boughs provide canopy and comfort. They—like the houses—encourage us to slacken our pace, to admire and feel proud that our city is so idyllic, so right.

A couple blocks' walk from the park, further up Jewett Parkway, before we reach Summit Avenue, stands a house so incongruous with its surroundings it demands attention. With its long, thin Roman bricks, banks of horizontal windows, and auburn-shingled, nearly flat roofs, the Darwin D. Martin House complex stands before us. Some argue it is the most architecturally significant house in the state. Majestic when it was built from 1903-1909, the house spent decades as an empty, leaking reminder of Buffalo's lost turn-of-the-century wealth. In the 1990s, preservation advocates took note and began campaigning to have it renovated. They succeeded. The price tag is largely accepted at $50 million. It seems like a lot of money, particularly for a city where 47 percent of children are growing up in poverty. But, the visitors and tourists the house will attract will make the money back, will make Buffalo a destination. So advocates say. Jack Quinan's *Frank Lloyd Wright's Martin House: Architecture as Portraiture* can tell you about this remarkable house and its history.

What we're seeking we can't find here.

As we cross over Summit, the Richardsonian Romanesque Church of the Good Shepherd—a charming neighborhood church—greets us. Its scale is appropriate to the dignity of the neighborhood. Its radiantly detailed Tiffany windows serve as a counterpoise to the austere, gray stone exterior.

As we keep walking east past Crescent Avenue, we notice folks sipping drinks on their porches and others who push mowers over their lush front and side lawns. We also notice a steady but infrequent parade of men and women of color walking westward, some handling basketballs and headed for the park. They come from where we're going.

The drink sippers and lawn mowers notice them, too. Some of these young men and women are walking or bobbing their heads to rhythms unheard by us. These two groups don't speak to each other, although they are neighbors. I wish they would. If they did they would know more about each other and our city could be less broken.

I've thought about brokenness a lot over the past five years as Kelly and I have walked the city's streets as she has recovered. On this street we've measured healing in distances—mailboxes reached, cross streets conquered. I remember how in the spring of 2011, Kelly gripped my arm and clung to me as we shifted along these sidewalks. She was fighting to recover from acute disseminated encephalomyelitis (ADEM), an auto-immune illness in which the myelin, or nerve insulation, in the brain and spinal cord is damaged.

The illness began in late winter 2011 and caused Kelly to temporarily lose her hearing, sight, and balance. Kelly, who was twenty-nine, lost her sense of self and her ability to trust herself. For weeks, she woke up wondering which part of herself would fail next. The disease actively attacked Kelly's nervous system for three months. Then, for the next six months she worked to recover. We ambled along these sidewalks searching for signs of recovery—balance, stamina, any façade of normalcy.

At first, from 22 Jewett Parkway—our former apartment—we could only shuffle along a few houses; Kelly's slippers sounded like sandpaper against the concrete. That's all she could manage before becoming too tired. We hoped short walks would build her resilience for longer ones, so we kept to the nearer passages of Jewett, Crescent, and Oakwood. As Kelly gained trust and confidence, our walks took us to Woodward, Russell, Greenfield, and eventually the blacktopped spine of the city—Main Street.

We walked straight into summer as Kelly regained her hearing, sight, and balance. When our walks increased in frequency and distance, her steps became more assured and her grasp less desperate. Today, she is hearing, seeing, and walking much like she did prior to her ADEM illness. Now, our ghosts perambulate these sidewalks; the trees' rustling reminds us of our vulnerability.

On today's walk Kelly and I cross Main Street. Here, Jewett Parkway changes names to become Jewett Avenue. Kelly and I noticed this curious shift during our recovery walks. The slowness of our pace gave us time to think, talk, and wonder about the sort of details we overlook in our daily hustle and the implications those details have for the people of these streets. The street still leads to the park, we reasoned as we walked. It's still a parkway. So why was the name changed? In what ways has this name change affected the relationships of the people who live on opposite sides of Main Street?

Today that's not the only change we notice. As we continue to walk eastward on Jewett Avenue, the street narrows so much that parking a car against the curb obstructs traffic. Ahead on the left looms the five-story, former Ford factory, now the Tri-Main warehouse, ribboned with alternating rows of red brick and industrial glass. We've hit an industrial area.

After we cross railroad tracks and Halbert Street, we reconnect with residential elements—ones conspicuously different from those we left behind. These houses encroach the street. The lots are narrower and more numerous. With the roofs lacking steep pitches, the houses slouch. As we approach Fillmore Avenue, houses have vanished from lots. We see the approaches cut from the street; we see the beginning of driveways leading to grassy lots and wonder about the families who lived here, the lives they led. The young men and women we passed on the Parkway heading to the park are from this neighborhood. Every day they pass these empty lots. Some of them are part of the 47 percent growing up in poverty. They walk through the more affluent neighboring area to reach the basketball courts. Yet they don't talk to the people in the yards and the people in the yards don't talk to them. If we could find a way to strike up spontaneous conversations, maybe we could build better, more cohesive communities, instead of disparate islands separated by our streets and our suspicions.

We cross Fillmore and continue east on Jewett Avenue. On this stretch of the street, the cracked wood, chipped paint, and loose shingles of the tight doubles hint at lives more hardscrabble than those of the inhabitants of the doll houses of the Parkway. Some homes have plywood nailed across their windows and doors. Others have had the plywood breached. "No Gas" is spray-painted in hasty scrawl on one home's plywood coverings. The siding of these houses are covered in a type of gritty tar paper trying to evoke stately brick.

On our right, two abutting lots are empty and we see through to Leroy Avenue. Kelly and I wonder about the houses that used to stand here and about the lives lived inside of them. What forces caused these lives to be so different from those of the Parkway less than three blocks behind us? Why do the lives lived here seem worlds apart from the drink sippers and lawn mowers of the Parkway?

We continue and Kelly stumbles over the cracked, uneven sidewalks. Unlike the smooth, unbroken sidewalks of the Parkway, here every block is a new challenge. We gird ourselves against the next unstable step. The sidewalks are patched with blacktop. The effect is rumbling mounds, unsure footing, and a reminder of Kelly's struggles and the neighborhood's disjointed past.

We keep walking and notice the addresses tick up rather than tick down like they do on the Parkway. The address system has changed. Starting at Main Street the addresses run away from each other in opposite directions. How did that come to be? Who made that decision? What were the motivations?

The trees lining the street are nearly all lindens. Along the south side their branches have been hacked off and disfigured to make way for the power lines. Wooden power poles line the street. The few houses on the north side have power and cable lines strung across and above the street. There are no such lines on the Parkway. There, power poles and black ropes don't crisscross above; they are camouflaged along the rear and the expansive trees are unencumbered.

After we pass 216 Jewett Avenue—a white and red double—stretches of thick grass run for a few contiguous lots. For half a block and all the way to the next cross street, Holden Avenue, only a single house interrupts the field. At the corner of Holden, the north side of Jewett mirrors the south's grass-covered yards. We wonder what happened here. What got erased? Where are the houses and the people who lived in them?

As we continue, the cut-throughs become more frequent. We see narrow houses adjacent to strings of empty lots. It's discordant. The song of the street has had its notes removed. The harmony gets picked up in a couple of houses, but then is lost. Kelly and I have pondered how our neighborhoods could be more tightly knit together.

The empty spaces on Jewett and Leroy give us a view of the cross atop Blessed Trinity Church's polygonal tower.

We keep walking east to where Jewett Avenue ends at Hill Street. Heading south we take Hill toward Leroy. We enter Blessed Trinity Church, walk past the symmetry of lacquered pews, and find the array of candles. After filling the box, we put flame to wick, consider our own story, the story of the Parkway and the Avenue, and hope for a better version of ourselves.

**Scott Reimann** has lived in and around Buffalo most of his life. He received a bachelor's in English from John Carroll University, a master's in English from Stony Brook University, and an advanced certification in English education from the University at Buffalo. Presently, he is an English instructor with Bryant & Stratton College. He is one of the founding members of the Western New York Network of English Teachers (WNYNET). He lives with his wife and daughter in University Heights.

# Tailgating at the Gates of Hell

## Justin Karcher

After swapping spit and getting cozy with a strung out snowman,
I'm in the bathroom and see a suicide note written in barbecue sauce on the
mirror:
"You're killing me climate change with all this cold and snow. After the plows
Got through, nothing left of me but a bag of bones and credit card bills."
Even when the truth stares me in the face, I'm still in denial.
I find some baby wipes in the medicine cabinet
And try to make the mirror gleam, a desperate bid to swallow the stuff
Nobody else cares about.

Then there it is: my reflection, plucked out of the grayness of limbo.
A man-child wearing a red devil mask and an old Bills jersey
With hands the size of Homeland Security. I'm shaking like slow thunder.
I want to grab life by the horns. Suddenly the bathroom feels like a cocoon
And my old body parts undergo a mint julep metamorphosis
So I exit the bathroom and make my way to the living room.

The house party's still in full swing. Unemployed hipsters bobbing
For dead starfish in large buckets of ice water. They're hoping to regenerate
Their missing parts. This one bedroom is crammed to the ceiling
With greasy auto parts. Two of my exes are making love on a bed
Of senile carburetors and bitter spark plugs. Fireworks are flying
Off the pillows, the force of the blasts knocking my heart off its feet
And it's like I'm stranded on a small life raft in sex-infested waters.
Eventually I'm rescued by addiction and find peace outside smoking with
strangers.

In the secondhand moonlight, it feels like we're all headlong out of orbit,
Like a planet, toward some terrible cataclysm. I truly enjoy the camaraderie
Of people slowly killing themselves. People from Buffalo are strange
And intimate creatures, grinding their bodies against each other
While tailgating at the gates of hell, hooting and hollering and cheering,
Drinking cheap Canadian beer and maybe some strong drink and persevering,
Like pint-size fish that refuse to be swallowed up by a whale or the heavens.

**Justin Karcher** is a poet and playwright. Recent works have appeared in *The Pickled Body*, *3:AM Magazine*, *Plenitude Magazine*, and more. He is the winner of the 2015 Just Buffalo Literary Center members' writing competition and has been nominated for Best Writer and Best Poet in *Artvoice Best of Buffalo* the past five years. He lives on Buffalo's West Side.

# When the Prize is Meat
## A Look at the People and Inner Workings of a Meat Raffle in WNY

## David J. Hill

You truly have not lived until you've seen a grown man triumphantly hoist a pork shoulder over his head as if it were the Stanley Cup.

It's actually a scene that plays out in church, VFW, and fire halls across Western New York nearly every weekend at something called a meat raffle. Attending one of these fundraisers is quite possibly the most quintessentially Buffalo thing you can do. Western New Yorkers love their meat, and these raffles prove it.

I experienced a hearty helping of meat raffles—and the colorful characters who often attend them—while writing a magazine article on them in 2013.

The idea arose from a conversation I had with a friend I hadn't seen in some time. We were catching up and I asked what he'd done the previous weekend. When he said he attended a meat raffle and that it was the greatest thing he'd ever been to, my jaw dropped. I didn't know how to respond, other than to repeat, "a meat raffle?!" The phrase alone piqued my interest. I had to know more. I started asking friends and co-workers about them with mixed results. Some hadn't heard of them at all; others said they went all the time.

I came across a website—wnymeatraffles.com—that compiles listings of upcoming meat raffles and picked a few across the region, from Depew to North Tonawanda. I interviewed attendees and observed the general goings on at seven or eight meat raffles. I felt like I had collected enough insight and material for my story, but I was struggling with the intro. I decided to go to one more, the AMVETS Post 72 Fall Meat Raffle in Lackawanna on a chilly November night in 2013. There were more than 300 people sitting around round or rectangular tables, eating snacks and unfurling wads of dollar bills.

I arrived about twenty minutes early and scouted out a few tables before one caught my attention. Several middle-aged men and women, all clearly friends, were laughing and enjoying themselves. At 7:00 p.m., just before the event was to begin with the first spin of the wheel, the group I was observing raised their plastic cups of draft beer in unison and said cheers.

Linda Kreutzer, an East Aurora resident attending her first meat raffle, shouted, "I want some meat! Mama needs some meat!" The prospect of spending a few bucks to go home a couple pork loins richer transformed

Kreutzer into her carniverous-crazed alter ego.

Similar to bingo and bowling leagues, meat raffles have been a part of Western New York's social landscape for decades. But unlike those first two, meat raffles have been exploding in popularity in recent years.

You can find at least a couple happening just about every weekend throughout the year, but the peak seasons are right before Thanksgiving and Easter. That's when you'll find multiple meat raffles occurring Friday, Saturday, and Sunday.

There's a reason they've become so prevalent.

Most charge $2 to $5 admission and include a door-prize ticket and all the draft beer, pop, and snacks you can consume. Participants are encouraged to bring their own food and snacks. I've seen people show up with whole pizzas, meat and cheese trays—you name it. And with more than a thousand pounds of meat up for grabs, the odds of winning are pretty good.

"Where else can you go for $5 to eat and drink all you want?" said Fred Schmitt, who emceed the Polish Falcons October meat raffle in Depew in 2013, which drew about 300 participants.

**"Beats sitting in the recliner."**

Meat raffles raise money—often $5,000 or more—for a wide range of organizations, from youth sports teams to charitable foundations. They're particularly popular in Minnesota, where they tend to take place in bars, and even in England.

Hams, steaks, pork tenderloin, shrimp, turkeys, and breaded chicken breasts are the most commonly raffled items, but I've seen organizations mix it up with bacon, or even non-meat items; the first prize I ever won was an autographed print of Buffalo Bills defensive tackle Marcell Dareus. It cost me $2.

The meats generally come from local suppliers and are either donated or purchased at a discount.

Doors usually open at 6:00 p.m. and the first spin is at 7:00 p.m. If you don't have a presale ticket, arriving early is a must. In winter 2015, I tried taking a few friends to their first meat raffle, only to be denied entry—all the tickets were sold presale and there wasn't any more room to safely fit tables and chairs in the place.

All it takes is one and you're hooked.

Meat raffles are great for people watching. "It's a nice night out. It's better than sitting at home in the recliner," Joanne Trzewieczynski, of the Town of Tonawanda, told me at a raffle in Depew.

Once the meat-crazed masses take their seats and the clock strikes 7:00 p.m., the action begins. Before each round, the emcee announces the prize, or prizes, that will be raffled off. Volunteers then fan out across the room, selling tickets for $1, $2, or sometimes $5 apiece, depending on the number of items to be raffled. Each ticket has three numbers on it, giving you three chances to win per round.

When the wheel's about to be spun, you'll see people doing drum rolls on the table, or hooting and hollering in excitement. I've even seen people pass around a package of freshly-won sausage to rub for good luck.

You're also bound to see some engineering ingenuity.

Sam Steinmetz, a bow hunter, and his wife, Sheri, used old arrows with clothespins affixed at one end to hoist dollar bills in the air to catch the attention of volunteers selling tickets. They told me they attend six to eight raffles a year, and usually fare well. "We still have meat in our freezer from last year," Sam said after Sheri collected her winnings, a Smith's ham, pork loin and a package of hot dogs. (Pro tip: bring a cooler to store your haul.)

"Some of them win three pounds of Sahlen's hot dogs and you'd think they won a million dollars," Schmitt, who emceed the Polish Falcons' raffle I attended in 2013, told me.

## Master of meat

Arguably no one knows more about meat raffles in Western New York than Mark Demmin. The Lackawanna resident who works in sales full-time has been coordinating the benefits for organizations across the region since 2010, when he took over for the late Dick O'Donnell, a legend who spent nearly three decades orchestrating raffles for the South Buffalo Lions Club before offering his services to other groups. When O'Donnell, who died in 2011, fell ill, he asked Demmin to carry on the tradition.

For Demmin, meat raffles are a family affair. His wife, Heather, their children, and O'Donnell's daughter, Linda Voit of West Seneca, help. Organizations "hire" the team, but Demmin says that after supplies and travel, he's not making much. The joy is in doing good for the community.

In 2013, Demmin's team coordinated twenty-seven raffles for more than a dozen different organizations, raising over $120,000. "That's why I do it," he proudly told me.

Demmin orders his meat from Will Poultry and picks it up the morning of the raffle. For the AMVETS 72 event in November 2013, he ordered more than 1,500 pounds of meat, including 900 of turkey and 210 of chicken breast. He arrives an hour and a half before the first spin to set everything up, including the custom-made 240-number wheel he got from O'Donnell; most wheels have either sixty or 120 numbers.

Voit, who coordinates the ticket runners, says she's happy to continue her father's work. "Every time I come to one, it makes me feel closer to my dad," she says. "That was his legacy. Mark and his family have come to be very, very good friends of mine."

Although my assignment ended several years ago, I've continued attending meat raffles. And every time I explain to friends what these events are like, I end up bringing more people with me.

Mark's meat raffles are the only ones I'll go to, because they're so well run—and I've had the most luck at his. Eight friends joined me for one over the winter. None of us left empty-handed. In fact, a few needed extra hands to help carry out our winnings.

Mine included a three-pound Smith's ham. I was so overcome with joy when I won it that I damn near Gronk'd the thing.

It brought me back to that very first raffle I went to three years earlier, seeing a pot-bellied middle-aged bald man lift the pork shoulder he just won over his head in triumph.

At the time, I thought the guy was either really crazy, or really drunk. But now I know exactly what he was feeling: the joy of meat.

**David J. Hill** is a news content manager in the Division of University Communications at the University at Buffalo. A graduate of Canisius College and a lifelong Western New Yorker, he's lived in Buffalo's Elmwood Village for the past ten years. He loves, in no particular order, tacos and summer and fall. His original article about meat raffles appeared in *Buffalo Spree*.

# Protests at Buffalo State College

## Stan Searl

On May 7, 1970,
stranded in a phone booth on Elmwood Avenue
between Rockwell Hall and the Albright-Knox Art Gallery,
I fought to breathe
after the tear-gas attack by the Buffalo Police,
called into action by President Fretwell
to stem the civil unrest.

I walked arm-in-arm with my fellow students and faculty,
striding out together,
calling on President Nixon
to stop the invasion of Cambodia,
imagining how we would encircle Rockwell Hall
as if we could levitate this administration building
by pouring out young hearts, mystically powerful.

As I stood there in the phone booth,
the tear-gas swirled around and
the booth vibrated from windy puffs
to blow the thickening gas clouds
back towards the police lines
while the gusty winds clarified the air and
I drifted into another kind of seeing,
transparent, open to mystery and the past,
hallucinating like entering into
the electric brightness of another May day
from the Pan-American Exposition of 1901.

I walked into the midst of Lombardy poplars
and enormous Cedars,
surrounded by thousands of pulsating electric lights,
flowing into the Exposition
from a newly constructed power plant at Niagara Falls,
illuminating the entire southern edge of Delaware Park,
open to an electric frequency,

these thousands of bulbs churning
powerfully as if Niagara Falls itself
offered a hidden illumination,
illustrating the power of saying no
together to the Vietnam War and
yes to the power of love,
now blossoming
from this intense array of new power
from mighty Niagara Falls,
telling me that
it's ok to teach from the soul—
to demonstrate who you really are and
follow the alternating currents,
be willing to be led
into dreams with my students ...
but then things blurred
as the tear gas had
drifted over again and
seeped into the phone booth and
made it impossible for me
to see or remember anything else.

**Stan Searl** lives in Culver City, California and for many years taught as a core faculty member at Union Institute and University, a self-directed, inter-disciplinary doctoral program. In 2014, he published *Quaker Poems: The Heart Opened,* and in 2016, Foothills Publishing will bring out *Homage to the Lady with the Dirty Feet and other Vermont Poems.* He has two books of poetry under development, including *Poems of Love and Work in Buffalo,* and a chapbook, *North Fork Poems.*

# The Rise and Fall of the Buffalo Mafia

## Lee Coppola

When it comes to the Mafia, Buffalo and the Niagara Frontier have a long and storied history. Much of it revolves around a single person, Stefano Magaddino, who for more than sixty years ruled a criminal empire that stretched from Pennsylvania through Western New York to Ohio and into Canada.

But the birth of the Mafia in Buffalo preceded Magaddino's arrival in the region by almost fifteen years. The roots were formed at the turn of the century as immigrants from Sicily and southern Italy crossed the ocean for a better life. Some of them were immersed in the criminal practices of the Mafia, which actually was created centuries earlier to protect Sicilians from invading forces.

At first the criminal-minded immigrants were a loose band of hoodlums using the threatening name "Black Hand." That changed when Guiseppe DiCarlo, skilled in the ways of the Mafia from his native Villalunga, Sicily, moved to Buffalo from Manhattan in 1908. DiCarlo organized the gangsters and created a criminal "family" that lasted for more than eight decades.

Magaddino entered the picture in the early 1920s, when he moved to Niagara Falls from New York to escape the city's Mafia warfare. It was the height of Prohibition, and he used his organizational skills and business-like demeanor, coupled with his Mafia upbringing in Sicily, to create an enterprise that made untold millions by illegally providing the public what it could not get legally.

After all, Western New York was a mere stone's throw from Canada, where alcohol was legal, mapping a path for smuggled goods through the region to the eastern seaboard. And along with the liquor came underground nightclubs dubbed "speakeasies" and illegal gambling on cards, dice, and horse races, all run by or with approval from Magaddino's criminal network.

One 1950s police report during Magaddino's reign indicated his weekly cut from an illegal, high-stakes card game was $25,000.

Magaddino's empire grew so powerful that it was one of the twenty-six criminal families across the nation summoned by famed mobster Lucky Luciano to New York to form what later became known as La Cosa Nostra. The national criminal organization was spawned after Prohibition ended, sparking Mafia wars over what territories and what activities various families could control. Luciano's commission ended the warfare and divided New York City into five Mafia families and recognized controlling families throughout the United States.

More than twenty years later, Magaddino ascended to the throne Luciano created, becoming the "capo tutti di capi," the boss of all bosses. But by the time he died at eighty-two of a heart attack in 1974, his empire was but a shell of what it had been.

Following the end of Prohibition, the Buffalo Mafia, like other families in the Cosa Nostra, had to find new ways to make money. Gambling was a continued revenue source for the Buffalo family. Magaddino's men ran illegal card and dice games, took bets on horse races and other sports, and loaned money at exorbitant interest rates to gamblers and others.

The family, which went by the nickname "the Arm," also found another revenue stream—labor racketeering. Its hierarchy formed Buffalo Laborers Local 210, giving "the Arm" a legitimate entry into the construction industry. The men who ran Local 210 reflected the power structure of the Buffalo family.

Many members of the union were hard-working laborers, but others connected to the higher-ups were given no-show jobs forced on builders by the union. For tax purposes, that gave them legitimate income while freeing them to carry on the mob's business.

Magaddino ran his empire first from Niagara Falls, where he operated a funeral home, and then from Lewiston, where he lived in a simple ranch house on a street with similar houses occupied by his adult children and their families.

He kept a low profile, preferring to send emissaries such as his brother, Antonino, to pass on his orders. When necessary to discuss mob business, he convened his top lieutenants at the Como Restaurant on Pine Avenue in Niagara Falls or at Andy's Café on Lower Terrace in Buffalo.

One of his underbosses, John Montana, owned the largest taxicab company in Western New York and was a Buffalo community leader who was a city councilman and ran unsuccessfully for Congress. His connection to the underworld was revealed in 1957 when he was caught at the infamous meeting of mob bosses in Apalachin, New York.

During the height of his empire, Magaddino, according to sources, ruled a Mafia army of ten to fifteen high-echelon leaders and up to 200 soldiers spread throughout three states and Canada.

Magaddino's family thrived for several reasons, primary among them the public's insatiable appetite, first for alcohol during Prohibition, then later for gambling, and then the illegitimate gains from labor racketeering. It also thrived because federal law enforcement officials refused to recognize the existence of an organized criminal network while local authorities often looked the other way at illegal gambling or were handicapped by lack of evidence when trying to solve the gangland murders that erupted during power struggles in the family.

Those marked for death were often gunned down in daylight or their bodies left in fields as examples of what happened for choosing the wrong faction in a power struggle. John Cammilleri, for instance, was shot to death in 1974 on his sixty-third birthday outside Roseland's, a popular Italian West Side resident. He purportedly was angling for more power in Laborers Local 210.

William (Billy the Kid) Sciolino was forty-three in 1980 when he was killed by two gunmen inside a trailer on the city's rapid transit construction site. He was suspected of being an FBI informant.

"The Arm's" first major clash with law enforcement helped spawn what today is known as the Witness Security Program. It happened because an underling mafioso, Pasquale Calabrese, held up at gunpoint the treasurer's office in Buffalo's City Hall in 1964. Outraged officials pressured mob bosses to force Calabrese to surrender.

He did, but when the mob failed to take care of his family, as promised, he agreed to testify against his bosses about a Los Angeles jewelry heist he was assigned as long as he and his family were relocated and given new identities. His testimony sent the top echelon of the Buffalo Mafia to jail, some for up to twenty years.

No formal government program was in place when Calabrese was relocated. In fact, he and his family obtained their new names when a Buffalo police detective prevailed on his parish priest to issue them phony baptismal certificates. Still, what happened with Calabrese was a precursor for the government's program to protect witnesses. It was also a significant dent in the Mafia's code of silence, or "omerta," an element of the criminal organization that helped sustain it for centuries.

The crumbling of Magaddino's empire started in 1968 when federal agents searching his son's house found nearly $500,000 in the attic after Magaddino had complained to underlings he had no money to pay them. No longer did his lieutenants in the widespread area he controlled pay tribute or respect to him.

Other forces also came into to play to help sound the death knell for the Magaddino family. State lotteries and off-track betting took away profitable mob enterprises. Casino gambling was introduced, eliminating another revenue source.

Then, finally, federal legislators took notice, and in 1979 passed the Racketeer Influenced Corrupt Organization Act, RICO. It provided stiff sentences against Mafia family members and allowed federal prosecutors to obtain convictions by reaching deep into a defendant's criminal history.

Faced with lengthy prison sentences, family members, many in the upper echelons of their organizations, abandoned the Mafia's code of silence to testify against their cohorts.

The last bastion of Buffalo's Mafia collapsed in 1995 when the federal government took control of Laborers Local 210 after the national laborers organization admitted the local had been influenced for decades by organized crime.

Today, the Buffalo Mafia family, like the national La Cosa Nostra syndicate, no longer exists. It withered when the Mafia's staples of loyalty to the family, silence, and fear, diminished as revenue sources dried up and law enforcement officials took action.

(Author's note: I've been often asked how I came to cover the Mafia during my twenty-five-year career as a journalist. As the grandson of Sicilian immigrants, I was raised on Buffalo's West Side and listened to stories as I grew up about speakeasies, "bathtub gun," bookmaking, and numbers racketeering. Some of my childhood friends took a different direction in life than I did so I was familiar with the names as I did my reporting. And others proved valuable sources when I sought to find out what was happening in "the Arm.")

**Lee Coppola** attended Holy Angels Grammar School, Bishop Fallon High School, and graduated in 1964 with a journalism degree from St. Bonaventure University and from the State University at Buffalo Law School in 1983. He worked for the *Buffalo Evening News* for sixteen years and was a television investigative reporter for nine years before being appointed an assistant United States Attorney in 1992. In 1996 he was named dean of St. Bonaventure's journalism school and retired in 2011. He lives in Hamburg with his wife, also named Lee.

# Neighborhood Stories

# From Buffalo to Washington and the Piano Lessons that Paid Off

## Marcus Joseph Ruslander, Jr. AKA Mark Russell

When my parents and my brother and I set out from Buffalo and headed to Washington D.C., in 1950, there was no Canalside, Solar City, or restaurants featuring tilapia avec morels on a bed of Swiss chard. There was Skid Row, Lackawanna Steel, and the Catholic obligation of fried perch on Fridays. For a teenaged future political satirist to move to our nation's capital made good sense, but I didn't know it at the time.

We moved to Washington because my parents heard that it never had a depression. Congress saw to that—even mandating that D.C. would have the cheapest retail liquor prices in the country. As the great Irish comedian Hal Roach put it, "We drank to forget we were alcoholics." And as it has turned out, my heart is in Washington, but my soul is in Buffalo.

We have all had to suffer the inane comment when we tell people where we are from: "Lotta snow, heh, heh." When people meet people from Venice, do they say, "Lotta water?" When people meet people from Washington, do they say, "Lotta bullshit?" Well, yes, actually. How about a sign at the airport: "Welcome to Buffalo—where the weather keeps out the riff raff." However, I must confess to laughing at a *New Yorker* cartoon a few years ago in which a priest at a funeral is looking down at the casket and saying, "He has gone to a better place. No offense to Buffalo."

Here are random thoughts that flow through my once Iroquois-beer-soaked brain as I drive around my native city. Canisius High School—the stately edifice was originally a Masonic temple. Before the Jesuits moved into the place, my father would tell people, they had it hosed down with 10,000 gallons of holy water. Adjacent to the school was the Milburn House. Its namesake was president of the Pan American Exposition, where President William McKinley was assassinated in 1901. McKinley was taken to the Milburn mansion, where he died. By the 1940s and through the 1950s, it was the rectory for the priests on the Canisius faculty. I could look out of my classroom window and see the beer truck pull up behind the mansion every morning to drop off three or four cases of Iroquois. A few minutes later, the milkman showed up and left a bottle of cream. The good fathers had a cat. I was bored in school, and the Milburn House is a parking lot now.

Moving north on Delaware Avenue, we come to Delavan. On that corner once stood a Mobil station where my father pumped gas at the time I was born. He made $15 a week, not bad for 1932. Next door was Meyers Tavern, a regular recipient of a portion of that $15. As high school kids, my buddies and I frequented the joint illegally. Later, I once took my ten-year-old daughter there for a Shirley Temple on the rocks—just to continue the family line of succession. The saloon has had a few different names since then. Last I saw it, in 2015, it was boarded up and seemed slightly haunted. The Mobil station is long gone, replaced by one of those generic self-serves, but it too, looked to be shuttered. Alas, the last time I looked, Delaware and Delavan was a total eyesore.

Continuing up Delaware, we come to Bird Avenue. Two houses to the left lived the popular Buffalo orchestra leader and piano teacher Irving Shire. His son, David Shire, went on to compose movie scores, including those for *All the President's Men* and *Norma Rae*. I was Irving Shire's worst pupil, but you can accomplish a lot with three chords and a little help from the politicians.

Going downtown in the late 1940s, we could have popped into the Vars building, at Delaware and Tupper, for a twenty-five-cent sandwich at my mother's snack bar in the lobby. A few years earlier, she'd been in the legion of Rosie the Riveters at Bell Aircraft, in Tonawanda, where she worked on the tail section of the P-39 Airacobra fighter plane. President Roosevelt never thanked her.

And while we are downtown, may we have a moment of silence for the dear departed "Shelton Square Opera House"? Also known as the Palace Burlesque Theatre, it represented a popular occasion of sin for generations of connoisseurs of the stately art of the ecdysiasts. I snuck into the Palace a few times, but of course only to see the comedians.

I recall the Town Casino, a spacious Vegas-style nightclub where I once saw the Duke Ellington band. With my parents. On a school night. (My education took many forms.) Shea's Buffalo, where I would stand at the stage door to get autographs. Kleinhan's Music Hall and a concert by Miss Ella Fitzgerald. My love of jazz would preempt homework for the Sunday afternoon jam sessions at the African American musicians' union hall, which may have had something to do with my maintaining a solid C- average. A place on Hertel was called the Everglades and featured the great Jackie Jocko.

Then there is the Father Baker Bridge, named after the legendary Reverend Nelson Baker, a beloved man who built a basilica and established an orphanage, among many other charitable deeds. I mention him because for years there has been a movement afoot in Buffalo to get him canonized as a saint. I imagine that one of the required miracles would be for the potholes on the bridge to heal themselves.

Let me close with a final bit of Buffalo and personal family lore. In the late 1800s, my great-grandfather, Abraham Samuel Ruslander, emigrated from Russia, eventually establishing Ruslander & Sons, which existed for more than 100 years. The company manufactured commercial kitchen and hospital equipment, including items for use in morgues. Today, the exact spot where Ruslander & Sons once stood is the site of WNED-TV, creator and producer of my public-television shows, "The Mark Russell Comedy Specials," which ran for thirty years.

So to WNED, thank you for a career, and to Buffalo, thanks for the memories.

And what better background for a comedian than cadaver trays?

**Mark Russell** left Buffalo in 1950 as an eighteen-year-old. Prior to that he led the Mark Ruslander Orchestra, consisting of four members. He returned to Buffalo in 1974 to tape the pilot of what became "The Mark Russell Comedy Specials" that were broadcast live from WNED in Buffalo from 1975 until 2004. He has also written both the lyrics and music for "Teddy Roosevelt and the Treasure of Ursa Major" and "Teddy Roosevelt and the Ghostly Mistletoe," which both had their premieres at the John F. Kennedy Center for the Performing Arts in Washington, D.C.

# North Park, With and Without Hate

## Jeff Z. Klein

Walk down Hertel Avenue and see the mix of cultures: hipster cafes and old Italian red-sauce restaurants and halal butchers and louche interior design stores and pubs where young Americans have decided they're huge Barça fans. Maybe even a rainbow flag here and there. Walk down the side streets. The houses are filled with young families, different cultures—middle class, not rich, not poor—fresh ground coffee, organic groceries, craft beer.

Funny, though—it still looks exactly the way it did half a century ago. All the two-story houses. The attics topped by the same triangular or square roofs. The little backyards. The narrow driveways just wide enough to accommodate a Model T (from another fifty years before, when the houses were built). The five- or six-stair stoops. The trees shading the street, almost as tall and domelike as the elms whose arching boughs formed vast, block-long ceilings, like a great green cathedral. Late at night the train horns, blaring distant and lonely from the raised embankments on either margin of the neighborhood.

The winter. Walking to school on the snow banks. Bombing cars with snowballs. Grabbing the rear bumper of some unsuspecting Dodge and po-geying down the snow-covered street.

*Jew.*

Buffalo, the United States, the world was different. Pinched. Small. Mean. North Park was made up entirely of white people—Catholics, Protestants, and a significant minority of Jews; no one else—and that made it just about the most diverse neighborhood in the city. There were two cuisines: regular food (meat and potatoes) and Italian food (spaghetti and pizza). We had a third, kosher. Separate sets of dishes and silverware, no mixing of milk and meat, no pork, no ham, no bacon.

That was one of the things that set them off.

*You've never had ham? You think you're too good for it, don't you.*

I had two best friends when I was a little boy, James M. and Freddie C. They were cool with me, but their brothers called me Hambone, in honor of the dietary habits of the Jews. Freddie was a couple years older than me. He and I would debate who was better, the Beatles or the Dave Clark Five. He loved the Beach Boys, and we both thought "Help Me, Rhonda" might be the best song ever. James was a good football player, touch or tackle. We followed the Bills closely. Jack Kemp or Daryle Lamonica? Against the

Boston Patriots, should they give the ball to Cookie Gilchrist on every play?

The other sport that mattered was baseball. James and his family liked the San Francisco Giants. My family and I liked the L.A. Dodgers. My father was from Brooklyn. My sister was born there. And I liked Sandy Koufax because he was the best pitcher in baseball and wouldn't play that World Series game on Yom Kippur. I had his baseball card. So James's older brother John is standing next to the stoop and asks if he can see my Sandy Koufax card. I hand it down to him. He takes it and rubs the face of it, hard, on the iron railing, up and down, several times. *Here*, he says, handing it back to me. Koufax's picture is still there, but it's got black streaks all over it.

The food especially seemed to get to them. The older C. and M. brothers simply could not get over their impression that keeping kosher meant Jews thought Catholic meat was inferior and couldn't be eaten. One day when my mother wasn't home, the M. brothers asked if they could come inside and get a snack out of the kitchen. I let them in and they descended on the fridge and cabinets like locusts, devouring all the Wise potato chips and Ritz crackers and Hershey bars they could find. But their real motivation was simply to see what the kitchen of Jews looked like.

*Not so different*, one of them said. *Where's the kosher stuff?*

I don't want this to sound like a bitter catalogue of slights from the musty scrapbook of my childhood. That's not my point. It's just that we've gotten into the habit of extolling the tight-knit ethnic enclaves of long ago, conveniently omitting one of their distinguishing characteristics—they could be snake pits of hatred. It didn't matter who the majority was, and it didn't matter who the Other was. The majority actively hated the Other. That's the way it was in most neighborhoods, in most cities. Yet, despite that, those neighborhoods could be wonderful. North Park—the old North Park, not the one now, which I like, but I'm talking about the old one—that North Park was a great place to be a kid.

But there was this one thing. It kept coming up.

Once I went over to Freddie's house down the block, the C. house. His two or three older brothers seemed surprised to see me.

*Hambone, what are you doing here?*

They stood around in the living room, ostentatiously discussing politics. *Hitler, he was bad. But he had some good ideas.* A look at me to gauge my reaction. These were fifteen-, seventeen-, twenty-year-olds talking in front of a nine-year-old. I think one of their parents told them to stop, but I might be making that part up. I do recall unmistakably their banter, their laughter, and how it went on long enough to make me uncomfortable. I knew full well what Hitler had done. It had happened only twenty years earlier.

My mother could sense the anti-Semitism in the air of our neighborhood, and she hated it. She'd grown up in Toronto when Toronto was the polar opposite of what it is today. When she was a girl, there'd been a riot, Gentiles vs. Jews, at the Christie Pits playing fields over the display of a swastika flag. At the beaches on the other side of town, some swim clubs flew swastikas to keep the Jews out. "No Jews need apply" signs at job sites were common. All that institutionalized anti-Semitism when she was growing up, and then the Nuremberg Laws and World War II and the camps. She had reason to suspect Jew-hatred everywhere she looked, but I scoffed—I thought what she experienced had gotten to her and made her obsessive. Many years later, we were watching TV together, and we saw a universally respected statesman disembark from a plane for a peace-keeping mission at some international trouble spot.

"Look at that anti-Semite," she said.

"What are you talking about?" I said dismissively. "That's the secretary general of the UN."

It was Kurt Waldheim. Later we learned he'd been an SS officer during the war. My mother was right; the old world was full of them.

She'd claim that things in our neighborhood got worse around Easter. I never noticed, but I do remember the only time in my childhood that I heard the phrase "You killed Christ." It came from one of James's older brothers on a spring day. I didn't understand. What?

*You killed Christ. Well, not you, but your people.*

I was completely baffled. I didn't know the story. I asked my mother.

"This is what they teach them in their churches," she said. She named the church down the block. "They teach this every Easter, and people like the C.'s and the M.'s come out and act worse than they usually do."

I asked my father too, but he just shrugged it off. He'd grown up in a place where all the ethnicities blended without incident, and he simply didn't care. He was an architect and an FDR Democrat through and through, and he never had a bad word to say about any group. (The last job he did was to convert an old East Side church building into a mosque, and that was after 9/11. He was friendly with the imam. I thought the whole thing was pretty remarkable. I wanted to write an article about it for a Buffalo magazine, and after much hemming and hawing the magazine editor got back to me. "Well, it's like this," the guy said. "A lot of people we talked to don't think what your father did is necessarily a good thing." Jerk.)

If you weren't around in the 1960s, you may not truly understand how pervasive this stuff was. People then didn't veil their prejudices—they were all out in the open, and nothing to be particularly embarrassed about. This was a time of ubiquitous Polack jokes, or, as sanitized on TV by famous comedians, "Polish jokes." No Asian immigration was allowed, so there simply were no Asians around, but there was plenty of talk about the Japs in World War II. And the N-word wasn't something you heard on TV, but it was pretty common in casual conversation. One of the older M. brothers spoke of a kid he knew who was a great football player. "He's a n--, but I tell you, I respect him," he said.

We grunted gravely in agreement, acknowledging how sincere and important an assertion this was. I tried saying the word a couple of times, but even back then it sounded foul; now I can't even type it, and you'd be mortified to see it in print. I can't remember the kid's name, but he came over once and played football with us. He was the only black kid who set foot in our neighborhood in the thirteen years I lived there.

One day when I was eleven or twelve, I went out our front door and heard a tremendous amount of yelling from the C. house. It seemed to be directed across the street, where a family of Hasidic Jews was moving in, although I didn't know the term at the time. They looked exotic. We and all the other Jews we knew were totally secular and assimilated—no yarmulkes, no outward sign of Jewishness. But these guys in their black suits and black hats, they stood out. Still, I couldn't figure out what was going on.

I walked over to the C.'s porch. The older C. and M. brothers were there, huddling behind the railings, yelling Get out! Get out! They'd spring up and throw small stones at the Hasids hauling chairs and couches into their new house, then duck down again behind the cover of the railing. I can't remember if James or Freddie was there. Maybe I don't want to. But I do remember, quite vividly, asking, "What are you doing? Why are you doing this?" One of the older brothers answered.

*Look at them. We don't want them living here.*

He seemed to forget that I was one of them too. He sprang up and threw another stone, and so did a couple of others. They yelled across the street. Get out, you Jews!

For many years I blamed myself for not saying anything at that moment, but now I understand that I responded within the boundaries of the behavior that had always worked for me: I simply left the porch and walked away. They kept screaming at the Hasids, who kept moving their furniture in without responding to the taunts or the stones, and they were still screaming as I stepped through my front door. But something in me had changed. I never talked to the C.'s or the M.'s again. Not even James or Freddie, even though I thought then, and still think now, that they never shared the hatred that their older brothers spewed.

The Hasidic family moved away just a month or two later, and after another year, so did we, to Eggertsville. Officially we could be counted as part of the white flight fleeing Buffalo, like all the whites leaving cities for the suburbs across late-'60s America. But in our case, that'd be misleading. We weren't fleeing black people, or poverty, or crime, or declining city services. We were fleeing the M.'s and the C.'s, to the northern suburbs, where the other Jews lived.

So the first week I'm at my new suburban junior high school, and a kid comes up to me and asks, "Are you Jewish?" Uh-oh, here we go, I think to myself.

"I am—does that affect anything?" I answer, challengingly. I think at this point I'm finally ready to fight.

But the kid was totally normal. "Oh no," he said. "I was just curious."

And that was it. From the moment we moved to Eggertsville, I never heard an anti-Jewish slur again. And in the five decades since, living in Manhattan and L.A., and now, just off Allen Street, nothing. I've heard Jews say bad things about other people, but never the other way around.

It seems like everything turned way back there in the 1960s, thanks to Vatican II, which changed church liturgy to stop blaming the Jews for the crucifixion of Christ; and thanks, too, to the civil rights movement, the feminists, new immigration laws that permitted Asians and Africans to come to the United States, Stonewall and the gay rights movement, and, all in all, to the very slowly dawning recognition that everyone deserves dignity and respect.

I recognize that what I experienced in my childhood was not all that difficult, and certainly nothing compared to what most black people can tell you about their experiences—or First Nations people, or Latinos, or Asians, or those in the LGBTQ community. And as I write this, a guy running for president wants to ban Muslims from entering the country. I recognize that we're definitely a long way from utopia.

But now, when I walk down Hertel Avenue, I feel all right. My old neighborhood may look the same, but it has definitely changed. No slurs, no hate, no threats. The only sounds are the music streaming from the bars, the happy shouts of the soccer fans, and the rustling leaves in the boughs arched high overhead, the great green cathedral that shelters everyone.

**Jeff Z. Klein** is a former editor and sportswriter at the *New York Times* and the *Village Voice*; currently he writes and produces the Niagara Frontier Heritage Moments on WBFO radio. He went to Sweet Home Senior High before moving to New York to attend Columbia University, and has written several books about sports, including *The Death of Hockey*, with his Sweet Home classmate Karl-Eric Reif. Klein lives in Allentown and in Manhattan.

# Back In the Day: Remembrances of Black Buffalo from the 1940s and 1950s

Georgia Burnette

Sixty-one years ago, on a bright morning in May 1955, I carefully checked my cap and gown for the early afternoon graduation ceremonies at the University at Buffalo. It had been a long and tiring journey, but one I was determined to complete despite the color barrier, lack of funds, and a deteriorating marriage.

Back then, few professions were open to women, even fewer to African American women although teaching, nursing, clerical, social work, and dental assisting come to mind. Nevertheless, there were restrictions when applying for entrance to these schools and for jobs following graduation.

I had been denied entrance to all of Buffalo's nursing schools because they simply refused to admit Black students. The county hospital, while admitting Blacks, refused to admit married students and I had been married for two years. I did a brief stint in an all-Black school of nursing in New York City and then I returned home and was admitted to the newly-formed nursing program at the University at Buffalo, which did accept a few Black students.

At twenty-two, I was one of two older "non-traditional" students in our class; the second was a thirty-year-old white male. Out of the twenty students accepted, only two of us were Black and there was one Native American. Following graduation, I had no problem finding work at Buffalo General Hospital, which had refused me entrance into its nursing program. Through hard work, I rose in rank and was promoted to leadership and even teaching positions.

At eighty-seven, I am an Old Buffalonian, born and raised in this once-bustling flour and steel town, but invisible to many because I was Black. We lived in our own neighborhoods (the East Side and Cold Springs), shopped at nearby stores, attended the city's public schools, worshiped at our own churches and interacted with the larger Caucasian community only rarely.

Here is my story of growing up in this segregated community, back in the day.

# The Community and Neighborhood

The African American community of the 1940s stretched along William Street from Michigan Avenue to a few blocks past Jefferson Avenue. In the 1940s, our neighborhoods had a sprinkling of Italian, Jewish, and Polish families living and working among us.

Many African Americans owned their own businesses because we were not welcomed into businesses of the dominant white society. Our beauty and barber shops, restaurants, auto repair shops, newspapers, cab companies, funeral homes, and physician and dental offices were usually within walking distance of our homes and schools, since few could afford an automobile.

We took streetcars or buses when we needed to leave our area. In 1941, when I was twelve years old, streetcar fare for children was three cents, with free "transfers" onto a second trolley. Some street vendors still had horses, particularly the watermelon man and the ragman. Pushcarts rounded out the scene with the popcorn and hot tamale sellers and the man who sharpened scissors plying his trade.

Buffalo's housing was already "old" by the 1940s, consisting mainly of wooden one-and-a-half-story (two-flat) buildings on narrow lots. We lived in the "flats" of these old, but still sturdy homes. Often, there were no yards, so we played on sidewalks or in the street; automobiles were not plentiful. We enjoyed jacks, marbles, kick the can, hide-and-seek. The boys rode on wooden scooters made of two pieces of scrap-wood nailed together, with an old roller skate for wheels, and a stick for a handle.

We were all poor. Ice cream was five cents a scoop at Adams Drug Store, a short block away from my home on Pine Street. For lunches, my mom prepared mayonnaise and baloney sandwiches, potted meat, Vienna sausages and for a "sweet," a slice of white bread with butter and sugar toasted under the broiler.

## Everybody Attended Sunday School and Church.

Sunday dinner was always special with chicken or pork accompanied by a fresh vegetable (cabbage, greens, or string beans), hot biscuits or cornbread. Our moms prepared delicious desserts and best of all, fresh-churned ice cream, if you were lucky enough to own a hand-cranked churn.

The Chapel on Cedar Street, the "colored" YMCA on Michigan Avenue, and the Urban League on Broadway provided structure to our young lives. The "Y" was the only place with a swimming pool for Black children. It wasn't until the 1950s that the Masten Park Pool adjacent to the old War Memorial Stadium on Jefferson at Best streets grudgingly opened to people of color.

Even when we could go to the pool, my friends and I seldom attempted the long walk up the hill to the stadium. We didn't know what awaited us if we entered the pools since we knew Blacks were still not really welcome.

The "Y" camp was in the southern tier, near Strykersville, and I was fortunate to spend two weeks there in the 1940s. The weekly fee of $12 was a princely sum in those days. At the time my mom was a day worker, cleaning homes for $3 a day while my dad worked odd jobs.

## Schools

I attended elementary school #32, formerly, The Bennett Park School. It was four blocks from my home and I came home for lunch each day. We were expected to be home from school to complete chores and homework, and perhaps start dinner for the family.

Because senior proms were not as prevalent as they are today, we created our own celebrations with the girls in fancy dresses and dark suits for the boys. Curfews for these special dances were sacrosanct, and woe be to those who ignored them. On one occasion and one only, I slipped in at a VERY late hour. Next morning, my mom simply said to me, "Nice girls don't stay out until 2:00 a.m." That was enough to profoundly embarrass me and thereafter, I was home by midnight.

Nevertheless, behind the scenes, we also began to smoke and sample whiskey and beer. But we were as careful as could be not to get caught!

Generally, graduation from high school meant entry into the world of work with a selected few going to college. But again, college admission was limited by racial restrictions, lack of funds, and a dearth of scholarships.

For those wishing to enter the nursing profession, the hospital schools refused Black students altogether, while the County Hospital accepted single females, but denied entry to married applicants. Although the city's vocational and technical schools prepared boys for employment in the automotive field, major car companies and automotive shops refused to hire them if they were Black. In the clerical field, however, I do recall that two of my friends received certificates from Bryant Stratton Business School and found work immediately in the local business community.

Following graduation from high school in 1946, I worked briefly at unskilled jobs, married in 1947, and shortly thereafter gave birth to my son, Dale. The following year I began work as a nurse's aide at the Buffalo General Hospital on High Street and was assigned to a unit for private patients. There were at least four such "floors" within the hospital and these floors did not admit Blacks as patients. People of color were sent to the multiple-bed wards, which offered little privacy and had communal bathrooms.

Black nurses were also not employed nor were Black students admitted into Buffalo General Hospital's School of Nursing. It was accepted hospital policy to keep Black workers in service-related jobs that paid low wages. I recall that I received $25 a week for the nursing aide job at the General.

Patient contact at the hospital caused me to again consider becoming a registered nurse and despite the odds, I sought admission to three nursing schools within the city knowing that I would not be accepted. Nevertheless, I was brave enough to speak to the admissions clerk in the school-office of the Buffalo General Hospital, and will NEVER forget her sneering smile as she shook her head to indicate that I could not expect to be admitted to *their* school of nursing. Undaunted, I began to search for a school as close to Buffalo as possible, and Lincoln School of Nursing in the Bronx was my answer.

Six months later, longing for family, friends, and my son, I returned home, thrilled to learn about the new nursing school at UB. I was admitted in 1951 and my parents assisted with tuition. Still, I had to work and I found a job first as a barmaid, then later as a waitress.

## Employment

During the Great Depression, work for the unskilled population of the Black community consisted of jobs as maids, janitors, waiters/waitresses, nursing aides, and cab drivers. Blacks were not employed as bank tellers, clothing store salespeople, bus or streetcar drivers, policemen or corrections officers, or as clerical workers in offices. Most professions simply were not open to us.

With World War II however, work became plentiful, and Blacks worked on assembly lines alongside our Caucasian counterparts in airline, automobile and steel plants and at telephone companies. Most of my older cousins found work in the war plants at Westinghouse, Western Electric, Twin Coach, and Bell Aircraft.

Nonetheless, Black men continued to be assigned the dirty, dangerous jobs in the forge or the grease pits of the auto plants, in the molten metals processing areas, or the coke ovens at the steel plants. But wages improved exponentially.

With the steel industry booming, my dad obtained work initially at the Kennecott Steel Company and later with Bethlehem Steel, the latter an assignment to the coke ovens. A vivid and painful memory I'll never forget was the first time I glimpsed the numerous scars on my dad's chest and back from the hot sparks which had penetrated his garments. This work provided a living for our family, and the injuries were, as my dad said, "just part of the job."

## Entertainment

We often gathered in homes, but when time and money permitted, we took advantage of the lively Black entertainment district. During my freshman year, I worked weekends as barmaid at the Lincoln Club, which was in the heart of the Black entertainment district on Michigan Avenue.

Just across the street was the Vendome Hotel, its dining room one of the most sought-after for special occasions. The Sugar Bowl, famous for ice cream, anchored the opposite corner. But the jewel in the crown just a block away, was the famous Moonglow Night Club, sporting a fabulous mural of good-looking, scantily-dressed women dancing the night away. That exciting nightclub was the place to go for floorshows and comedians.

Nearby and equally as famous was Ann Montgomery's Little Harlem Hotel, where jazz greats such as Lena Horne, Sara Vaughn, Billy Holiday Cab Calloway and Count Basie all played or stayed. For us, this was the place to see and be seen during special occasions and major holidays.

More recently, from the 1980s-1990s, the Buffalonian's Dinner Dance occurred every three years in August. This was an extraordinary weekend when more than 1,000 Buffalonians gathered at the Convention Center to reminisce about growing up Black in Buffalo from the 1920s through the 1950s. These reunions spanned a period of eighteen years and during those eventful weekends, the Little Harlem was again packed to the rafters.

Just around the corner on Broadway at Michigan Avenue was the Colored Musicians Club, formed in 1935 when the all White Local 43 refused to include African American musicians. Offering the "best jazz in an intimate setting," the club was known for good food and its Sunday evening jam sessions.

## Dan Montgomery's Steak House: Uniforms, Wages, Food, and Ambience

My job at Dan Montgomery's Steak House, on Exchange Street, got me through my second year at UB—first as a hatcheck girl, then as a waitress working weekends from 7:00 p.m. to 3:00 a.m.

As a new waitress, it was thrilling to join the ladies in those lovely flowing gowns. We were required to wear floor-length skirts or dresses, buoyed by stiff, starched "under-slips" which rustled as we walked. These slips were usually made from a bed sheet starched so stiff it stood alone when placed in the corner at the end of the day. Later, waitresses wore hoops, which also rustled with movement and took the work out of starching that under-slip.

I remember receiving wages of $2.78 per evening. Steak, fries and cole-slaw were the most popular fare, accompanied by rolls and butter. The price was between $1.50-$1.99 per meal.

The restaurant was beautiful. As you entered the seldom-used "Piano Room," the handsome mirrored walls caught your eye, as did the lovely black chairs and tables. The bar area on the lower level sported an elegant lighted ceiling, accenting the stunning floor that depicted the kings and queens as from a deck of cards. The Wurlitzer jukebox sparkled in the glow of the ceiling and was reflected in the large mirror behind the bar. The main dining room contained a skylight in addition to lovely stained glass windows.

Professionals of all races and from all walks of life frequented the restaurant; physicians, prominent attorneys, politicians, and businessmen came for the steak *and to be seen.*

Ships plying the Great Lakes from Cleveland and Detroit directed their passengers to our door each Wednesday evening. We could count on that being a wild and wooly evening when we expected and received good tips. This was also true for sporting events and Thursday evenings when the downtown clothing and department stores remained opened until 9:00 p.m.

Longtime manager Herman Harrison, the evening bar maid, Bernice, daytime waitress Muriel, and Paul, the cook, were the constants on the scene. I believe all (except Muriel) were relatives of the legendary owner, Dan Montgomery, who was married at an earlier time to Ann, who owned the Little Harlem Hotel.

## Memories

In 1955, following graduation, I moved into the professional world of nursing and enjoyed a successful career until retirement in 1993. My divorce became final in 1958 and shortly thereafter, I moved to Chicago to explore life and work in "the big city." In 1966, my son Dale was fatally injured in an automobile accident and I returned home for good to Buffalo.

By that time the Lincoln Club, Vendome Hotel, the Sugar Bowl, and Club Moonglow had all been demolished. The Little Harlem succumbed to a massive fire in February 1993, but The Colored Musicians Club remains a gathering spot for great music and fond memories. It also has a museum offering a historical perspective of the club and its musicians.

The city of Buffalo declined as industry moved to Mexico, India, and China, but is now striving towards a renaissance. Remnants of our segregationist past still linger, but hopefully new thinking will prevail.

My reflections are of a time long past, where the good and the bad blend. They are stories of comfort and despair to make me laugh and cry.

These are the stories that keep me company while I sit in my wheelchair.

**Georgia Burnette** was born in Buffalo in 1929, attended School #32, Hutchinson Central High School, and the University at Buffalo School of Nursing. During her thirty-eight-year career, she served as associate director of nursing at the Buffalo General Hospital, assistant professor of nursing, Niagara University; director of nursing at Roswell Park Cancer Institute, and the Buffalo Psychiatric Center. At age seventy-two, she began writing and has published articles in the *Buffalo News*, the *Officer* and *Reunions Magazine*, among others. She lives in Wheatfield.

# The Rise and Fall of Lackawanna

## Dick Hirsch

The municipal personality of Lackawanna, New York, a small city on Lake Erie, adjoining Buffalo, has always been defined by two prominent qualities: the huge steel mill that operated there for some eighty years and the spectacular Our Lady of Victory Basilica which attracted both religious pilgrims and sightseeing tourists from around the world. It was an odd partnership. The steel mill sprawled over 1,500 acres and at times employed members of nearly every family in Lackawanna. As the major employer and taxpayer it exerted tremendous influence on the city and its government, while at the same time fouling the atmosphere with acrid residue from its blast furnaces and open hearths. There were other Roman Catholic parishes in Lackawanna, but Our Lady of Victory and its legendary pastor, the Reverend Monsignor Nelson H. Baker, vied with the steel plant for the role as the city's most iconic institution. The steel plant was abandoned and closed in 1982, a major economic blow to Lackawanna. The Basilica endured, and Father Baker, already a mythic figure in Western New York, embarked on the long path to potential sainthood.

But Lackawanna has always been more than steel and Our Lady of Victory. It was a rough and tumble community, a workingman's town, where a shot and a beer were often served as a breakfast appetizer for nightshift workers. Over the years, many languages were spoken along Ridge Road and South Park Avenue, two of the major thoroughfares, as Lackawanna became the home of generations of new Americans who were drawn there, as if by a magnet, attracted to the steel. Steel promised jobs for men of strength and endurance, men who could do the demanding and exhausting work. These were men with little occupational skill, other than a strong back, but they proved to be quick learners.

Census takers would find residential neighborhoods dominated by pockets of second-generation Irish and Polish families, as well as a melting pot of others, relative newcomers, including Italians, Macedonians, Serbians, Iranians, and Croatians, to mention a few. They all got along, most of the time. Sometimes they didn't. Those new Americans and their descendants helped define what became the Lackawanna polyglot persona.

One of the major players in the history of Lackawanna was a man rarely associated with the city, a man of the upper crust, most often recognized as one of the leaders of high society in Buffalo, a man whose name still resonates, John J. Albright. Albright was the benefactor who provided the original money in the early twentieth century that led to the construction of the Albright Art Gallery in Delaware Park. The institution grew from a provincial art museum to an internationally-known art center, evolving into the Albright-Knox Art Gallery. Albright, a man with diverse business interests, was selected for a significant mission by the Lackawanna Iron and Steel Company of Scranton, Pennsylvania: search for and quietly acquire property on the shore of Lake Erie that would be suitable for a major steel mill.

The property was originally called Limestone Hill, a section of what was then the town of West Seneca. It was essentially an agricultural area of truck farms, although records indicate a few Buffalo executives established vacation homes on the precipice overlooking Lake Erie.

As the century drew to a close, industrialists were considering the opportunities offered by the Buffalo area, with its location on the Great Lakes and its notable booming economy. The city was already a railroad center, second only to Chicago. Among those who proved to be most interested were the managers at the Lackawanna Iron and Steel Company. Anxious to find a more suitable location for their business, they retained Albright with the mission of quietly buying property for an undisclosed client. Albright did his job, acquiring the necessary land.

All the land had once been home to the Seneca Indians, the strongest of the six tribes of the Iroquois Nation, whose members settled there around 1655. The Senecas established villages along Buffalo Creek around 1780. By the mid-nineteenth century the Indians began to sell land to developers and in 1851, the Erie Board of Supervisors approved the establishment of the Town of Seneca. A year later, the name was changed to West Seneca to eliminate confusion with Seneca settlements elsewhere.

It is unlikely that any of the property owners considered that the land, more than 1,000 acres, was destined to become one of the world's largest steel plants. A new corporation, the Lackawanna Steel Company, was formed. Construction began in July, 1900, and by the following spring, several buildings had been completed and men and machinery began to move from Scranton. The plant incorporated the latest manufacturing techniques. The first two blast furnaces began operating in early 1903 and the rail mill began functioning later that year. With each passing year there was further expansion of capabilities.

A sales brochure issued by Lackawanna Steel in 1910 contained this description:

"The location of the works affords unlimited facilities for transportation on the Great Lakes. A large canal, extending into the grounds of the plant, 4,000 feet long, 200 feet wide and twenty-three feet deep, has a dock frontage of 8,000 feet for receiving and shipping material. These docks are amply protected by a government breakwater, 2,500 feet long, making a perfectly safe harbor."

It was a time of great migration to the United States, with a growing number of European families deciding to seek the better life and the prosperity which were supposedly the standard in the United States. Many went to major east coast population centers like New York, Boston, and Philadelphia. Word about Lackawanna Steel must have reached the promoters whose specialty was selling steerage accommodations on steamships leaving Europe. After passing through Ellis Island, many set out by train for Buffalo, having heard that there were jobs available at the steel plant. The company never encountered a shortage of job applicants and most settled near the plant.

The presence of the huge factory in the Limestone Hill area was a source of friction between the eastern and western parts of West Seneca. Those living in the eastern part of town could see no benefit to what was developing at the steel plant. They objected to the cost of municipal improvements needed around the plant and urged formation of a separate community. That happened in 1909 when the City of Lackawanna was formed, adopting the name of its biggest corporate citizen. It covered an area of about six square miles, including the steel mill.

The plant was acquired by the Bethlehem Steel Company in 1922 and the name was changed. Years of expansion followed, with the site growing to over 1,500 acres. The plant's products included bars, sheets, rails, tie plates, structural shapes, sheet pilings, and a variety of other materials. It had its own railroad on the property, the South Buffalo Railway, and it operated 24/7 decades before that term was invented. Employment at peak periods was over 20,000. For many, the work was demanding and dirty, yet generations of Lackawanna men sent their sons to the mill to follow them and become steel workers. Some left the steel company and opened taverns on Steelawanna or Electric Avenues, or on intersecting side streets, believing they could have a better life by providing a spot where the plant workers could relax before and after their shift. There were many taverns in the city, but some of the proprietors eventually embarked on other careers which led their families to lives in other places, mostly nearby suburban communities with new homes on larger lots and greener grass. But a special place in their psyches was reserved for Lackawanna.

After years of rumors, the Bethlehem Steel Company shut down the plant in 1982, depriving Lackawanna of its namesake and its original reason for existing. There was great sadness when the end came. True, the sky would be brighter, the air cleaner, and the traffic less congested on the Hamburg Turnpike during shift changes. But still, there was enduring sadness.

**Dick Hirsch** is the author of eight non-fiction books and has been writing the weekly "BfloTales" column for *Business First of Buffalo* for over thirty years. He claims he received his advanced education in journalism while a reporter and columnist at the *Buffalo Courier-Express*, after he graduated from Trinity College in Hartford, Connecticut. He also had a nineteen-year engagement as producer and moderator of two weekly public affairs programs at WNED-TV.

# Walking Away in Riverside

## Patricia Sweet

A boy crouches behind a parked car and motions for another to join him. The streetlight glares down at them. The corner looks ancient, used up. Even the kids look old. They freeze as I approach. I wonder what they're up to.

My husband hates me walking down Niagara Street alone. Too dangerous, he says. But my cousins and I ran this block like wild ponies fifty years ago. That was then, he says.

The DNA of my ancestors, the dust of their flesh, is embedded in the concrete. Their ghosts linger in the burned-out lots at Niagara and Austin, in forgotten attics farther down toward Squaw Island. For over 100 years they tramped these cracked slabs up to the streetcar, and later, to the #5 bus. Leo Zahn, my maternal grandfather, lost his business in the Depression and ambled up Hertel Avenue to Geltz's or Mike's or one of a dozen taverns to play his accordion to make a stab at supporting eleven kids. Catherine Mooney, my paternal grandmother, waited for the street car on the very spot on which I stand to get to Woolworth's, downtown, where she was a shop girl. Generations of uncles caught the bus to Chevy, where they built cars few of them could afford.

Now, most residents of Black Rock and Riverside drive to work. The sidewalk belongs to the very old and the young. To immigrant families who walk in a line, father first, mother and children steps behind. To chubby or tattooed American girls rolling their babies in strollers and droopy-pants boys like the ones I'm watching.

My father transplanted our family from Riverside to Grand Island in 1961. Not a clean break for me. I missed my little gang on Chadduck. I longed for the park, the playground, the good old days of walking down Tonawanda Street to buy popsicles and comic books. You couldn't walk anywhere on Grand Island and there was no one to play with.

We did visit my grandparents in the old neighborhood. On those days I noticed everything. How the elm trees were dying, how Reiser's (the best candy store) had boards over the windows, how the edges of the sidewalk stuck up, causing me to trip, and even the occasional pennies and stones trapped in the concrete. My father said that prisoners made the sidewalks but I'd never seen any guys in striped suits.

As my grandparents died, the houses were sold to investors who divided them into apartments and rented them out. Multiply that by thousands and you have the Black Rock and Riverside of the new millennium. Few landlords live on the premises. Tenants have invested little in the apartments. Crime rates have soared.

In 2007, as empty-nesters, my husband and I bought a little cottage on Niagara Street. What possessed us, I don't know—maybe the world-class view of the river, maybe the rumor that Buffalo was on the rise. My husband liked the low taxes. I liked getting back to my roots. My cousins thought I was crazy. Most of them grew up here, attended Riverside High School, and fled to the suburbs as soon as possible. The buzz in the extended family was that I was dumber than I looked.

Maybe so. Two months after moving in, my husband called me at work. I didn't know what was up but could tell from his voice that it was bad. I arrived home to find the back door kicked in and clothes strewn everywhere. The top of a chest I'd used to store quilts was ripped off its hinges. The thieves must have thought it was where we hid our treasure. Only there was no treasure. Just stuff, a TV, a laptop. The door was locked but one frame had given way to a simple kick.

After venting for several days, we reinforced the door frame and bought security cameras. Within two weeks, a window we'd thought too small to be breached was smashed in and whoever had been there before brought a child to crawl through and open the door so they could steal the few things they'd missed the first time: a DVD player, a remote control, and the TV in the bedroom.

It was December. As Detective Martinez from the "D" district took fingerprints, he joked about thieves needing to do their Christmas shopping, too. When no one laughed, he added that a lot of people in the neighborhood were desperate.

That year, I joined them. I became desperate not to look at every kid walking by as the one who cracked my quilt chest, or as the one who was watching and waiting until no cars were in the driveway to make a second hit.

My feelings of losing control have vacillated with the seasons, but in nine years, we've lost two bikes, a camera, two laptops, a VCR, two TVs, and some decent jewelry to thieves. We've had windows, doors and furniture smashed. For a while, I looked for my earrings on every woman I passed on the street. Every blue bicycle was the one boosted from our garage.

Forgiveness is key to freedom and in the spring of 2014, we began attending Renovation, a new mega church on Hertel Avenue, formerly St.

Florian's Parish. I introduced myself to the pastor as someone who lives in the neighborhood. He said, "Bummer." They used to run four services, but I notice, it's been reduced to two.

My husband and I have gotten better at securing our property. We've had glass block windows installed that we're told it takes a jack-hammer to break. We've established a routine of locking doors, and I like to think after nine years we no longer draw much attention to ourselves. I no longer wear suits or carry a briefcase. Maybe, I thought, we could belong after all. It takes all kinds of people to make a world, right?

But on March 3, 2016, after working out at the neighborhood gym, I returned to my car to find the windows smashed and my purse, which I'd hidden, stolen. Out of all of our thefts, this one was the most random, occurring in a crowded parking lot. It led me to decide that the stress of crime is more than I can take. The idea that I can be hit at any moment, and that people may actually be following me, tracking my movements, has made me paranoid. Like a combat veteran who freaks out at the explosion of a fire cracker, I have sacrificed a bit of my mind to this battle.

In fifty years of life spent in other places, I'd never been ripped off. As kids we never had much to steal. The concept of needing to lock and guard and worry was foreign to me. In Grand Island my father left his keys in his car. I don't think my parents even owned a key to the house. This didn't make living in suburbia exactly thrilling for me in the 1960s and 1970s. I never lost a chance to complain about the sterility, uniformity, and all around unhipness of the scene. My parents knew I wished we'd never moved out of the city. Riverside was cool. Where we lived was phony and stuck-up.

When my husband and I bought our little cottage on Niagara Street, I felt like I'd come home. I would endear myself to those around me by performing acts of kindness like picking up trash, raking leaves, stopping to chat. One of the first comments I got was "You paid how much for that house? You were robbed." A neighbor knocked on the door and shouted at us in a drunken rage. People stared out of upper apartments when we hung out in our back yard. Our front window got covered in spray paint.

Now I avoid looking people in the eye. The glass isn't half full. It's empty. My cousins were probably right. I look smarter than I am.

Dumb, maybe. But teachable. I have learned something. My white privilege, or whatever you want to call it, goes beyond having benefitted from a two-parent home and decent schools. It goes beyond never experiencing racial prejudice. It took a series of thefts for me to realize the extent of my privilege. Getting ripped off blew my mind because it was something I'd never had to deal with. The reality is that thieves are victims first. When you grow up being stolen from, it's likely you will steal. The lifestyle perpetuates itself.

This might sound elementary, but for me it was a revelation. The moment I could hear sympathizers say, "At least no one got hurt," and accept it as a genuine cause for gratitude, I began deflecting the instinct to hate.

On my lonely walk down Niagara Street, I look again at the boy behind the parked car. The windows of my SUV are still blown out, so I am walking, rather than driving to the grocery store. I assume he's hiding because he and his friends are planning to break into the car or maybe key the paint or slash the tires. My heart pounds.

In a move that would horrify my husband, I prepare to interject myself. *I'll give these kids a piece of my mind and then call 911.*

But a girl runs around the corner. She looks up and down the street. One of the boys glances at me and puts his finger to his lips. *Quiet.* I realize they're playing Hide and Seek, like I'd done fifty years ago on that exact spot.

I put away my phone, smile, and pretend to zip my lips.

Thank God, some things never change.

**Patricia Sweet** spent many years teaching English, first at Holy Angels Academy, then at PS 81. More recently, she has taught at Buffalo State and Canisius Colleges. In 2014, she published her first novel, *The Code.* Her second, an historical coming of age novel about a girl obsessed with Jimi Hendrix, is nearing completion. She still lives on Niagara Street.

# I Haven't Met the Old Woman in the Knit Sweater Yet Because Life Is Disappointing

## Cayli Enderton

I always wonder about the buses outside the window
I always wonder where Main Street is and if the old woman in her knit
 sweater
is going to meet a friend or going to do shots
I wonder if the boy with short black hair has parents
who get along and if he has money for the bus
Did he run out of nickels? Or did he borrow 3 from the woman carrying
a paper bag filled with bread, eggs, and milk
all she needs to survive the week
I wonder if the two women with doe eyes can smell the wolf
of a man who watches them from behind
The way he licks his lips hungrily as they chatter away, following them
down the block
I wonder if the man who looks like Clarke Gable is really in love
How is it possible that this city is so small, but so large at the same time
and how is it I still haven't met the old woman in the knit sweater?

**Cayli Enderton** is fifteen years old and a sophomore at City Honors School. She writes poetry, prose, and songs. She's published work in *Wordplay*, various JBWC zines, and was a runner-up for the first JBWC poetry contest, and opened for Colum McCann at BABEL in 2014. She is interested in writing, art, music, and photography/filmmaking. Cayli has been a Youth Ambassador at the Just Buffalo Writing Center since April 2014. She lives in an apartment in downtown Buffalo. She wrote this poem on Mohawk Avenue.

# Manufactured Articles

## Crystal Ockenfuss

There are concrete ghosts
grain elevators standing
guard over Lake
Erie, sentinels watching
over a past
obscured by smoke
Bethlehem burning
steel saviors—Buffalo
1927 I see them streaming
out with the whistle
into our windy, dirty
city—*Belle Fleuve*
no beautiful
river now
nor then. Buffalo
shaggy industrial
beast, your proud dead—
rusty hulks gone to meet
their mortal
animal namesakes.

**Crystal Ockenfuss** was born and raised in Buffalo and did her undergraduate studies at the University at Buffalo in German and cultural anthropology. She was first exposed to modern poetry by Robert Creeley and wonderful people at Talking Leaves...Books. After many years' residence in Europe, she currently lives and writes in the San Francisco Bay area.

# A Long Journey: Proud to be Arab

## Sara Ali

It's September 11, 2001. I'm eleven years old and the only Arab girl in my class. My family is Muslim, which makes me even more different.

Kids at my Grand Island school routinely make fun of me for my thick eyebrows, prominent nose, and olive skin. I act like I can handle the bullying. It doesn't bother me one bit, I tell myself.

I'm wrong.

I'm sitting at my desk in my fifth grade class feeling sleepy when my teacher, Miss Graziano, briefly walks out of the room. I wonder where she's going and if I have time for a little doze before she returns.

She walks in a short while later and tells us some planes have just hit the World Trade Center in New York City.

She asks us to write how we feel about it in our journals.

I don't know how I feel.

I'm eleven years old and have never been to New York City. I'm helpless to change what happened. Although it makes me sad, it's not connected to me. I shake it off and go back to my daily routine.

What I don't know is that people are going to blame my family and me for what terrorists from the other side of the world did. It's not going to go away like regular bullying.

It's the end of the next school day and I'm climbing my way up the steps of the bus. I am eager to get home. And then I hear my classmate who lives a few houses down from me yell from the back of the bus.

"Terrorist!"

Not thinking he's talking to me, I turn around to see what all the commotion is. Terrorist is a bad word, I know that much. I also know terrorists flew the planes into the Twin Towers.

"It was you! Your family did it. Osama Bin Laden is your uncle. Terrorist!"

*Is he talking to me? Is he saying that my parents are related to the founder of Al-Qaeda? Why?*

Muslim extremists blew up the buildings. But for some reason, people in my class assume my family and I were to blame.

The bus driver doesn't do much. She vaguely tells him to "stop," but she doesn't tell him he's wrong. No one does.

The kids keep laughing.

I try to make myself small. I'm anxious to get off this bus and go home.

I contemplate whether I should tell my parents. I do and they're unhappy. They call the school and talk to the principal.

The following morning at school, my mom drives me in and we sit down face to face with my classmate, his mother, and the principal.

We sit across from them.

"Brandon, apologize for what you said to her."

"I'm sorry, Sara."

*Fuck you. No you're not.*

The adults talk. Brandon and I sit in awkward silence. He won't look at me. I know he hates me.

He stays out of school for a week.

He never calls me a terrorist again.

But he finds other ways to torment me. So do others, both at Veronica E. Connor Middle School, and then at Grand Island High School.

Today, I am proud to be Arab—part Jordanian, part Palestinian American. But saying so didn't come easily.

I spent years—really until I turned twenty, four years ago—hating a part of myself and separating from my parents' religion. As a teen, I considered myself an atheist. Now, I'm agnostic. I question all beliefs and wonder if there really is a supreme being.

My Grand Island neighborhood was predominantly white and closed-minded. I felt like I was the only brown girl in the school. I wasn't, but I can count on my two hands the people of color who were in my middle school and high school classes.

You would think we all would have banded together for moral support, but we didn't. We barely talked.

I didn't want to communicate with *them*. *They* were *other*. The minorities. The colored kids.

They were too much like me.

Kids laughed at me for being brown. If I was friends with brown people, I would get made fun of even more.

I'm a poster child of a brown girl who internalized racism so much I no longer needed the white kids to bully me, because I did it myself. I would start cracking jokes about my parents' religion and my skin color before they could. I went around the halls shouting "A-rab," in that stupid, phonetically incorrect way some people like to say it.

I figured if I showed them it didn't bother me, they would stop. Right? Wrong.

I've gotten called a "sand nigger" and a "towel head." I've been told to vacuum the sand out of my vagina. A kid once drew a picture of me flying into the Twin Towers. The racism was constant.

I was an easy target. I made fun of myself back, which unleashed the worst in everyone.

Once, three girls I grew up with IM'ed me, calling me "a stupid Arab," among other things. Then they chatted among themselves about me. I'll use fake names for the sake of their dignity, as I'm sure they've grown up to be better human beings now.

Ashley: Ew…Do you smell that?

Kayla: Ewww! Smells like shit!

Jenna: No, it's just Sara. Brown Arabian piece of shit.

I was in the seventh grade. I didn't cry. I almost didn't even care.

I was made fun of so much, I was numb. Being called a piece of shit wasn't half as bad as what I'd been called before.

At twenty-four, I now realize that my biggest struggles weren't the name-calling and constant bullying. It was growing up with a bicultural background.

At home, I wasn't Arab enough. I couldn't speak Arabic and I was not a practicing Muslim. As a teenager my parents were still teaching me Arabic words I should have already known, and I knew little about the culture. In school, I wasn't light enough or savvy enough about pop culture to know what the kids were talking about.

I wasn't Arab enough. I wasn't American enough. I disappointed everyone.

I'd go to school where my peers would don Pink Floyd shirts and talk about "old" rock and roll; I'd go home to my mother making baklava and kanafa, speaking in Arabic to my father and talking about the Israeli-Palestinian conflict.

Should I be more like my family, or should I be more like the kids in school?

Around my thirteenth birthday, I visit my family in Jordan.

It's my first time meeting my mother's family. They greet me with hugs and happiness.

I meet my grandmother, my aunts, my uncles, and my baby cousins. I taste freshly slaughtered lamb and I watch camels roam free on the dirt roads and treeless desert. I wake up to the prayer echoing from the mosque and through the capital, reminding everyone to wake up and pray. It's incredible.

I come home and none of my peers care about my cultural experience. It's too brown, too Muslim, and too un-American for their fragile whiteness. Things go back to how they used to be.

These days, the bullying is gone, but the racism still exists. I see Islamophobia in the media every day, especially in the rhetoric of Donald Trump.

It doesn't diminish my pride. The fight for acceptance wasn't with my peers; it was a fight within myself.

Today, I am the editor in chief at *Karibu News*, a refugee and immigrant newspaper on the West Side. I write articles that focus on Buffalo's newest community members and their lives. Sometimes I try to bring that "betweeness" I always felt into focus. Mostly, I want to contribute to preserving the culture of others, and making sure newcomers and their kids are proud to be who and what they are.

Although it came with a struggle and endless bullying, today I identify as a brown Arab girl of Middle Eastern descent. I like my big nose and thick eyebrows. I enjoy my darker complexion, although I am pretty fair-skinned for a brown girl. I feel lucky to say I have family in the Middle East, and I'm proud to defend my parents' religion and my culture.

As for the kids who bullied me, I no longer despise them. The anger has dissipated. My biggest wish is that young Muslim and Arab kids will read this and understand that the bullying comes to an end.

Ignorance is not worth your hate.

**Sara Ali** is the editor-in-chief at *Karibu News*, a multilingual newspaper enriching the refugee and immigrant community. She attended Buffalo State College for communication studies and graduated in May 2015. She currently resides in the Town of Tonawanda.

# Korey's Story: How I Survived Life on Buffalo's East Side

## Korey Greene

I was born and raised in Buffalo's notorious East Side.

Some people or Buffalonians would say, "Why would he say 'notorious?'" Others would say that sounds pretty accurate.

If you watch the news, every few days, there's a story about a killing or a crime on the East Side. It's the most crime-ridden area in the city. When I say East Side, I mean the the area bordered by Main Street to the west, Winspear Avenue to the north, the Buffalo River to the south, and Cheektowaga to the east. It's a large community and most of its inhabitants are African American.

I used to be one of them.

But I got out. Kind of…

When I was twenty-three, a childhood friend of mine killed a man during a robbery. Another friend of mine called that day to say his friend had been killed.

My friend had killed his friend.

We could barely talk about it. It was so raw.

It was an ugly time. A lot of people I knew were doing dumb things and making mistakes to get money or drugs. Some of my family and more of my friends landed in jail. I had a job working as a debt collector, but I didn't love it or want to stay in it.

I kept thinking about my neighborhood, what was wrong and why.

In 2005—four years after my friend became a killer—I wrote and filmed a documentary called *The Forgotten City*, which talks about the murder and tries to get at the root of the violence and crime and lack of hope on the East Side. We found some answers, some truths, and a lot of questions.

The film took my mind and circumstances to a different place. Many people ask me how I did it. How I turned something so negative around, how I became a Buffalo filmmaker. How I left the danger, but stayed in Buffalo.

I always thought the better question was, how did I make it into the neighborhood in the first place?

In 1987, my mother, my brother and I lived on Navel Avenue in a small downstairs apartment. Most people on our block were black and everyone rented their homes. Some of the houses had upper and lower tenants. There were a few single-family homes, but not many. There were trees and small front porches and some lawns were manicured. Others weren't.

Prior to living there, we had lived on Woodlawn and Saint Louis Avenues. These were some of the best years of my life. I remember playing street football and basketball with other neighborhood kids and running between houses and back alleys, which we called "shortcuts."

It was the late 1980s, a time when black people weren't afraid of each other; in fact we protected each other. I remember when my mom would go to work, we left our doors open and three or four different neighbors would come in to check on us. The entire community was involved in day-to-day activities in the neighborhood. If an old lady couldn't cut her grass, we would. If you were acting up, a neighbor had the right to correct you, and what you didn't have, you could borrow.

But over time, through the 1990s, joblessness really took root and then the crack came in and things really declined. Some of my family members fell along with the neighborhood. Like most of my friends, I only sporadically saw my dad. Most fathers didn't stick around long enough to be role models. Most of my friends and I had single mothers raising us.

It wasn't always this way. Buffalo was once a boomtown for blacks.

Some came after World War I for jobs. Others came later when jobs in the steel and flour mills and other industries were plentiful. Families stuck together because life had rhythm and regular Friday paychecks.

But that wasn't my Buffalo.

Coming up, I saw my hard-working mother, who worked a bevy of jobs, survey the neighborhood and watch people getting addicted to drugs, see how trash littered the yards, and how homes all around were abandoned and started to get boarded up. She knew she had to get me and my brother out, before we became what our neighborhood was becoming.

She'd been thinking about a move for a while, but in 1988, after the drug addicts who lived upstairs broke into our apartment looking for cash or anything of value, my mother knew it was time.

Our next journey would be different from all of our priors. We moved onto Wright Avenue, which was still the East Side, but it was a predominately white neighborhood. It was right on the border of Cheektowaga, which is also heavily white.

We were the second black family on the street.

For me, it was like a dream—a beautiful home, quiet suburban style street and kids everywhere. People actually cared about their houses—they kept them up. And the yards were manicured and attractive. People put trash in the bins. They didn't just drop it on the street. The kids didn't shoot hoops or play football like we were used to. They played street hockey, a game my brother and I had never seen before. We were blown away what a difference a few streets could make.

As we settled in our new life, we started to notice signs we were unwanted. That's how I learned about racism.

It was a hot summer day and my mother and I decided to go for a bike ride around the neighborhood. I was about eight years old and I had my brand new Huffy bike.

We made it only to the next block over, to Eggert Road, when a group of white men in their early twenties started throwing rocks, ice, and bottles at us from their red pick up truck and yelling, "Niggers go back to where you came from."

I would be forever changed.

My mother was livid, but all her rage quickly turned to sadness and tears. She had thought this new neighborhood would keep us safe.

We sat in my bedroom and she explained to me how things would be different now.

I had to be stronger and resilient to survive in this neighborhood.

This first incident was followed by many more. I quickly realized how much the color of my skin mattered.

Some neighbors didn't want me and my brother playing with their kids, especially if they had boys our age. They kept them in when we were playing outside. The father of the family next door let out all the air from our basketball when it accidentally bounced into his yard. They moved away less than a year after we arrived.

To make some extra money, I got a neighborhood paper route. I walked up to one house and got ready to lay the paper on the porch when a man appeared at the door with a gun. Because I was black, he assumed I was there to steal something.

This gets back to my better question: how did I make it into the neighborhood? How did I survive in that all-white racist environment?

I just lived day by day. I kept to myself. I played with my brother.

And then, within a few years, the neighborhood changed as more blacks came.

Today, that area is mostly black.

So I made it in with the whites who all eventually moved away and then had to make it in with the blacks and all the street life activities that came into play in the 1990s and 2000s.

Today, I see some progress on the East Side. The good people are as decent and caring as ever. Most of my family and friends live there. I'm there visiting every day. It's my place in Buffalo and I can say our community is still struggling. The schools are bad, the families are torn apart, and drugs, alcohol, and violence are the result.

Sometimes, I think we are waiting too patiently for people or politicians to help us.

That's honestly not going to come just right now. Buffalo's primary focus is on making downtown and our waterfront area better. I do feel the East Side will get its turn and there are *some* things in place, but until we are the primary focus, we just have to do it ourselves.

We need jobs and education and role models.

That's what I am trying to do and be.

I am using my childhood experiences on the East Side to tell stories about people who feel they don't have a voice in the world. My documentaries are unscripted. I just take a camera into the neighborhoods and ask questions. I try to get at the truth about the underserved and undereducated in this city. The tagline for my company, "Knuckle City Films," was "Every frame on par with reality."

Filmmaking saved my life.

*The Forgotten City* helped me channel the frustration I had at my friend and at all the wasted life and hope on the East Side. If I hadn't made it, who knows where I would be? Statistically, my chances of being dead or in prison were (and still are) high. A lot of my friends didn't make it.

The film won awards but it also made me realize that my experiences matter. People want to know about them.

The film thrust me into the ever-growing Buffalo film community and introduced me to independent filmmakers who are generating jobs and buzz about our city. Several Hollywood studios have also come to film in Buffalo and they have brought massive budgets and created jobs for locals.

I'm trying to do my part, too.

In 2014, I directed a feature narrative film called *The Romans* which I co-wrote with former Sabres general manager Larry Quinn, now a Buffalo school board member. The film created over 300 jobs including cast, crew, extras, and helped local businesses. The best part is we even hired people from my neighborhood.

The film was picked up by the distributing company Indican Pictures and will be released in summer 2016.

My latest work is a feature documentary called *The Blackness Project*, which talks about culture and race in America from the perspective of African Americans and other minorities. It was inspired from conversations about *The Whiteness Project*, which is a similar documentary discussing race and the perceived loss of white privilege by white Americans.

*The Blackness Project* is still in production under Black Rose Films and looking at a winter release in 2017, with some post-production help from my friend Addison Henderson. He's the one whose friend was murdered in 2001.

We could have gone the other route. Addison and I could have been enemies. But we are still friends and still do business together.

We still talk about problems that plague our city and the tragedy that sealed our friendship. It's the first scene of *The Forgotten City*. We came together out of regret.

My friend is still in jail. Addison's friend is dead.

But from that sadness and misfortune, we are building, dreaming, inspiring, and producing.

We've found hope.

Filmmaker **Korey Green** was born and raised on the East Side of Buffalo. He attended Seneca Vocational High School and then Alfred State College, where he pursued his interest in creative writing. In 2005, he wrote and directed the documentary *The Forgotten City* and has since directed more than a dozen short films and a host of music videos, commercials, and a feature documentary, *The Experience,* which was shot in Ghana, West Africa. Green just completed the narrative film *The Romans*, which he directed and co-wrote, and he is working on *The Blackness Project* for 2017. Green has won numerous film awards, in New York, Los Angeles, Denver, Chicago, San Diego, and at Miami's American Black Film Festival and the Buffalo Niagara Film Festival.

Photographer Milton Rogovin has iconic stature in Buffalo. An optometrist and social crusader, he documented the lives of Buffalo's poorest residents, many of whom lived on the Lower West Side. In 1972, he began photographing family groups. He and his wife, Anne Snetsky, photographed the same families over thirty years and created evocative photographic testaments to time and life across generations. Rogovin's photographs provide insight into the lives of Buffalo's Puerto Rican, African American, Native American, Asian and Italian families. Rogovin's photographs are in the permanent collections of over two dozen prominent museums around the world.

(opposite page)
Untitled
Lower West Side Quartets, 1972-2002
Photographs by Milton Rogovin (1909-2011)
Courtesy Center for Creative Photography, University of Arizona Library

(this page)
Untitled
Lower West Side Quartets, 1972-2002
Photographs by Milton Rogovin (1909-2011)
Courtesy Center for Creative Photography, University of Arizona Library

# The Way We Were

## Ronald Wendling

My wife Mary and I, both well into our seventies, live in a ninety-seven-unit condominium near Philadelphia, where we moved years ago, from Buffalo, for my job. A number of the other residents are our age and older. Most have children, whether local or out of town, but I rarely see even the locals unless one of the parents is seriously ill. The parents generally drive themselves to doctors' offices. A few of the healthier seniors drive their friends to the supermarket or church, but for the most part they must depend on themselves for whatever physical or spiritual sustenance they need.

All of this presents a picture far different from my years growing up in Buffalo in the 1940s and 50s, when the care of older people—of almost everyone for that matter—was among the main responsibilities not only of the family, but sometimes even of the neighborhood.

The contrast between now and then, of course, reflects changes in American culture. But for me, the North Park neighborhood I grew up in represents the "then" especially well.

Mary and I raised our children in a middle-class Philadelphia suburb during the 1970s. It was more like the North Park of my boyhood than the condominium, townhouse, or gated-community culture that has developed in so many places since that time. Then, if the man down the street was known to be good at repairing bicycles, we didn't hesitate to send one of our daughters to his garage to have her bent handlebar fixed, for free. Today, for fear that the man might be a sexual predator, many parents would probably take the bike to a shop or simply replace it with a new one. Expense aside, the more important cost is the lost opportunity for the family to become better friends with the man down the street.

North Park offered many such opportunities, one being during the snowstorms. When the snow started in the later afternoon or evening, other neighborhood boys and I would shovel half-circles by the curb big enough for our dads to park their Fords and Chevrolets in for a reasonably cleared getaway the next morning.

My mother never thought twice about borrowing a cup of sugar from Rita G. next door because it gave them time to talk. Neither did I mind toting a large bag of sugar in my bicycle basket the several blocks from the corner store to Mrs. G's side door to replenish her supply, especially during a strike at Bethlehem Steel, where her husband worked. The number of cups was never an issue because so many household necessities were flying back and forth all the time that it was too much trouble to keep count.

My mother may have picked up this financial casualness from her father-in-law, whose management of his Black Rock grocery store often involved waiting to be paid for a cut of beef or a ham until payday or, in the years before unemployment insurance, keeping a running tab for a neighbor who had been laid off from the Wickwire plant.

My fondness for Rita G. was not unselfish—she was a better pie maker than my mother, who specialized in cakes, especially chocolate and carrot. One summer afternoon when I was about nine, Mrs. G caught me gawking from our breakfast-room window at a banana-cream pie with graham-cracker crust that she had placed on her porch to cool. From then on she never made another one without sending me over a piece, even though she had four children and a husband to feed.

I was reminded of Mrs. G. shortly before Thanksgiving this past year when Mary and I found one of those small specialty-store bags hanging on our doorknob with four carrot cupcakes with white frosting nestled inside. The note was from a lady on the floor above us. We hardly knew her, but it said simply that she thought we might like them. The spirit of Rita G. lives on, if only occasionally.

Families in trouble were all the more eligible for such generosity. My father, who was addicted to alcohol, had two married sisters who heartily disapproved of his drinking, but that did not stop them from putting my sister and me up for a time when Dad was driving my mother mad. Mom had two sisters of her own who also took us in. Only one of these aunts lived in North Park; the others were in Riverside, Kenmore, and Kensington—places I came to regard as extensions of North Park.

But North Park itself shored up families like mine that were under threat of collapse, though it did so indirectly. My dad's "troubles" never were the local secret we tried to pretend they were. That was why the men of the house on either side of us would, once in a while, give me a hit on the shoulder a little bit rougher than it needed to be: "You're a strong guy," that shove told me unmistakably, "You'll get through this."

I am not sure the condominium or townhouse culture that we have now still offers youngsters, or adults for that matter, such natural acceptance of grief. A certain intimacy was present in the spaces that separated the homes in North Park. Now the closer our property abuts our neighbors', the more remote our lives seem to become from theirs. Most of the condominium residents I talk with in the elevator (usually about nothing more than the weather) I have rarely seen anywhere else in the building, except at the twice-a-year "meet your neighbors parties" that never quite manage to fulfill that expectation.

The intimacy is vanishing, I think, because it has become so institutionalized that it feels fabricated, like church membership that has less to do with religious faith than with tithing (now available online) and a sense of obligation. Calling a hotline when one's thoughts are getting suicidal or one's spouse is becoming abusive is no doubt valuable. But having a brother or sister or the lady next door over for a candid talk might have been better.

Dating services may occasionally work well, but a chance meeting at a friend's backyard barbecue might feel a little less formalized. Meals on wheels, visiting nurses, fifty-five-and-over communities, assisted living facilities, and hospices can all provide care and healing companionship, but perhaps a little less naturally than the conversation of a family member, a friend, or a longtime neighbor.

Two incidents epitomize my experience of Buffalo.

Both were in the vicinity of Main and Jefferson. When I was still in grade school, I was riding the Parkside bus on my way home to North Park one dark winter evening about 8:30. There were high snow banks on either side of Main Street, which was eerily empty of traffic. The bus itself carried no more than eight passengers. A little less than a minute after one street corner stop, the driver braked in front of Paul's Pies, its marvelous reddish sign blinking smartly against the white facing.

He announced that he was going in to buy us one dozen jelly doughnuts and one dozen peanut sticks. Two men in the bus insisted on accompanying him to help him with the bill and, over the driver's resistance, they did. So there we all sat, the dreariness of a routine NFT bus ride suddenly interrupted by fresh doughnuts for the remainder of the ride.

The second experience was of the sudden intimacy Buffalo could create among strangers. This was in the early 1960s at a small bar on the corner of Jefferson and a side street a little further down from Main than I was used to venturing. I had arrived early, but still had to stand in a longish line of other jazz fans who had shown up to hear the great jazz trumpeter Maynard Ferguson. There was no one at the door collecting a cover charge because there was no cover charge. There was no doorman making sure that people outside could enter in a timely fashion. The traffic in and out was nevertheless steady, constant, and most surprisingly, voluntary.

Black people and white people sat at the bar drinking, chatting amiably (very few overstayed their welcome) and passing beers behind them to the listeners who had to stand. People drank, listened to the jazz, and left after a reasonable time, as if instinct told everyone not to monopolize music like this. Ferguson himself was still finding his way from Big Band music toward the newer forms, but you wouldn't know that to hear him play on this magically integrated night.

An economic resurgence is taking place in Buffalo, and my hopes for it are largely based on an article I read recently about a program inviting entrepreneurs to undertake start-ups there. One young man among them remarked that what most motivated him was the unpaid mentoring that he got from experienced businessmen. That is the generosity I remember coming naturally to so many Buffalonians. If solid prosperity does materialize, it will probably owe more to that spirit than to state and federal funding.

**Ronald Wendling** grew up in Buffalo and attended Canisius High School. He taught English at Canisius College as a member of the Jesuit order who had not yet been ordained to the Roman Catholic priesthood. He left the Jesuits in 1965 and left Buffalo that same year. Philadelphia, where he married, raised a family, and taught English at Saint Joseph's University for over forty years, has been his home since then.

# The Lemon Street Connection

## Jennifer Connor

Shaketa Redden's grandmother Olivia spoke fast, with a thick Arkansas twang. Now thirty-three, Shaketa remembers having to occasionally translate for friends who didn't understand. Olivia was tiny, at most five feet tall, but what she lacked in height she made up in determination. And she was generous, despite the fact that she didn't make a lot of money baking cinnamon rolls at Sibley's Bakery.

"People knew if they came to her house they could stay there…Whatever she had she would give or let people borrow," Shaketa said. "Every weekend and every summer I would be over there. I called it the fun house."

The neighborhood was Buffalo's Fruit Belt, named for the orchards planted by the Germans who first settled there at the turn of the century. It was there that Olivia, over generations, fostered the idea of a family as an act of love that transcends name and blood.

Today, some in the Fruit Belt worry the neighborhood may lose its identity as a historic, tight-knit community of mostly people of color.

Shaketa's family moved back to the Fruit Belt in the 1990s. While their home on Lemon Street was being built, Shaketa would take pictures to document the stages of construction. She remembers her parents photographing the foundation being laid, the walls going up, and the roof, which would become her secret perch, being built.

"There were times in the summer, especially, when our parents would be sleeping and we would be hanging out on my porch or on my friend's porch," which was just across the street, Shaketa said. She named the long list of cousins she grew up with—cousins by upbringing, not by family name. "It was a very carefree time because I didn't have too many restrictions. There were just a ton of kids playing sports, riding bikes, and running in and out of houses, just because—who knows why? It was just a Lemon Street connection."

Her recollections are marked by an air of security and trust. For example, she remembers the night when they forgot to close their front door and someone came and yelled her father's name from the porch until he went out and closed it.

Her father's given name is Larthonia Redden, but everyone calls him Squirt, since he was the youngest in a large family. His house today is quiet and well-kept; the plants and trees are neatly mulched, and an air of contentment pervades the groomed yard and white-railed porch. There is an audible, steady hum of people coming and going in the neighborhood, which is quieter during the day, but soon is enlivened as the sidewalks and yards fill up in the afternoons and evenings. Many children play out in the yard and gardens at Futures Academy 37, the local school, where community members have replanted fruit trees in the past few years through a partnership with the University at Buffalo Center for Urban Studies. People trickle in and out of the Moot Community Center and the New Zion Baptist Church across the street. The historic churches, dating back to the 1800s, are quiet during the week and remain in good condition. People drive slowly down the streets, kids ride bikes, and people are out mowing lawns, stacking firewood in their yards, unloading their cars, or just sitting on the porch.

Like his daughter, Squirt grew up in and out of homes and yards in the neighborhood. He liked to pick plums from the neighbor's tree and one time broke the gate during a hasty exit; another time, he had to jump out of a pear tree after getting stung by a bee. Neighbors would put whitewash on a tree out front as a signal that they wanted someone to help them plant grass in the yard. Squirt and other kids would go dig the yard up for a few dollars and spend the money on marbles and penny candy. He remembers a childhood filled with after-school and summer programs.

At the basketball court behind the Neighborhood House, set up by the Buffalo Federation of Neighborhood Centers, the children played first, then the teens and adults would tell stories and offer advice to their juniors. Squirt remembers listening to old-timers in the neighborhood. "All we did was sit around and talk, after we played basketball," he said. "We would hang at the courts when they wasn't running us off and we'd sit right up on 'em and listen."

It used to take Squirt two hours to walk the two blocks up to High Street with his brother, because so many people wanted to talk to him. Shaketa also remembers his slow drives through the neighborhood marked by conversation stops to the chagrin of his teenage children. People have always gone to her father for help navigating everything from employment to personal issues to a pothole in need of repair.

Today, Lemon Street is only three blocks long. In the 1950s, it went several blocks longer, both to the south and the east. But construction of the Kensington Expressway in the 1960s cut off those blocks and then in the 1970s, the city's urban renewal policy led to bulldozing in the western half of the Fruit Belt. Some of the land went to the Buffalo Niagara Medical Campus (BNMC); some was left vacant. At its largest, the Fruit Belt was half a square mile. It is now half that size, which contributes to its vulnerability during the current, extensive phase of construction of the BNMC.

It also leads residents to worry that they will lose their neighborhood.

"What does a person of color or their home or space equate to in the establishment of wealth?" Shaketa asked. "There are lots of people in this neighborhood who have invested their lives. It makes me angry that now that [the Fruit Belt] is a place where professionals and white people want to live, our land or our wealth is worth more, and all of the other richness in the neighborhood may be swept away."

On official documents, the city has begun calling the neighborhood "Medical Park," rather than the "Fruit Belt," which some view as a demeaning move of erasure for a culturally vibrant place with multi-generational roots. For residents, though, the neighborhood will always be the "Fruit Belt."

The connections travel far beyond those who still live in the neighborhood since many more return daily or weekly, with even more coming in the summer for the famed Fruit Belt Picnic. The impact of the place extends well beyond its land, but there's no neighborhood without the land, and the people who have always lived in the Fruit Belt fear they will soon lose it.

"I mean, I still say I live in Fruit Belt, and I don't even live over there," Shaketa said. She hasn't moved far, only a couple of miles. "But I am also over there all the time. I was there today."

For Squirt, the connection is simple. "My heart is here," he said.

**Jennifer Connor** is a freelance writer who examines the relationship of people and place. She has written for Buffalo publications over the last three years and her story, "In the Shadow of the Sacred Heart," was chosen as one of *Block Club Magazine*'s Top Ten Stories. Her writing is informed by her background in social justice, her study of the natural world, and her many years as an educator of young children. She received her bachelor's in English from UMass Amherst. She lives on the West Side.

# Food, Art, Books, & Music

# The Armies of the Nightlife:
# A Requiem for the Wild, the Innocent, and the Old, Weird Buffalo

## Jeff Miers

They started arriving five years back.

New faces around the city: Kids who'd gone to college here but had broken with tradition when they didn't bail on Buffalo immediately following graduation. Folks who'd lived in the suburbs and had ventured into the city only for the occasional musical at Shea's, or perhaps a hockey game, and then hauled ass right back home.

Now they were moving into the heretofore abandoned downtown, attracted by the new builds, the lofts, the artisanal restaurants, the façade of an urban bohemianism that in fact wasn't bohemian at all, but rather a suburban attitude and world view transplanted a few miles away.

They seemed an innocuous enough lot, this influx of millennials and older working professionals. Was it just the Pegula money that attracted them? Was it the fact that there had been a city peppered with magnificent architecture lurking here all along? Was it the possibility of forcing Buffalo to conform to an image of hip urbanity borrowed from, say, Portland?

Maybe it was all of these. Maybe it was none.

These new arrivals brought with them many things—energy, attitude, music, beards, money. But they threatened to take as much as they gave.

They were after Buffalo's cultural underbelly, its old, weird, blurry blend of avant-garde art and punk rock, its boozy clubs that smelled like stale cigarette smoke, sweat and urine, its cheap apartments in Allentown, its air of artistic permissiveness, its ghosts of Mark Freeland and Paul Sharits, its acceptance of the fact that nothing was guaranteed and everything was allowed.

They were after its very soul.

## A Terrible Beauty

I moved to Buffalo in August 1990. I came here for the music. Born in the Berkshires, Massachusetts, transplanted to the Capital District for my teen years, and landing eventually at SUNY Fredonia, intent on blending my love of reading, writing, and rock into an enlightened state of unemployability. Buffalo struck me as the closest I was likely to get to the image I'd conjured of the New York City milieu that had produced Patti Smith,

Basquiat, Television, and Talking Heads.

I met Buffalo people at Fredonia, heard them speak of this mythical place called "the Continental," listened to them riff on the actual chance of getting a locally-recorded original song into rotation on this thing called WBNY-FM, a college radio station that didn't look down its nose at the talent in its own back yard.

They mentioned, jealously, a pop-punk trio on the ascent called the Goo Goo Dolls, who they said sounded like the Replacements, which struck me as something worth sounding like. They talked about a band playing art-punk known as the Ramrods, and that band soon came to Fredonia to play in our rathskeller, and a bunch of us got drunk and made the gig. These guys seemed like gods to me, even though they were my own age. They were smart, and they were roughshod, and I was hooked. A town that could cough up musical miscreants like this—guys who read books, drank a lot of beer, liked the Sex Pistols and jazz and the Violent Femmes—simply had to be cool.

I graduated in '89, went back to Albany, wasted a year on a doomed relationship, took some graduate classes, drank too much, nearly starved. I fancied myself entering a Rimbaud phase. But I was just denying the inevitable. I needed to be in Buffalo. So I packed my records and guitar and books and crappy clothes in my '82 Dodge Omni with the cassette player and the slipping clutch, and hit the Thruway. And I never looked back, fearing that I'd turn to a pillar of salt, or worse—end up stuck in Albany, a town with shopping malls in place of a discernible music scene.

The first band I saw when I arrived in Buffalo was Squid. They were deafening, horrible, and awesome, Captain Beefheart played as prog-punk-atonal noise, a sound I'd recognize over more than a decade later when I heard a group called Mars Volta. There I was, in this Continental I'd heard so much about, watching a band of freaks making a noise that both frightened and invigorated me. I glanced around the shadowy club. Everyone looked cool, like art school drop-outs with motel tans. And they were into Squid, this band of jesters who clearly couldn't care less about commercial success, only the awful beauty of this moment and the one right after it.

My fate was sealed.

## This Dead City

Your ancestors, all ye new arrivals in the downtown Buffalo arts subculture, were adventurers, rebels, narcissists, drunks, druggies, thinkers, fools, dreamers, and freaks. They suffered for this place, trying to pull from its barren landscape something meaningful, while simultaneously avoiding "real" work and refusing to grow up. Patti Smith wrote a song about them and those like them, called it "Dead City": "Is it any wonder they're spitting at the sun? God's parasites in abandoned sites, and they never have much fun." But she was wrong about the last part—we had fun. Too much.

Of course I joined a band. That was what I came here for. Soon I was playing the Continental. I'd made it. Everything else would be gravy.

We bought a dilapidated van, drove it to NYC and went to CBGB, but we were too late, for that dream had died, and all that was left was a punk-rock hangover. We played clubs in the West Village, we partied, we slept on floors. We got up and drove back home with all our gear and not enough, and then the next weekend we went and did it all over again, and it was heaven and it was hell.

When we were here in town, we played a lot, at the Continental and Nietzsche's and the Cabaret and Mohawk Place and these bars in the suburbs where metal and pop cover bands normally played, and the bar owners hated us, and they usually didn't pay us what we were promised. When we weren't playing, we went out to see our peers perform—Lollipop, Space Monster, Blue Whale, Girlpope, Towpath, the Waz, Ansley Court, the Groove, Moe, Michelle Weber, Monkeywrench, Doombuggy, the Splat Cats, Marvelous Sauce, the Headhunters, Scary Chicken, Phonkbutt, Dark Marbles, the Steam Donkeys, Tugboat Annie, the hippie bands, the metal guys, hip-hop djs, those enthralled with the burgeoning Seattle-based post-punk/hard-rock scene, the jazz players, the funk bands, the singer-songwriters—because they were all here.

We drank—there were no IPAs, a PBR was seen for what it actually was (a third-rate brew), and our favorite brand was "cold"—and we chain-smoked right there in the clubs, and some among us went too far and took up drugs, and we stayed until they threw us out at 4:00 a.m., and then we went out for breakfast or took the bacchanal back to someone's apartment. We threw parties, and the main attraction at these parties was the stereo, which we'd gather around and blast, dissecting and discussing the latest album from whoever it was, and this and the promise of an endless flow of drinks was enough to pack the place. We met the dawn in the previous evening's clothes, and knew a poor man's satori, clinging to the illusion of hope, unaware that our situation was hopeless, for who knew that the music industry was only a few years away from dying, and that no one would want to stand around drinking and listening to full albums at high volume for much longer? It was ending, though we thought that it was just beginning, that things would always be this way, that artistic people our age would be able to afford to work and live in Buffalo, poor but able to get by.

We played. We partied. We played some more. Sometimes we paused to eat. But not always. We didn't live a healthy life. And we didn't care.

How do you defend this irresponsible, largely hedonistic lifestyle? You don't, you can't, you shouldn't.

But it doesn't need defending. It is what it is. And it's always like this.

## Displaced and Disappointed

"Gentrification," they call it. "The process of renewal and rebuilding accompanying the influx of middle-class or affluent people into deteriorating areas that often displaces poorer residents," according to Merriam-Webster. Areas like ours, buried and forgotten in the detritus of abandoned industrial economies, are an easy mark for developers because we are so desperate for the whiff of something resembling success that we sell out to the first bidder, unaware that in doing so, we give away so much of what it is that makes us who and what we are.

It's happening here in Buffalo now. It starts with the housing in the less seedy urban areas becoming unaffordable for the artsy types who have long called those areas home. Soon clubs and art spaces are pushed out by raised rents. Suddenly there's nowhere to park when you want to go out to see a band. Newer residents in the Allentown district—the central music hub for our city—start complaining about the noise, the late-night gigs, the giddy and often inebriated denizens of those clubs emerging at 4:00 a.m. looking to continue the party. Transported suburbanites don't see the music scene as an essential contributing factor to the city's character. They think this is their city now. "Thanks for keeping this alive while we ignored it, but we've got this now, you can leave," their version of a Buffalo renaissance implies. As is always the case, this supposed renaissance is not likely to cross color lines, economic divides, or Main Street.

Change is necessary, inevitable, constant, and not always for the better.

The bands and artists working here today—more of them than ever—are threatened by the fine print in this renaissance, whether they know it or not. Our music scene is at the heart of our cultural identity. It's ours. And it's not for sale.

Stay weird, stay edgy, and stay idiosyncratic, Buffalo. You wear it well.

**Jeff Miers** is a musician and music journalist, and has been the pop music critic at the *Buffalo News* since 2002. A graduate of SUNY Fredonia, Miers did graduate work at University at Buffalo, and following college, went on to act as editor-in-chief of WNY weekly paper *Buffalo Beat*, and as co-founder of all-music fanzine *Rockstar Magazine*. Born in the Berkshires, Massachusetts, he spent his teen years in the Saratoga Springs region, before moving to Buffalo in the summer of 1990, and lived in the city until 2002. He served as guitarist with touring and recording indie-rock band The Tails from 1990 until the group's dissolution in 2000. He still performs regularly with several ensembles around Western New York. Miers has won several Associated Press awards during his tenure at the *Buffalo News*, and in 2008, was nominated for a Pulitzer Prize. He lives in Snyder with wife Kim, son Declan, and golden retriever, Melody.

# Down Beat

## Mitch Gerber

I found a piece of my father's past, after more than sixty years, in the stacks of the Library of Congress.

It happened this way.

In the early 1940s, when he was an eighteen-year-old kid in Buffalo, working as a copy boy at the *Courier-Express*, he got a press pass from *Down Beat*, the national jazz weekly. Years later, when I was a kid in Buffalo, he told me stories about flashing the card to get into downtown nightclubs, where he'd stand at the bar to hear Teddy Wilson and Gene Krupa and the other gods when they came to play.

He still had the pass in a dresser drawer, under a little box that held cuff links and tie clips. The pale green pasteboard with barely shriveled edges and art deco lettering had the managing editor's scribble at the bottom and was marked to expire in December 1943.

By that time my father was in the Army.

I wondered if he ever wrote about all that good Buffalo jazz.

"Nah," he said. "I just went to hear the music."

I didn't quite buy that. He had loved to write. After the war, he produced good stuff in a nonfiction-writing course at the University of Pittsburgh, which he attended on the GI Bill.

But by that time he was married, and I was on the way, followed by my sisters. Dad, responsible and self-effacing, spent most of his working life managing the menswear department at Hens & Kelly. He was content, but he didn't write anymore, except sales reports and letters to his kids at college.

Dad didn't talk much about himself or his feelings unless prodded. But he did tell magnificent bedtime stories about his childhood. He always loved words and taught me to use them honestly and sparingly.

When I went to work for the *Courier* in 1977 as a reporter, I walked along the same hallways that he had, saw stories impaled on the same spike on the city editor's desk, walked out into the night, after deadline, through the same polished brass doors. It felt good—Buffalo is a place of strong, deep roots.

And financial uncertainty.

The paper went out of business in 1982, and I eventually landed in Washington, D.C., editing for the *Chronicle of Higher Education*.

I had a good family, a rewarding job, and the years went by.

Then I came upon Dad's pale green card again, now squirreled away in a box of ephemera my parents left me when they moved to Florida. Again I wondered about my father's writing life.

The box contained short pieces of writing Dad had done for a 1943 college writing course. One piece was about his city editor at the *Courier-Express*, a man who was still working there—and still wearing the same green, anti-glare eyeshade—when I started as a copyboy in the summer of 1968. Another was about a hamburger joint. Another was about his father, a pharmacist, who ran Holzman's Drugs at Delaware and Chippewa in the 1930s. Spot Coffee is there now. My grandfather never raised his voice, Dad wrote, except once, when there was a fire in the store.

I read Dad's pieces and wondered if he had ever been published in *Down Beat*.

I was in an ideal place to find out. Washington, D.C. offers easy access to resources that even the internet can't yet match. The federal government has preserved a lot of paper. At the Library of Congress, I applied for a reader identification card and turned a couple of corners to the Performing Arts Reading Room.

Yes, they said, the library had every issue of *Down Beat*, the oldest on microfilm. I handed in the call slip—Volumes nine through twelve, January 1942 to December 1945—threaded the film into a viewing machine, and advanced to 1943.

The machine whirred in the darkened little room as I maneuvered through the weeks of that wartime year.

February 1: "Tex Beneke Joins Heidt's Band."

March 1: "Niteries Face Race Problem" and "'God Bless America' Puts American Band Leader in Jap Jail in Shanghai."

May 1: "Dooley Wilson Plays Village."

June 1: "How Columbia Bagged Sinatra."

Below that big story was a brief item, just two paragraphs: "Blackout No Bar to Solid Buffalo Bash."

I stared at the page for a few moments, drinking it in, hearing Krupa and Wilson in my head.

Then I went home and phoned my father.

"Dad," I said, holding the copy I'd made of the *Down Beat* story, "I want to read you something."

*BUFFALO – A blackout halted traffic and put out lights in four western New York counties May 5, but it didn't turn out the lights of Memorial Auditorium or stem the frenzy of jive and jitterbugging that went on at the annual Musician's Union Parade of Bands.*

He interrupted me: "Did I write that?"

*More than 7,500 jammed the huge Madison Square Garden-like struc-*
*ture to dance to the music of 25 bands, headed by Mitchell Ayres, and ap-*
*plaud the rhythms of the Andrews Sisters.*

"I wrote that! I wrote that!" Dad hardly ever raised his voice.

*Continuous music was provided by local bands that alternated from*
*stands at opposite sides of the auditorium. The music started at 7:00 p.m.,*
*and at 5:30 a.m., when this correspondent was leaving, reluctant but beat*
*to his size nines, the session was still going strong.*

I paused before pronouncing the last line:

—*Saul Gerber*

**Mitch Gerber** grew up in Kenmore, where he graduated from Kenmore
West Senior High School. In school and college he spent summers working at Rugby Knitting Mills, on Seneca Street.; the New York Central
Railroad, at the Central Terminal; AM&A's, downtown; and the *Couri-*
*er-Express*, all of which are now out of business. After several years away,
he returned, worked for a sports magazine called *Buffalo Fan*, bought a
house on Granger Place, and landed back at the *Courier-Express*, where
he expected to stay until it folded, in 1982. Several stops followed; for
the past twenty-one years he's been an editor at the *Chronicle of Higher*
*Education*, in Washington, D.C.

# Finding the Words We Do Not Have Yet at the Just Buffalo Writing Center

## Robin Lee Jordan

Yesterday, I listened to a group of young writers record a pre-apocalyptic summit set in the year 2666 for an episode of their podcast, "This Buffalonian Life." Two days prior, I listened to this same group of teenagers turn each others' fears into comics and their dreams into poems.

> Once I dreamed
> the sky was red
> The red sky
> came creeping in
> staining white cotton
> blue.
>
> *—Eden (age fourteen)*

A few weeks earlier, award-winning Norwegian memoirist Karl Ove Knausgaard told them to "F*#@ everything. Just write."

A few months earlier, some of these same young writers were walking up the stairs of the Just Buffalo Writing Center (JBWC) in downtown Buffalo for their first workshop. Some already identified as writers and strode right in, chapters of their first novel in hand. Some, coerced by a parent or teacher or counselor, trudged up the stairs, heads hung as low as their expectations. Some tiptoed in, not sure if they belonged, not sure where, exactly, they were. Regardless of how they come to us or where they're coming from, most of the young people who discover the JBWC quickly realize they've found something extraordinary: a safe place to search for the words they do not have yet.

> When I first came to the center I didn't know who I was or even what to do with myself. I didn't talk to anyone. I didn't know what to make of it all...I talk now, probably way too much. I don't just know *what* to make of it all, I know that I can make it all.
>
> *—Hemingway (age fifteen)*

I'm the coordinator of the Just Buffalo Writing Center (JBWC) and, each week, in a loft overlooking downtown Buffalo, I help show young people how creative writing can alter the way they see and interact with

158

the world. Through workshops, students learn to approach writing in new ways. They write comics about their random daily interactions, create plays inspired by "mystery bags" of props, and are reminded of the poetry within music. They generate text from paintings and make paintings of text. They are introduced to "new" tools with which to write. For instance, ever since our opening in the spring of 2014, we've speckled our center with typewriters for collaboration, creation, and play. One typewriter sits on a pedestal in front of our windows, encouraging young writers to describe a slice of Buffalo as part of an ongoing collaborative poem. Each line marks a different voice, a new perspective, creating a poetic dialogue about our city.

> A seagull on the head of a streetlight radiating.
> Clouds working as love letters.
> Teenagers in hoodies growing their fingernails. Growing their fingernails.
> Summer is locked inside every parked car.
> Iron skeletons woven together with rust.
> We forget what it's like to swallow bugs on our bicycles.
> You must believe everything is real.
> It is not fake. The cars, the people, the buildings.
>
> —*JBWC visitors*

The way literature can strengthen our understanding of our identities and the identities of others has never been clearer to me. Our shelves are packed with books donated by the community and some of the literary scene's most innovative small presses like 1913 and Rescue Press. These books have introduced our young writers to voices that often go unheard or unnoticed in schools and the literary world. Alongside established voices, our library celebrates emerging local and international voices, indigenous writers, writers of color, and queer writers. Our students are thrilled to find their own complex identities and the lives of their friends and community mirrored in these texts. One week, these writings might inspire us to debate the cultural value of memes or turn snowflakes into language. Other weeks, they might teach us how to grapple with some of the ugliest realities of Buffalo (and humanity) through story. Racism, sexism, homophobia, war, climate change, greed; our students process these difficult realities using words they didn't know they knew.

> Turned tables, unfair laws;
> hypocrisy—be an adult, be a child.
> Be both...be none.
> Try again and again,
> but no one can hear you through the dirt.

Expectations, helplessness
collide together in a daunting world,
like a universe of helpless stars
set on a crash course..."
  —*Lucy (age sixteen) in response to Louise Erdrich's* The Round House.

In the middle of the night when I'm watching TV,
sometimes I wonder why there aren't characters like me.
And when there are,
why are they often not like me?"
  —*Darren (age fifteen) in response to Claudia Rankine's* Citizen.

In a city like Buffalo, which continues to deal with poverty, drug abuse, crime, and low graduation rates, a safe, empowering space for students can mean secure footing towards a promising future. While many of our young writers are loved and carefree, others face difficult challenges. For some of our students, they find refuge in a safe space free from racial/sexual/gender discrimination, difficult home situations, or the stigma of living with mental illness. For all youth who pick up a pen and write with us, JBWC is a place to speak freely and take imaginative risks without the fear of judgment.

now we glow
light flows like waterfalls

  —*Robin (age fifteen)*

Unexpected exhales fill
the air above the
table top, floating between the
vowels and consonants that we have
learned to call home.

  —*Hannah (age sixteen)*

What's it like to become a family?
It's like seeing starlight.

  —*Birch (age fifteen)*

Something magical is happening here.
  I don't hesitate for a moment when I say that Buffalo will be better for it. I love watching how the exploration of words connects young people to their local and global community more deeply. Four walls cannot contain these teenage writers. They've read before large crowds at climate justice rallies, voicing their anguish at the fast destruction of our fragile planet.

Right now,
we are coughing carbon through catacombed lungs
the smoke crystallizing into chaos
It is easy to watch the icecaps melt
when you will not be the one drowning in the sea
It is easy to justify the means
when you will not see the ends
When you put a price tag on every seed
and tax on every drop of water
you won't be the ones paying

*—JBWC Young Writers*

JBWC writers have raised funds for the Buffalo "bookbike," which delivers books to kids in neighborhoods without libraries. They have set up our typewriters on the busy sidewalks of Main Street and Elmwood Avenue in order to turn the concerns of their community into poetry. As part of our made-to-order poem project, "customers" request a poem on any topic and our young writers type it while they wait. The students then proclaim these poems from our custom-made JBWC soapbox.

War is a terrible thing
A combination of dyslexic
weapons
shrinking the future into a
pinhole of dehumanized humans.
A fire stealing people out of
homes that were never really
theirs.
Cattle cars through market places of
fruits never to be purchased.

—JBWC Young Writers

broken hearts matter
we shouldn't hold fear
let black lives blossom

*—Robin (age fifteen)*

Every day I wake up feeling grateful; grateful to be taking part in the formation of young citizens and trailblazing artists through the celebration of literature; grateful, to borrow from the amazing Audre Lorde, to help them find "the words they do not have yet."

I have no idea how to paint you the picture of
my hopes and dreams
because I cannot speak using words I don't know.
I am feeling...
This is what I think...
I didn't want you to go, but...
I have no idea how to complete these sentences.
I have no description for the thoughts,
no approximation for my love, no alternate word for my dreams.

—*Hemingway (age fifteen)*

As the lucky teacher of these students, I am learning how eager some Buffalo teens are to awaken and how crucial art is within that messy growing process. I am learning how quickly young artists develop when offered the time and place to play, share, and struggle. I am learning that a good teacher balances humor and tragedy, seriousness and play. I am learning that there are hordes of undeveloped, talented writers who have no idea they are writers because no one has introduced them to the art form's true possibilities.

But perhaps the most important lesson my students have taught me is that I don't have the words yet either. What a privilege it is to search alongside these remarkable young people.

**Robin Lee Jordan**'s creative nonfiction, fiction, and poetry have been published in various publications, including the *Buffalo News*, *alice blue review*, *H_NGM_N*, *Puerto del Sol*, and *Paper Darts*. She received her M.F.A. in poetry from Oregon State University and was an editor for Toe Good Poetry. Robin is the coordinator of Just Buffalo Writing Center, a free, creative writing center for teens. She also runs the community art project (B)uffalo (A)rt (D)ispensary, a coin-operated, mini-art exchange that repurposes toy vending machines. She lives in the Delaware District of Buffalo and can see Forest Lawn Cemetery from her front porch.

# I am a Buffaholic

## Andrew Z. Galarneau

Hi. My name is Andrew, and I'm a Buffaholic.

By day, I write about restaurants for the *Buffalo News* and Buffalo. com, a daily newspaper and website that serve a metropolitan area of about one million people. By night, I roam the streets of Buffalo and its environs, looking for the best meals possible.

In 2016, Buffalo is experiencing a restaurant gold rush. From downtown to the suburbs, new places are opening at a pace that industry veterans call unprecedented.

I recognize some of the main reasons. A generation raised on the Food Channel has taken up restaurant-going as daily sport. They roll their eyes at Guy Fieri but are hungry for the satisfaction of discovering an authentic place around the corner. Their smartphones are alive with others having better times than they are, and they will spend to close the gap, and plant their Instagram flag.

Restaurant-makers have noticed. Decades of population loss and economic stagnation have put restaurant-capable real estate within financial reach of a broad group of operators. They include the usual suspects, established restaurateurs expanding their portfolios and opportunistic business types hoping to turn a buck.

They also include families who settled here after fleeing war or worse in their native lands, blessing their new neighbors with the flavors of Burma, Iraq, Bosnia, and Ethiopia. Then there are the sons and daughters of Buffalo who left town to grow up in kitchens in Manhattan and Aspen and Washington, D.C., before coming back to stake their claim.

Trying to keep up with Buffalo's new places and dishes of the moment is pleasantly impossible. It's the best job in the building, the best job I've ever had. Except when it's the worst.

Cry me a river, I know. But hang on and hear me out.

My name is Andrew, and I'm a Buffaholic.

Buffaholism's core condition is an abiding sense that your town will always be ranked among the losers, synonymous with failure. It manifests in different ways. One symptom is a tendency to scoff at any development news touted as a Sign That Things Have Changed. Having heard announcements of Signs That Things Have Changed for most of my adult life, I have developed a severe allergy to municipal cheerleading.

My Buffaholism manifests in a severe reluctance to believe that things have changed, or make proclamations to that end. I don't want to contribute to an air of false optimism, believing that, like the overuse of antibiotics, it weakens natural defenses so infections can run wild.

Over the last two or three years, I have seen glimmers of something remarkable happening in Buffalo restaurants, but I've kept it mostly to myself. A part of me wanted to shout my head off about it years ago. I did not.

Why? Because I love my city, and I hate to see it let down. Monday morning at the office after a Bills loss is a black hole that no tonnage of Timbits can lighten.

I'm a Buffaholic. But I'm getting better.

I'll start with this: my job is changing my life. The restaurants of Buffalo are forcing me to confront my illness. Plate by plate, meal by meal, they are feeding me the antidote, the medicine that's helping me believe in my city again.

## Does God Hate Buffalo?

I wasn't born this way. I grew up out in the woods, in Indian Falls, a Genesee County town without a stoplight. If I climbed to the top of the maple tree across the street, I could see the Marine Midland Tower's lights on the western horizon, marking downtown Buffalo.

My understanding of the world beyond the cornfields came from two sources: Buffalo television stations watchable on our twelve-inch black-and-white set with improvised coat hanger antenna, and the *Buffalo Evening News*, delivered by car each afternoon to the tube next to our mailbox.

Screen time was limited by the benevolent tyranny of parents hung up on homework, but primarily because being the 1980s, it was our only screen. The newspaper was a much more powerful influence, pumping a river of daily information into my developing brain. Which brings us to the sports section.

Other pages held my interest—the comics first, of course, and I treasured the "A" section for its staging of dramas and tragedies from writers around the world: earthquakes and floods and revolutions.

But the sports pages were where the champions lived. Every fall, the Buffalo Bills and Buffalo Sabres embarked on the road to glory, chronicled in loving detail by writers and photographers serving as surrogates for a community that had suffered so much loss and heartbreak. Loss and heartbreak, the province of the local news and business sections: companies bleeding away to Mexico, entire industries that defined the city skyline crumbling into ruin.

No matter how grim the local news section was, the sports section had a different tone. Every season, the Bills and Sabres offered hope. That was how I got hooked.

From 1990 to 1993, the years the Buffalo Bills went to the Super Bowl, I was working at newspapers in Concord, New Hampshire, and St. Petersburg, Florida. As the guy from Buffalo, I made a point of frying up chicken wings and inviting people to my apartment to watch the game four years in a row. For four years, I hosted celebrations that morphed into wakes, during which I redefined the term "poor loser."

That was a long time ago. Not long enough. My left eyelid still twitches every time I hear "wide right."

In 1997, I was hired by the *Buffalo News* and returned to the city in time to experience several Sabres playoff runs. I did not host any parties. When Brett Hull ended the 1999 Stanley Cup finals with his skate in the crease, I was sad but not surprised. The next year, John LeClair put a puck through the side of the net during a playoff game and the National Hockey League said it was a good goal. I was starting to feel like I deserved it.

On May 13, 2006, when Jason Pominville went coast-to-coast short-handed in overtime to assassinate the Ottawa Senators, and Rick Jeanneret howled "Now do you believe?" I did. I did believe.

Sixteen days later, on June 1, 2006, I woke to learn that bedrock Sabres defenseman Jay McKee could not play in the game that decided if the Sabres would play for the Stanley Cup because of a previously unknown knee infection. I started to reassess a few things.

What if God did in fact hate Buffalo? If it really was the Nineveh of the Great Lakes, what would the signs be? When Brian Campbell was whistled for delay of game and Rob Brind'Amour ended the Sabres season on the power play, there was no conclusive proof that Campbell's puck didn't deflect off God's shoulder before going over the glass.

Rock bottom. The little boy fan in me died that season. The fact that the Buffalo Bills have not been to the playoffs since 1999—before two of my three teenagers were born—feels, at times, like a kind of mercy.

I still go to Sabres games, sharing a pair of season tickets with colleagues. I sit in the same seat I was in the night I fell in love with Dominik Hasek. I'm paying $75 per game, call it $100 with snacks and drinks.

This year, I thought of how far that C-note would go in a Buffalo restaurant. Go to one of the better places, and I'm all but guaranteed an experience that will not only leave me satisfied, but proud to live in Buffalo.

Proud. To live in Buffalo.

My name is Andrew, and I'm a Buffaholic.

But I'm getting better since I found a new team to root for.

Every week, I choose a restaurant and write a review that tries to tell people what it's like to eat there. I'm the only person who gets paid to eat in all of Buffalo's new places and tell everyone what I think. That's a lot of responsibility for a kid from Indian Falls.

I have no taste for leading cheers of municipal greatness. I have a gut fear of getting people's hopes up. But it's my job to tell the truth as I see it. So here goes.

Something remarkable is growing in Buffalo. Already, today's Buffalonians can explore the city's greatest burst of restaurant investment in modern history. An established roster of fine and casual restaurants has been joined by a plethora of places offering choices Buffalo has never gotten before. In the last five years, restaurants have opened across Western New York that have fed me some of the best dishes of my life.

I can still step into Duff's for a double hot and a pitcher. A fish fry at Wiechec's in Kaisertown, spaghetti sausage parm at DiTondo's, pasta that makes me want to hug the chef at Ristorante Lombardo.

What's new is hidden in a former Kenmore pizzeria turned into a sweet little restaurant called Balkan Dining. Ask for "pita." (Elsewhere it's known as burek.) Whereupon a Bosnian woman makes a sheet of fresh phyllo dough, fills it with meat, cheese, potatoes, or spinach, curls it into a snail, bakes it to a flaky golden-brown, and gives it to you. For $7.

Over on Grant Street, West Side, a place called West Side Bazaar is, dollar for dollar, the most fun dining room in Buffalo. Eight or nine families who came to the United States in search of a better life are making a run at their own American dreams, but it's disguised as a scrappy little food court. Two kinds of Burmese, Ethiopian, Laotian, dim sum, Thai, all cooked to real ethnic standards because they're feeding their cousins but the new neighbors get to horn in on the action. Prices top out at $12.

There's Five Points Bakery, where two former gutter punks have built a place making bread from Hamburg wheat that makes toast that stars in tourist guides. Or Essex Street Pub, the scruffy West Side bar where Ani DiFranco and the Goo Goo Dolls played some of their first sets, now offering legit barbecue and vegan club sandwiches with Buffalo-brewed beers, another homegrown duo honing its chops.

There's even a Spanish restaurant in Buffalo now (Amherst, actually), for the first time in forever. At Aro, a young man from Clarence, back from a stint with one of the best Spanish chefs in America, is cooking with his wife, a pastry chef. Their tapas and creative desserts have city dwellers headed for the suburbs to eat.

Meanwhile, downtown, Toutant is making Buffalonians relearn how to make a reservation. Its jam is homegrown versions of Southern classics with killer hooks; Louisiana-born chef James Roberts' stage is a building that would probably have been torn down otherwise. Because of his decision to plant his flag in Buffalo, on Mother's Day I got to take my mother to a place with the blue-collar classics she loves, made with fine-dining focus. You can get your mom roses. I took mine downtown for the best chicken and waffle brunch ever.

In East Aurora, a couple who fell in love with an old bakery in Paris has aimed to recreate its best features, down to a wood-fired oven where most of its twenty-eight breads are fired. Then Elm Street Bakery adds first-class sweets and rustic dinners. On Hertel Avenue, Craving is offering carnivores and vegetarians old-school dishes made with a new appreciation of local ingredients. Chef Adam Goetz has been working out deals with local farmers to grow vegetables and raise animals that go directly to dinner plates in Buffalo, New York.

I have taken to calling such places New-School Buffalo. They could put Buffalo on the nation's culinary map, I think. Not by out-fancying anyone, but by making food you can only experience in Buffalo. By devising myriad ways to show eaters that Lockport pork and Lewiston peaches are eats to brag on just as much as Carolina shrimp or Vidalia onions; that there is an indigenous Buffalo cuisine that goes beyond chicken wings.

Not that there is anything wrong with deep-fried bar snacks. At a New-School Buffalo place like Steven Gedra's The Black Sheep, your $10 can get you crispy nuggets of luscious T-Meadow Farm pork grown in Lockport and swaddled in kimchi barbecue sauce. With housemade Ranch dressing. Made in Buffalo. Only in Buffalo.

They taste like victory.

These new places are just starting, really. They're investing time and money in developing relationships with farmers, working out how to get more of the good stuff when it's never going to be as steady as the Sysco truck's rounds. You'd have to call them underdogs, especially when you drive down Niagara Falls Boulevard at dinnertime and count the full lots at chain restaurants with multi-million-dollar television ad budgets.

If we support these sons and daughters of Buffalo with our money, and our attention, I think to myself, we could win—national recognition, anyway. Respect.

My name is Andrew, and I may always be a Buffaholic. But I'm taking recovery one meal at a time.

Perhaps a football or hockey team will bathe Buffalo in reflected glory one day. My money is on Buffalo's restaurants. At their best, I'll put 'em up against anybody.

**Andrew Z. Galarneau** was born in Chicago. A 1983 graduate of Pembroke High School, he graduated from the University at Buffalo in 1988 with a diploma that says Journalism despite the fact that the University at Buffalo does not have a journalism major. After reporting for the *Concord Monitor*, *St. Petersburg Times*, and *Lowell Sun*, he was hired by the *Buffalo News* in 1997, and became food editor in 2012. He is a Duff's guy.

Photograph by Julian Montague

# let love be at the end:
# Lucille Clifton's literary legacy

## Barbara Cole

Buffalo is known for chicken wings and epic snowstorms, for losing four NFL Super Bowls in a row and still having one of the most dedicated fan bases. The locals might wax poetic about Frank's RedHot® Sauce, butter lambs, sponge candy, or the whiff of Cheerios wafting on the breeze, but beyond these indelible edibles, one of the greatest points of Buffalo pride still remains a secret. Even among those who were born and raised in the city of good neighbors, few diehard residents realize how many great writers have called Buffalo home.

Some Western New Yorkers might know that Mark Twain lived here for a few years or maybe they are vaguely aware that the award-winning novelist, Joyce Carol Oates, grew up in Lockport. Perhaps they've heard of Robert Creeley, the influential twentieth-century poet who resided in Buffalo for nearly forty years. But how many know the full extent of Buffalo's literary legacy?

How many realize that F. Scott Fitzgerald spent part of his boyhood living in what is now known as the Hotel Lenox or that he went to school on Cleveland Street at Nardin Academy? That William Wells Brown, considered the first African American to have written a novel, worked on the steamboats along Lake Erie, helping fugitive slaves escape through the Underground Railroad? That two-time Nobel prize winner J.M. Coetzee taught here; that Bollingen Prize winner Susan Howe spent formative years here and later returned as one of the founding members of the University at Buffalo's Poetics Program; that her younger sister, Fanny Howe, who went on to earn the Ruth Lilly Poetry Prize for lifetime achievement was born here; that path-breaking literary critic Leslie Fiedler called Buffalo home for nearly four decades and is buried at Forest Lawn cemetery; that playwright and labor organizer Emanuel "Manny" Fried spent the majority of his life in Buffalo; that best-selling Jewish author and rabbi, Chaim Potok, was born here; that African American visionary Ishmael Reed grew up here.

And the list goes on: John Barth, Charles Bernstein, Alexis De Veaux, Raymond Federman, Leslie Feinberg, Eric Gansworth, John Logan, Nnedi Okorafor, Charles Olson, Elizabeth Willis. Research any of the names and discover the monumental bodies of work, the astonishing range of accomplishments. Walk the streets contemplating whose footsteps came before. Open your eyes and you might discover that the gentleman standing behind you in line at the Lexington Co-op is Pulitzer Prize winner Carl Dennis or that the neighbor you see jogging down your block, best-selling author Brian Castner, was just interviewed on NPR's Fresh Air by Terry Gross. There's yet another Buffalo connection: Gross earned her bachelor's and master's degrees from The University at Buffalo.

Like so many before, I came here in 2000 because, back then, if you wanted to devote your life to poetry, Buffalo was the place to go. I came, specifically, for the UB Poetics Program, but the community I found here kept me from leaving. Still, even after my extensive studies, it took nearly a decade before I discovered that Lucille Clifton had a Buffalo connection.

Born in Depew on June 27, 1936, to Samuel, a steelworker, and Thelma, a laundress, Thelma Lucille Sayles grew up on Purdy Street on Buffalo's East Side. At the age of ten she began writing her first poems. At sixteen Lucille graduated from Fosdick-Masten Park High School—now City Honors—and was headed to Howard University on scholarship to study drama. After two years, she transferred to SUNY Fredonia and then made her way back to Buffalo where she became involved with a local theater group. But it would take me years to learn all of that.

In April 2009, I was working as the Education Director of Just Buffalo Literary Center, a not-for-profit organization whose mission is to create and strengthen communities through the literary arts. One of the education programs I collaborated on was the Buffalo-Williamsville Poetry, Music, Dance and Art Celebration—a showcase bringing together students from the city and suburbs through the arts. Every year, this event features a nationally-renowned poet whose work inspires students to create musical compositions, visual artworks, choreographed dances, and their own original poems. Lucille Clifton was selected as that year's featured poet. I was surprised to learn that she had spent so much of her life in Buffalo; growing up in Philadelphia, I always thought of Clifton as a Baltimore poet. Pleasantly surprised, I was even more thrilled at the prospect of meeting her.

After the event—a lengthy affair which included performances by nearly 200 students from more than thirty high schools—the line of people waiting to talk to Ms. Clifton was long. While waiting, I found myself shaking hands with a poet named Kazim Ali who, at one point, mentioned that Just Buffalo had been a defining force in his life.

"Being a teaching artist for Just Buffalo really inspired me to go on to be a poet," he told me.

It was a claim I wouldn't forget. As my conversation with Kazim concluded, I glanced over at the line again, still swarming with eager-faced students. "This is their night," I told myself. "I'll meet her some other time."

But there wouldn't be another time. Lucille Clifton died less than a year later—exactly fifty years to the day of her own mother's death.

Four years later, when I became Artistic Director of Just Buffalo, I often found myself thinking back to what a missed opportunity that night had been. And so, when it came time to select a writer to receive Just Buffalo's Literary Legacy Award, I decided to track down Ishmael Reed, a contemporary of Clifton's who had, like her, grown up in Buffalo and gone on to make a name for himself as a highly-acclaimed writer and leading voice in defining African-American literature. As much as I might have known about Reed's work, it was only after meeting him that I fully grasped the pivotal role he played in Clifton's life.

On the morning before the awards ceremony, I took Reed over to the Willert Park housing development on the East Side where he lived as a young boy. Afterwards, we visited old haunts and he reminisced about the early days of the Buffalo Community Drama Guild Workshop—the same theater group Clifton had been involved with after she returned from Fredonia. It was through this collective that Reed introduced Lucille to a young philosophy professor named Fred Clifton. Soon enough, Lucille Sayles became Lucille Clifton. The contrast between the vibrant arts community Reed described around Michigan Avenue and the buildings we confronted now was stark. Few of the places Reed described still existed. Formerly bustling neighborhoods had become abandoned, seemingly forgotten sections of Buffalo.

Story after story circled back to Clifton—how much Reed had always admired her work, so much so that he sent some of her poems to Langston Hughes in 1967. Hughes must have shared Reed's admiration for the quality of her writing because he included her poems alongside the likes of W.E.B. DuBois, Countee Cullen, Richard Wright, and Gwendolyn Brooks in the groundbreaking anthology, *The Poetry of the Negro, 1746-1970*. What a life-changing moment that must have been for the young mother who now had four daughters and two sons with Fred. Just as the growing family left for Baltimore, Clifton won the YM-YWHA Poetry Center Discovery Award, which subsequently led in 1969 to the publication of her first book of poems, *Good Times*. By year's end, it was named one of the *New York Times* best books of the year.

For the next four decades, Clifton continued to break barriers and make history. The poet laureate of Maryland from 1975 to 1985, her second collection of poems, *Two-Headed Woman* (1980), earned Clifton her first Pulitzer Prize nomination. Then, in 1988, she made history as the only author to ever receive two Pulitzer Prize nominations in a single year—one for *Good Woman: Poems and a Memoir: 1969-1980* and a second for *Next: New Poems*.

Over the course of her career, Clifton published fourteen books of poetry, a memoir, and eighteen books for children, including her much-loved

Everett Anderson series. Clifton's awards include an Emmy for her work with Marlo Thomas on the TV special *Free To Be...You and Me*, a Coretta Scott King Award for children's literature, the National Book Award for *Blessing the Boats: New and Collected Poems 1988-2000*, and the Ruth Lilly Poetry Prize—yet another historical moment as Clifton was the first African-American woman to win this award.

Despite all of the honors and awards, Clifton's poetic style, with its spoken word cadence (largely unheard of when she started writing) and noteworthy lack of capitalization remained unassuming, fully self-possessed but without any posturing or ego.

Toni Morrison, who edited Clifton's memoir, opens her "Foreword" to Clifton's posthumously published *The Collected Poems of Lucille Clifton 1965-2010* by noting that the "love readers feel for Lucille Clifton—both the woman and her poetry—is constant and deeply felt.... Accolades from fellow poets and critics refer to her universal human heart; they describe her as a fierce caring female. They compliment her courage, vision, joy—unadorned (meaning 'simple'), mystical, poignant, humorous, intuitive, harsh and loving." And yet, Morrison continues, "I am startled by the silence in these interpretations of her work. There are no references to her intellect, imagination, scholarship or her risk-taking manipulation of language."

Her themes tackle the most challenging issues—racism and bigotry, terrorism and violence, oppression and loss—while simultaneously reveling in joy and love, faith and spirituality. Clifton's poems are full of history—Native American and African heritage, biblical stories and mythology, iconic leaders—but are also deeply personal, chronicling her own hardships and heartbreaks: the loss of her beloved Fred to cancer when he was only forty-nine; the deaths of two of their children, daughter, Frederica, and son, Channing; and her own struggles with three bouts of cancer and a kidney transplant. And yet, Clifton's work manages to be full of humor and hope, the common thread an underlying affirmation of the human spirit.

In my work with Just Buffalo Literary Center, I've spent years thinking about how best to honor writers like Clifton who have called Buffalo home. I've collected images of how cities across the world identify literary landmarks—the striking blue circles of London marking the homes of writers like Charles Dickens, Virginia Woolf, and George Orwell; Dublin's bronze plates submerged in the sidewalks depicting key scenes from James Joyce's *Ulysses*; Paris's etched placards marking famous addresses such as 27 Rue de Fleurus where Gertrude Stein and Alice Toklas held their literary salons. As a team, we've discussed what Just Buffalo might do to increase the community's awareness of our literary gifts, met with colleagues in the literary world and leaders in city infrastructure, written grants and tried to cobble together funding, talked and dreamed and dreamed some more.

And then, quite suddenly, in December 2015, we received funding for the first phase of a public arts initiative honoring Buffalo's great writers. To my mind, there was no question that one of the first pieces would honor Lucille Clifton.

On January 26, 2016, our team reconvened to strategize. Towards the end of our discussion, Laurie Dean Torrell, Just Buffalo's Executive Director, opened a book and began to read aloud "blessing the boats"—arguably Clifton's most anthologized and well-known poem:

> may the tide
> that is entering even now
> the lip of our understanding
> carry you out
> beyond the face of fear
> may you kiss
> the wind then turn from it
> certain that it will
> love your back  may you
> open your eyes to water
> water waving forever
> and may you in your innocence
> sail through this to that

My breath caught in my throat as the last line hung in the air: "sail through this to that." We sat in collective silence, the power of Clifton's words washing over us. Breaking the silence, I gasped, "I have goosebumps," and others chimed in, too. The energy in the room was palpable. At the time, I thought it was just excitement at the prospect of creating some sort of lasting artwork that would pay homage to Clifton. But less than thirty hours later I came to understand that something powerful had been unleashed that day.

The very next night, just one day after Laurie read that poem aloud, Kazim Ali sent us an email. Since our initial minutes-long meeting in 2009, we had been in contact only once when, in the summer of 2015, I reached out to ask Kazim if he'd be part of a series of video testimonials I was curating for Just Buffalo's fortieth anniversary. Though we had not spoken in five years, I still remembered Kazim's passionate declaration about how Just Buffalo had inspired him to be a poet, and invited him to tell his story on film. Much to my delight, Kazim graciously agreed. Unfortunately, the day before the filming, a last-minute change in travel plans prevented him from returning to Buffalo from his current home in Ohio.

That was in August. And now, months later, an email arrived from Kazim letting me know that he was in town and ready to shoot his Forty Stories testimonial if we still wanted it. As if by magic, Kazim also mentioned that he had recently contacted Clifton's eldest daughter, Sidney, inquiring about Clifton's various Buffalo addresses. They were contemplating some sort of historical designation and wondered if Just Buffalo might like to be involved—our grant, our conversations, our dreams completely unbeknownst to them.

Breathless, I called Kazim, filling him in on the astonishing coincidence. We hatched a plan to go scout out Clifton's former residences the next day together.

"Who knows what we'll find," Kazim mused.

Clifton's body of work insistently circles back to her complicated childhood. She chronicles abuse by her father and recalls her mother—also a poet—setting fire to her body of work after Clifton's father denied her the right to be a writer. In her first collection of poems, *Good Times*, Clifton dedicated her book simply "for mama." Her poems pay homage to the denied ambitions not only of her own mother, but of the generations who came before:

> in the inner city
> or
> like we call it
> home
> we think a lot about uptown
> and the silent nights
> and the houses straight as
> dead men
> and the pastel lights
> and we hang on to our no place
> happy to be alive
> and in the inner city
> or
> like we call it
> home

On a cold, gray morning, Kazim and I drove around Buffalo's East Side, tracking down each address only to confront empty lots dusted with snow. Some houses on the street remained standing in varying stages of decrepitude, while others had been replaced by new construction. But Clifton's had been razed. There were no doors that we might hope to enter, no walls to press our ears against in an attempt to listen to whatever legends they might have to tell. Still, we photographed the emptiness, silently pondering what those streets might have looked like when little Lucille had looked out her bedroom window or when the young Mrs. Fred Clifton, wife of a university professor, brought their beautiful babies home.

At the Purdy Street address—arguably the most resonant in Clifton's poems which mention the street by name—Kazim and I snapped photos of what is now a driveway used as a makeshift parking lot for the house-turned-church next door. On the other side of the property, I noticed a woman's face at the window, peering at us through the curtains. Eventually, the woman stepped outside and Kazim and I explained our interest in this empty piece of land.

"A great writer grew up here," I offered, but heard the inadequacy of those words. "Multiple Pulitzer Prize nominations," I added. My voice trailed off, realizing that no label, no accolade could encapsulate the life that had blossomed from this location.

Standing there, I began to feel how inadequate a placard would be. How could anything so small evoke the largeness of Clifton's life? This, too, is the problem one faces when trying to talk about Buffalo. It's not about the food; it's not the football. There's no one thing you can point to that fully articulates its singularity.

At the next address, just a few blocks away on a small dead-end street, Kazim and I once again confronted absence. No house, no marker, no nothing. I photographed an enormous tree across the street that seemed large enough to date back to Clifton's youth, a projection borne out of the desire to hold on to something. I could almost hear her words:

earth

here is where it was dry
when it rained
and also
here
under the same
what was called
tree
it bore varicolored
flowers children bees
all this used to be a
place once all this
was a nice place
once

Why had I been thinking so strictly in terms of place? What had I been looking for? All this time I had regretted never meeting Clifton, never shaking her hand or asking her to sign my books when, in fact, she had been here all along.

The next day, I called Clifton's eldest daughter, Sidney—the one who provided Kazim with specific addresses. I shared with her the synchronicity of the previous days and my hope for some lasting tribute to Clifton. As we talked, a vision began to emerge of a sculpture or a fountain, perhaps a gate, something that might catch the light.

"You know," Sidney reminded me, "my mother's name means light."

As I hung up the phone I remembered that Buffalo does too. Or, once did.

It's been over a century since it was thought of as the City of Light but there are movements now to restore her former glory, to redefine what Buffalo might mean for the next century. Clifton's poems remind us that we still have much work to do—in Buffalo and beyond—to overcome our complicated past. But what a future we can dream of together:

let there be new flowering
in the fields let the fields
turn mellow for the men
let the men keep tender
through the time let the time
be wrested from the war
let the war be won
let love be
at the end

**Barbara Cole** is the artistic director of Just Buffalo and a 2011 fellow in poetry from the New York Foundation for the Arts. Born and raised in Philadelphia, she received her master's in creative writing—Poetry from Temple University before coming to Buffalo to earn her Ph.D. in English from the University at Buffalo. Since 2000, Cole has been writing the ongoing long poem project affectionately known as *foxy moron*. In addition to her poetic projects, she edited *Poets at Play: An Anthology of Modernist Drama* with Sarah Bay-Cheng (Susquehanna University Press, 2010). She lives in Elmwood Village.

# Rustling the Leaves in Buffalo: The Story of Talking Leaves...Books

## Jonathon Welch

*You think your pain and your heartbreak are unprecedented in the history of the world, but then you read. It was books that taught me that the things that tormented me most were the very things that connected me with all the people who were alive, or who had ever been alive.*

—James Baldwin

Kate Selover opened "everyman's bookstore" (named from this line in a medieval play: "everyman, I will go with thee and be thy guide, in thy most need to go by thy side") on Main Street in the University Heights neighborhood in June 1971, to provide Buffalo's book-buying community with a place to find those life companions, and a space to commune with fellow booklovers. In a few years she was successful enough to decide to try her luck in New York City, where her daughters were living.

When I, along with a small collective of fellow University at Buffalo graduate students and community activists, took over the store from Kate on January 1, 1975, we had no expectation that it would last beyond five years, let alone decades. We'd raised the capital by convincing friends, family, and strangers with a passion for books that we could last at least five years and pay back the loans we solicited from them (crowd-sourcing before there was a word for it). Some we approached turned us down, told us we were crazy, that the book business was dying, people weren't reading, television was ascendant, and the world didn't need another bookstore, especially one run by neophytes with no book business or retail experience.

But we still purchased the store.

We incorporated a cooperative, "everyone's book cooperative," envisioning a non-profit that would expand Kate's vision of books and reading as a form of guidance to something more inclusive and broader; not just a bookstore but a vital community space. We had a passion for books and reading, and a belief in their power to move people and the world, to forge understanding. Knowledge is power, we believed, and books, from the past or of the moment, are active forces in the acquisition of knowledge and the building of community.

Building on the inherited foundation of a small, general trade bookstore with a literary emphasis, we were keen to expand as a community and cultural center, a home for the disenfranchised, the alternative, the under-represented and underappreciated—a place where people and ideas interact, conversations across disciplines, cultures, and interests flow, and change is incubated. We aimed to create a place where the classic and the avant-garde, the reactionary and the activist, the reader and the writer, the materialist and the spiritualist, the learned and the ignorant, could gather, commune and communicate, and engage with the world to make it a better place. It was critical for us to provide a space for the explosion of important work being produced by small, independent, and university presses as changes in printing technology enabled access and affordability, and the growing concentration and corporatization of the mainstream publishing industry constrained innovation and risk-taking. Equally critical was to represent the diverse communities traditionally given short shrift in mainstream publishing and culture—African Americans, Latinos, women, gays and lesbians, Native Americans, prisoners, third world writers, and activists.

With volunteer help from a membership that soon numbered in the hundreds, and two, then three, part-time employees, "everyone's book cooperative" managed in a couple of years to greatly expand the inventory of the store and to program poetry and film events, and to forge relationships with other fledging arts groups and alternative businesses, including Just Buffalo (poetry), CEPA (photography), Hallwalls (art), White Pine Press, several theater groups, North Buffalo Food Coop and Lexington Real Foods Cooperative, and Great Arrow Graphics and New Buffalo Graphics (T-shirts), as well as with faculty members in the humanities and social sciences at the University at Buffalo and Buffalo State College, most of which continue to this day.

During the store's early years and now, Buffalo was in the midst of a dynamic, tumultuous, and often dislocating process of change—initially from an industrial and shipping powerhouse to a de-industrialized banking, education, and legal center, now morphing into a medical research and health care hub. Corporations moved south and overseas, factories closed, jobs disappeared, and people, retail, and the University at Buffalo moved to the suburbs or away. The multi-year process of building a subway along Main Street at the end of the 1970s had a devastating effect on "everyone's book cooperative." The complex reality of New York cooperative corporation law forced us to abandon the cooperative construct and become a "regular" business. Founding member Martha Russell, my life partner and the co-op's third employee, and I became the owners in 1979, adopting the name Talking Leaves...Books, with a logo created by New Buffalo Graphics founder Michael Morgulis, depicting the motto "Word Is Seed," to reinforce the emphasis on the power of books and reading to help us understand and shape the world.

Talking Leaves moved and shrank, moved and grew, again using community crowd-funding, remaining in University Heights even as the university gradually moved away. During each move, store customers did most of the work, a common occurrence in the world of bookselling that is not often seen in other businesses. In 2001, with a third round of community support, we opened a second location in the city's Elmwood Village, a neighborhood bereft at the closing of all its previous bookstores.

Through all the changes in our city and in the book business, we've tried to abide by some simple principles—to conduct business with integrity and common sense; to treat our customers and booksellers with dignity and respect; to listen and respond to their concerns and ideas without compromising our own principles and standards; to provide the best and most diverse literature, writing, and thinking of the ages and of our own age; to link past, present, and future in constructive, instructive, often provocative, ways; to provide a meeting place for people interested in books and ideas; and to be a productive and valued partner with other community-based organizations and businesses.

Words matter, language matters, poems matter, books matter, stories matter, relationships matter.

We have never wavered in this certainty, despite the multitudinous threats to such belief in a culture that too often seems to belittle, undervalue, undermine, and consume it. We wish to be a part of the dialogue and to further it as an independent, idiosyncratic, attentive, respectful, responsible, but never uncritical community voice. The resilient strength of the literary community here over our four decades, and the strong relationships and partnerships we have forged, indicate that we've managed some of that well, that we haven't overburdened or unduly strained or otherwise contaminated that fertile soil in which we first took root. Like good gardeners, we always strive to enrich it more than we exhaust it.

Change has been as constant as the daily opening of boxes filled with books over four decades—change in our city, change in our culture, change in the ways of doing business. Technological changes have enabled speedier distribution and more efficient buying practices, and give the promise of making the notoriously inefficient publishing industry more efficient. Urban and suburban real estate speculation and development, enabled by technological change in the financial industry, contributed to the rise and partial demise of the corporate superstore and bookstore chains. The localism movement is an outgrowth of those changes, with the potential to reshape communities and retailing in a more democratic way.

Concentration and consolidation in the publishing industry constricted the menu for readers, emphasizing the newest blockbusters and brand-name authors and ideas. The attendant growth in small independent and non-profit publishing has helped to expand this menu, but to a smaller and more disparate audience. The internet and now mobile technology are impacting how people shop and how they read, with wide-ranging effect. The anti-competitive practices of behemoth Amazon.com, in particular, have had a devastating effect on the book and publishing ecosystem and on local communities, eroding the tax base and displacing retailers from almost every sector of the economy. All of these changes have made bookselling more intimately connected to the world of commerce, and thus more impacted by the ebbs and flows of a consumerist society than it was when we began.

We are still often told the book is dead, the book business is fossilized, the internet is taking over, long-form reading is passé, print is moribund, brick and mortar retail is no longer viable. Yet we are still here, putting books into the hands of readers, providing a space for public discourse across boundaries, as are hundreds of other independent bookstores around the country, with more opening every year.

Bookstores, it turns out, are hospitable places to explore new ideas and experiences, both in the books one discovers and in the people one runs into and engages with while shopping or attending a reading, a book signing, an author talk, a forum, a book club. Reading is a private and personal activity, but also tends to reach outward, to fold readers into a web of interrelated activity that broadens and strengthens the deeply communal experience of living, of engagement with others.

The other constant of our existence is our customers. Local businesses like ours have relationships with those who choose our services that far surpass the ostensibly commercial transactions that begin them. We do business with, cater to, listen to, interact with, customers—real life humans—not consumers. Without customers, we don't survive, we fail to build the foundations that permit and extend our tenure. Our customers to a large extent define us. We are a center of interaction, not consumption. And we are a significant part of what defines community, if that word is to have any meaning. Over the years our customers have helped to move our books and our fixtures, raised money to provide us with vacations, financed our growth, enlightened us, and lifted our hearts. We have helped educate and care for their children, have helped memorialize and bury their loved ones, have helped launch their books. Together we have helped numerous schools, churches, hospitals, homeless shelters, and community and arts organizations raise needed funds to provide necessary services.

First-time visitors to Talking Leaves are often surprised to find a "store like this" in a place like Buffalo, surprised a blue collar town could or would support a literary/academic bookstore filled with poetry and philosophy and scholarly work from throughout the ages. "Stores like this" aren't supposed to exist in decaying Rust Belt cities; but then neither are multiple community-supported theaters, three world class art galleries, a philharmonic orchestra, a nationally-recognized, citizen-organized and run Garden Walk, a unique Literary Center, and all the other groups that enrich the cultural and social and political life of this city.

We survive because people took a chance on our vision and our passion, and thousands of customers have taken and continue to take a chance on books and reading to be sure, but also on the intimacy of a relationship not totally and solely defined by the commerce we are engaged in. Most local businesses and successful non-profit cultural organizations exist and survive in much the same way. We count on our community members to take a chance, to risk coming out to hear something new, something unfamiliar, something challenging. Remember that Alice Walker, Stephen King, Joyce Carol Oates, Toni Morrison, Margaret Atwood, John Grisham—all were unknown at one time. And remember too that plenty of wonderful writing and thinking goes on outside the radar of most of us. The new and unfamiliar can become familiar, a companion of sorts, altering one's thinking or one's life, but only if one takes the risk, gives it a chance.

We draw our sustenance from the willingness of customers to take such risks with us, and from our willingness to risk with and for them. When someone tries an unknown writer, explores a new area of interest, or visits a previously unfamiliar local business, she maintains and invigorates the local economy that makes her community a unique, singular place. Every visit to a chain or online store does serious damage to the smaller, locally-based, independent businesses that are the lifeblood of any community. In the long run, that damage threatens the vitality, originality, and unique character of that specific place.

Monoculture is life-threatening and life-defeating; diversity is the key to a sustainable future, in nature and in culture. Talking Leaves...Books and other locally-based businesses are both bastions of and portals to that diversity, that sustainability. The greatest honor one can give us is continued critical support—reading, writing, listening, buying books, attending events, engaging with us in the lively and animated conversations that help define who we are and lead us on our path to the future.

*Say that the leaves are harvested*
*when they have rotted into the mold.*
*Call that profit. Prophesy such returns.*
*Put your faith in the two inches of humus*
*that will build under the trees*
*every thousand years.*

—Wendell Berry

We hope we have contributed to that eternal process and will continue to. Time and history will determine whether we've enriched the soil of our community with the humus we've deposited so far.

**Jonathon Welch** moved from Wisconsin to Buffalo in 1972 to pursue a graduate degree in English at the University at Buffalo. He took a leave of absence in 1975 to help found Talking Leaves...Books, which he now owns. He and his wife Martha have lived in the same house in the heart of the city for the past four decades, and raised their two children there.

# Epitaph: Buffalo girl

## Mary Kane

If I die suddenly
by choking on a chicken wing bone
I hope you do not say
I did not live.
Because I have eaten wings
mild, hot, and must-sign-a-waiver first.
I have tried the precision of fork and knife
and eaten like a cavewoman, filling my nails
and face with chicken bits,
letting the smattered orange-red juice
burn my skin.
I have been to the Anchor Bar
Home of Buffalo Chicken Wing
and I have introduced more than one
to the delights
of a food that leaves you wanting one more always
and begging for a carrot, celery, blue cheese,
to extinguish the fire inside.
On summer nights, on Mrs. Person's porch
I ate as a child, not counting if I had had more than my share—
shoving them in guiltless.
On my 30th birthday I ate them
judiciously and blissfully
before singing The Gambler with my girlfriends,
to the room of clapping, hooting, hollering
chicken wing-eating drunkards.
Surely by now I have ingested a thousand wings
and have enjoyed each one.
So if I choke on a chicken wing bone,
say it's because a girl has got to know when to hold 'em
and know when to fold 'em.
Console them by saying in heaven
I will eat wings into perpetuity
like a child, a cavewoman, a sexy 30-year old wannabe Karaoke star
all at once.
And still love each one.

**Mary Kane** grew up in Tonawanda and spent many weekends and summers on Dover Road in Lakeview, where many of her ancestors had settled after coming from Italy. Mary earned an M.F.A. from Hamline University in 2012. Her work has appeared in *Murphy Square*, *Kaleidoscope*, *Burner Magazine*, *OVS Magazine*, *Sleet* and the *Vermillion Literary Project* magazine.

# Broadway: A Salute to Urban Markets

## Elizabeth Bowen

I had fallen in lust and maybe even in love with urban markets many times in my life, from San Francisco's Ferry Building Market, where I sampled mushroom ice cream, to the Reading Terminal Market in Philadelphia, where eating soft pretzels made by Amish people always reminded me of the little stake of central Pennsylvania that my parents (and I, at one point) called home. When I found myself planning a move to Buffalo in 2014, the Broadway Market, with its pastries and its fish vendor and its famous Easter butter lambs, spoke to me. *This is the right move.*

But before I got to know the Broadway Market, I had to visit another market in another city: Baltimore. My mother's brain tumor brought me there unexpectedly in 2013. One day she seemed essentially herself, smiling and chatting with the other teachers' aides at a training at school; the next day she got disoriented while driving, and later that night in the ER, my parents received the diagnosis: glioblastoma multiforme, stage four. Doctors recommended surgery, though only to buy time. And so we pulled into Johns Hopkins Hospital in Baltimore, ninety minutes from my parents' home near Harrisburg.

That week in Baltimore felt like a year—the meetings with the surgeon (and his frighteningly competent secretary), the MRIs, the endless blood drawing, the multi-hour surgery, the far longer recovery. Framing all this was the city itself, and in particular the hardscrabble East Baltimore neighborhood where the hospital was located, with its wonderful Northeast Market. The market gave us something to focus on other than cancer; here we could make decisions that had nothing to do with side effects, survival rates, or rare but possible consequences. All we had to decide was what to eat, Maryland crab soup or fried noodles or oversized yellow cupcakes. The hisses of food preparation, the clang of multiple languages, the smells of coffee and frying oil, screamed life to me at a time when death seemed to linger.

One year (and for my mom, six grueling weeks of radiation and six rounds of chemotherapy) later, I moved from Chicago to Buffalo. For me the year also saw the completion of my Ph.D., the dissolution of my nine-year relationship and a broken engagement, and the beginning of a dream job as a professor. The job drew me to Buffalo—a city I had never thought of visiting and where I knew no one. The only thing I knew about Buffalo was that it was famous for its chicken wings, which held little appeal for me as a sometimes-vegetarian.

It took me a year to visit the Broadway Market. It was a year of learning and meeting people and driving the mountainous miles between Western New York and my parents' house over and over. It was also a year of decline for my mom.

As she grew weaker, I realized that helping to bathe and dress and feed your parent, as she once did for you, is its own sort of privilege. I also had to adjust to knowing that canceling my wedding meant my mom would never meet the person I marry, if I marry. I came to terms with that truth because I had to.

And I learned to see the beauty in the fact that at least my dying mom knew this: that I had made a place for myself in Buffalo, that perhaps improbably given the snow and the rust and our family heartbreak, I was and am happy.

As I get to know Buffalo, the realization strikes me over and over. It might be while drinking cheap beer and dancing to a Zydeco band in a Croatian social club. Or while riding my bike with my new friends to a hidden clearing that overlooks the river near Red Jacket Park. Or eating the best fried rice of my life from a Burmese food stall at the back of the West Side Bazaar.

*Maybe my happiness here wasn't so improbable after all.*

One warm and clear Western New York morning the summer of 2015, I found myself with a fast, new bike and nowhere to be. So I set out for the Broadway Market from my apartment in Elmwood Village via the ribbons of the Olmsted Park System. These boulevards—in varying states of grandeur and decay—connect Buffalo's historic green spaces. My route took me through the center of the East Side, quiet that morning save for those buzzing insects that are the hum of summer even in the city. There was little traffic as I rode past the mix of vacant lots and boarded-up houses scattered between beautifully and perhaps defiantly maintained single-family and two-flat homes with well-groomed lawns.

Riding east on East Utica, I crossed over the wail of speeding vehicles on the NY-33, making me wonder once again what this neighborhood was like before urban renewal charged in in the 1960s and interrupted the elm-lined Humboldt Parkway with the highway, putting a wall of noise and pollution between former neighbors. A few blocks south of Utica I found the curving path through Martin Luther King Park. The park's massive splash pool was dry that morning, with not a child in sight (though on my ride back, a few sprinklers puttered and a gaggle of kids splashed through the languid days of summer). From the park I picked up Fillmore, its wide thoroughfare and bike lane making for a quick ride past houses that date back as far as the 1890s and now sell for as little as $10,000, along with the occasional deli or convenience store. Just left of the intersection of Fillmore and Broadway, the heart of old Polonia, I caught my first sight of the huge market building, the spires of grand, slightly crumbling Catholic churches framing it on three sides.

The Broadway Market can underwhelm at first. On this weekday morning, it was far from bustling. More people stood in line for the watch repair shop near the entrance than at any of the food stands. A third of the stands weren't even open.

But as I explored further, I saw signs of life. Senior citizens chatted comfortably at tables over coffee, clearly regulars in their usual perches. Old-time meat stalls decorated with Polish flags and featuring Polish sausages stood near a halal butcher's stand and a soul food restaurant. I enjoyed a flaky apple turnover from Chrusciki's bakery, and bought some frozen mushroom pierogies for dinner.

A photo exhibit along the side wall celebrates the market's heyday. I admired images of the beloved Sattler's department store that stood across the street and helped to define the neighborhood from its 1889 opening until it closed in 2002. Sattler's is so vaunted in Buffalo that just uttering its name inevitably triggers a warm nostalgia among Buffalonians of a certain generation.

There were also photos of the market's most famous product, Easter butter lambs, which are cubes of butter molded to look like lambs. The lambs reclined resplendently with tiny red ribbons around their thick yellow necks. I couldn't help but think: my mom—who so valued quirky holiday traditions, dairy products, and the history of underappreciated places— would love this.

At Easter, I learned on a later visit, Buffalonians flock to the market for those lambs and for the memories and old charm the market evokes. Ma Malczewski's Easter Stand even has cardboard replicas of the butter lambs, with a sign encouraging visitors to take selfies. Vendors sell Russian and Polish painted wooden eggs, pussy willow branches, and chocolates and cheeses and pierogies. Amid the bustle that consumes the market at Easter, the senior regulars still hold court, seemingly oblivious to the tourists or the business that for a few weeks a year, transform their market into what it used to be.

For me, just knowing that the Broadway Market exists, that it is still in operation and that life breathes between its walls, gives me hope—even in the wake of loss. My mom died, at home and at peace, in December 2015.

Losing my mom after her long illness has come with a sense of grief that is, for the most part, gentle and slow-moving. Her physical presence, I had already learned, does not dictate my sense of her presence in my life. I think of her as I continue to seek new experiences and tastes and places, and feel the waves of thrill, anxiety, and sometimes unexpected comfort that this can bring.

I think back now to when I arrived at Broadway that first morning. My mom is somehow in this memory, as she is part of many of my Buffalo experiences, though she never visited here. I remember parking my bike at one of the empty racks in front of the market. Pausing to wipe the sweat from my forehead with the back of my hand, I looked up and saw the large red lettering above the main entrance, confirming I was in the right place.

I did not know what to expect, or what might be waiting for me inside. But I immediately felt at ease.

*For Karen Simons Bowen, 1950-2015, with gratitude and love.*

**Elizabeth Bowen**'s love of all things Rust Belt dates back to her days as a college student in Pittsburgh. In 2014 she moved to Buffalo from Chicago. She is an assistant professor of social work at the University at Buffalo and enjoys exploring Buffalo by bike.

# Buffalo Artist

## Bruce Adams

"An Artist." That was my answer to the question of what I wanted to be in life. It was Al asking. He was the bigger and scarier of the two owners of the Shetland House, a greasy spoon at the corner of Sheridan and Bailey in Amherst, where at seventeen I was working as a dishwasher.

"Oh, an Artiste," he responded in a mock French accent while bouncing slightly on his toes and extending his pinky, efficiently combining both art and gender slur in one concise affront. Classic Al.

"Yes," I said, "a visual artist."

It had been my stock answer since fourth grade. Born in Buffalo, the son of a blue collar factory worker, I would soon attend state college here, marry local, buy a Westside Victorian house, and raise a family. I was entrenched in this Rust Belt town. So it would be in the "City of No Illusions"—as graphic artist Michael Morgulis once labeled Buffalo—that I would make my career. This wouldn't be easy of course; being an artist in Buffalo is no cakewalk.

Most members of the art community make their living at something else, often cobbling an income together from a hodgepodge of art-related jobs. Some drift through town like tumbleweeds. Some plan a brief stay, often to attend or teach at one of the region's colleges and universities, then unexpectedly settle down.

Some leave, typically migrating to The Big City to the East, only to return like Monarch butterflies in the spring. A few of us are born and spend our lives here. The list of sometime-artist-residents includes such notables as Cory Arcangel, Charles E. Burchfield, Tony Conrad, Hollis Frampton, Robert Longo, Robert Mangold, Spain Rodriguez, Milton Rogovin, Paul Sharits, and Cindy Sherman, among many others.

Being an artist in the land of beer and chicken wings has benefits and disadvantages. It just depends on what you value.

An obvious plus is the richness of the art community itself, beginning with our museums and galleries. The Albright-Knox Art Gallery—about to be renamed the Buffalo Albright-Knox-Gundlach Art Museum— arguably houses the finest collection of modern and contemporary art west of Manhattan. Artists from Mangold to Longo have cited it as a major influence.

In the 1970s, Albright-Knox curator Linda Cathcart began a relationship with the founders of the nationally-known artist-run space, Hallwalls.

Some of those founders were Longo, Sherman, Charles Clough, Michael Zwack, Diane Bertolo, and Nancy Dwyer. They brought cutting-edge art and artists to Buffalo during the near mythical 1970s, a period of super-charged creativity driven by social and cultural change, funding availability, barefaced ambition, and pure dumb luck.

Across from the Albright-Knox stands the Burchfield-Penney Art Center, a spectacular facility dedicated to the art of Western New York. Over the years, the Burchfield-Penney has edged away from its early staid reputation, adopting a more with-it approach. North of Buffalo, on the campus of Niagara University, the Castellani Museum boasts another world-class collection augmented by regional art.

The scrappy multi-disciplinary Hallwalls and its photography-based counterpart CEPA (Center for Exploratory and Perceptual Art) offers up innovative art and attitude. The list of artists who had early, and in some cases first, exhibitions at these non-profit art centers is impressive: Robert Irwin, Vito Acconci, Sol LeWitt, Chris Burden, Richard Serra, Jonathan Borofsky, Jeff Koons, Laurie Anderson, Karen Findley, David Salle and Jennifer Bartlett, Laurie Simmons, Barbara Kruger, John Baldessari, and Richard Prince, among many others. Early on, CEPA worked with the Niagara Frontier Transportation Authority to establish a "photo bus" that exhibited work of area photographers—including a young Cindy Sherman—in the advertising spaces above the seats. Since the 1990s, Big Orbit Gallery has mounted large-scale installations in a funky former icehouse setting.

Despite being a hotbed of progressive art activity, Buffalo is often perceived by artists as a launching pad to better things. But amid the big-hair, Big Brother Reaganomic days of 1984, some of us wondered if Buffalo could ever be the better thing?

Sculptor Stiller Dawson and I spent two months that summer leading an art-making meditation on the meaning of being an artist in Buffalo. We branded ourselves the New Artists' Alliance of Buffalo (NAAB), and labeled the work of the twenty-six participants the *Buffalo Artists' Metropolitan Project*. We improvised on-sight installations, put on readings, held forums, and just hung out. We asked some fundamental questions:

Is there economic opportunity for artists in Buffalo? (No.)

Does Buffalo art have a signature style? (Figurative was someone's best guess.)

Why do so many artists leave? (Duh. It's a short trip to New York City.)

I too heard the NYC siren song and, in the 1980s, rolled my unstretched canvases onto a carpet tube, slung them over my shoulder and crisscrossed Manhattan in search of interested galleries.

In 1986, I had a solo show at White Columns, an important non-profit gallery. This is the point when many Buffalo artists would pull up stakes and move east in search of fame and fortune. But for me, Buffalo was more than a struggling art community; it was home.

The Buffalo art scene had become, as former Albright-Knox curator Heather Pesanti put it in her catalog essay for the Albright-Knox exhibition *Wish You Were Here: The Buffalo Avant-garde in the 1970s,* "highly aggressive and political, even combative," displaying "a flamboyant disregard for taboos."

The University at Buffalo had gained a national reputation beginning in the 1970s as a nexus of contemporary art, particularly new media. Its Center for Media Study (later renamed the Department of Media Study) produced a slew of artists who seeded the community with a fierce spirit of creative freedom and innovation.

And there was Artpark in nearby Lewiston, which in the 1970s and 1980s was a living lab of experimentation for artists from across the world. Survival Research Laboratories—a performance art group that puts on noisy, often violent works of social and political satire using machines—was scheduled to come in 1990. It was seen as a return to the park's heyday, but officials canceled the show over fear of funding cuts.

Buffalo artists protested by building a "Trojan Bible," from which a brigade of performers planned to emerge and engage audiences outside the gates. Park police intervened before the colossal good book made it out of the Artpark forest. Over the next hour, while several of us video-recorded, police arrested eighteen artists for attempting to speak about censorship.

The charges were later dismissed.

Buffalo artists and galleries also championed a number of progressive social issues, including LGBT pride. Starting in 1988, Ron Ehmke produced the biannual Hallwalls festival *Ways in Being Gay.* A year later, as a Congressional debate over offensive art raged in Washington, the gallery defiantly mounted *Censored! An Evening of Objectionable Art* without opposition.

Hallwalls was also the first gallery anywhere to present the provocative work of performance artist Karen Finley. In 1981, as part of a collaboration with the Albright-Knox, Hallwalls and CEPA displayed Robert Mapplethorpe's explicitly sexual *X Portfolio*, which would later be at the center of the storm as the government axed arts funding. Mapplethorpe, too, attracted no controversy in Buffalo.

Not everyone loved Buffalo's challenging art scene. The city's cantankerous old-school mayor, Jimmy Griffin, was famously quoted by the *Buffalo News* as saying, "Well, they got this one thing in Buffalo, Hallways or whatever the heck it is. To me, that's strictly trash that they put out. And again, getting back to times when I was growing up, some of these things, they'd laugh those people right of the country. They'd put them in the psychiatric center over there. Who in common sense would do some of the things they're doing?"

Hallwalls put the quote on a mug. Some of Buffalo's artistic fire was undoubtedly stoked by a collective sense of betrayal. As artists raged, industry, wealth, youth, and jobs vanished from Buffalo. Some artists left for stronger markets. Those of us who stayed, found new purpose for the vacant buildings dotting the landscape, like using the H.H. Richardson Psychiatric Center and the Central Terminal as exhibition space. Postindustrial decay also became appealing artistic subject matter.

Perhaps the most inspired use of vacant factories, malls, roller rinks, and warehouses began in the early 1980s, with the *Artists and Models Affair*, a single night public party and salute to artistic excess. *A&M* took place every year in a different (often) abandoned Buffalo building and mixed high and lowbrow installations, performances, band and DJ sets, and thrills.

At one early *A&M*, artist Brent Scott shot a forty-foot column of fire with a homemade flame-thrower. Another time, he shrink-wrapped a woman in plastic and suspended her by block and tackle. At another, the Post-Modern Militant Sisterhood (PMMS) circulated among the crowd and spontaneously "made out" with random men and women. And then there was the chipper "Love Boat cruse director" who greeted partiers with white-powder-coated nostrils, leading them to Vanna de Milo, who struggled to turn *Wheel of Fortune* letters without arms. At the height of the televangelist scandals, Mark Joyce, Chuck Agro, and I created the parody of *Heretic USA* (after Jim Baker's Christian theme park, Heritage USA), to satirize religious hypocrisy in a loutish display of blasphemous mockery.

Hallwalls eventually took over *A&M* and the parties continue intermittently today. But empty venues with willing owners are harder to find.

As the global art market raged in the 1980s and 1990s, Buffalo experienced no bump in commercial success. You might say we are the Filene's Basement of art: fine quality, rock bottom prices. Yet everyone seems to be buying tube tops at K-Mart. Market wise, Western New York is a framed poster and Thomas Kinkade print kind of town. The buy local movement hasn't reached the art industry.

Anna Kaplan, Director of BT&C (Buffalo Trade and Commerce) Gallery, a contemporary commercial gallery, believes area art collectors often buy from centers like New York or Miami where sophisticated presentation impresses. "Buffalo is full of great art that should be part of public and private collections," says Kaplan, "but it's often not treated with the respect it deserves..."

Which brings up another ironic advantage for Buffalo artists; no market means no competition. Communalism is a way of life here. A spirit of cooperation and support pervades the art community, with little of the backstabbing one-upmanship that accompanies economic potential.

What Buffalo lacks in commercial viability, it makes up for in afford-ability. Housing is famously inexpensive, and thanks to a glut of vacant real estate, studio space is relatively cheap. For over twenty years, I've shared a studio with artist and art former *Buffalo News* art critic, Richard Hunting-ton. Our combined rent would get us a Manhattan janitor's closet.

These days, the art community—which has always bristled with hope and urgency—is undergoing another shift.

Galleries and other art venues are popping up like mushrooms after a rainstorm. There are light shows on the grain elevators downtown, instal-lations and public art at the airport and at Canalside. An empty Gothic church at Richmond and Ferry will soon become an art center with col-laborative art space, a contemporary gallery, offices, and arts management resources. The Albright-Knox is working with the city to increase public art. Outdoor murals are enlivening cityscapes.

In New York City, most artists are tiny interchangeable parts in a co-lossal art machine. In Buffalo, I've been a curator, art advocate, art critic, event coordinator, art educator, and mentor to young artists. My work is in museums: the Albright-Knox, Burchfield-Penney, Anderson, and Castellani.

I once heard a story in which members of an African tribal community asked a researcher where his home was. The researcher explained that he had no permanent residence; he lived all over the world. The tribe members expressed shock, profound sadness, and pity for the man. The African sense of self and security is rooted in identification with and within a community. You need to know your tribe's history to understand who you are. You need a sense of belonging.

My roots are in Buffalo. I know the history and legends of my tribe. Here, I belong.

**Bruce Adams** is a conceptually-based figurative painter, writer, and educa-tor. He as worked as a public school art teacher, college professor, installa-tion and performance artist, and critical and creative writer. His art has been exhibited internationally, and is included in numerous private and museum collections. He received his undergraduate and master's degrees from Buffa-lo State College in art education, and has lived in the Elmwood Village for thirty-nine years, while keeping an art studio in the Great Arrow Building. He was the director/curator of peopleart/bflo, and a past board member and president of Hallwalls. He has written art reviews for the *Buffalo News*, and is the longtime award-winning critic for *Buffalo Spree*.

Graphic artist Michael Morgulis is Buffalo's homegrown Andy Warhol. His buffalo-themed images, T-shirts, posters and slogans bathe the city in hope and pride. Trapped in his studio during the epic blizzard of 1977, Morgulis thought up the city's now- iconic slogan, "City of No Illusions," based on the 1967 sci-fi novel "City of Illusions." Brad Pitt has worn his T-shirts and his civic pride is legendary. These photos show part of his 1982 series of seventy billboards. He's pictured in the image on the upper left.

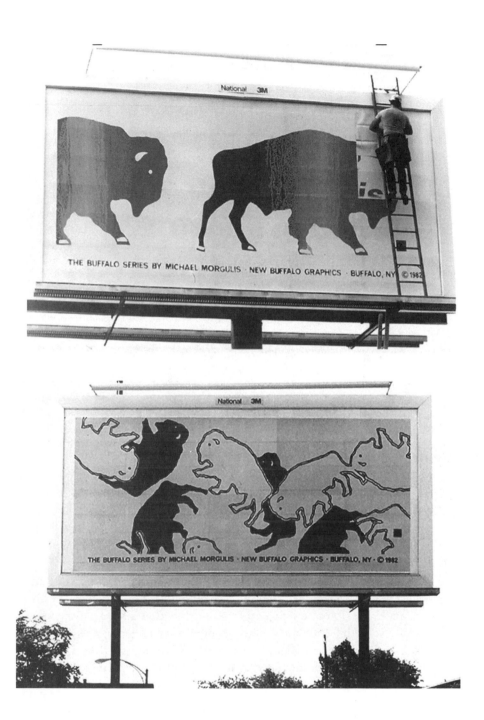

THE BUFFALO SERIES BY MICHAEL MORGULIS · NEW BUFFALO GRAPHICS · BUFFALO, NY © 1982

THE BUFFALO SERIES BY MICHAEL MORGULIS · NEW BUFFALO GRAPHICS · BUFFALO, NY · © 1982

# John & Mary—Notes & Harmony

## John Lombardo and Mary Ramsey

### John:

Our story begins with a chance meeting in Buffalo at Nietzsche's. It was a winter Sunday afternoon in 1988 and both of our groups were scheduled to play together. Mary's group was the Lexington String Trio, playing a collection of classical string pieces unamplified in a barroom setting. My band was the Billups, playing mostly original new wave tunes.

Mary played viola. I played bass. We started talking and hanging out. The cellist in the trio, whom I knew a bit, kept telling me Mary wasn't only a classical musician, but also had a great voice, and after a few weeks, I asked her to sing something for me. She took my guitar and played a beautiful rendition of the Acadian Ballad, "Un Canadien Errant," entirely in French.

My mind was made up. Here was an artistic opportunity that only comes once in a lifetime.

I was a founding member of 10,000 Maniacs. We formed on Labor Day of 1981 and I departed in the summer of 1986 to move to Buffalo and to begin a normal life away from the constant touring and pressure. After being in a group for many years in which collaboration was the key to our success, I wasn't sure if I would ever find another artistic partner whose talents would dovetail with mine.

Then I met Mary.

Mary and I started composing songs straight away and we performed in Buffalo to rather enthusiastic responses. Mary and I played together in Toronto, Pittsburgh, Albany, Rochester, and Nashville, and many other places.

We connected with Dan Griffin, an old friend from my 10,000 Maniacs days, whose faith and vision led to a recording contract with Rykodisc as well as a publishing deal with a division of MCA Nashville. We recorded our first album, *Victory Garden*, with Robert Buck and Jerome Augustyniak at Mitch Easter's Drive-In Studio in Winston-Salem. It was released in 1991.

Two years later, we followed with *The Weedkiller's Daughter* and basically hit the road. We played everywhere we could: New York, Boston, Chicago, Minneapolis, London, Amsterdam, Berlin, Vienna, all over. We toured with Warren Zevon and opened for Richie Havens, Laura Nero, Robyn Hitchcock, The Bank, Alex Chilton, Tom Rush, The Roches, Jules Shear, and Chris Isaak, among others.

We were invited on the final Natalie Merchant tour with my old group 10,000 Maniacs, and in 1990 we went all over the country as well as did a three-show residence at London's Town and Country. After Natalie's departure, Mary and I were invited to join the group proper and we got a record deal immediately with Geffen Records.

The 1997 release, *Love Among the Ruins*, fostered the hit single, "More than This," a cover version of Roxy Music's 1982 song. That led to TV interviews and another tour and we even played three United Service Organization shows in Bahrain and Kuwait.

We're still playing with 10,000 Maniacs, recording last year's *Twice Told Tales* and the band just released a live album, *Playing Favorites*. The band is celebrating its thirty-fifth year in 2016.

All these years later, Mary and I are still enjoying the fruits of that initial encounter on a snowy Buffalo Sunday late in the last century.

## Mary:

Buffalo has a magnetism that pulls me.

I think it is in part a pull from the great bodies of water that flow powerfully around the city. There is the constant flow of the Niagara River and the roar of the water crashing over Niagara Falls and the great Lake Erie itself; both at times are stormy and peaceful, which invigorates me and inspires my music. I am especially drawn to the power of Niagara Falls, a place of energy and restless creativity, a place that straddles two countries and where the genius of Nikola Tesla gave birth to the first hydroelectric plant, empowering the city with great energy and light. It was that energy that sent Buffalo into the spotlight of economic stardom, the remnants of which are still apparent in the historic architectural structures that still stand today.

Buffalo's old buildings have energy and tell stories. When I first came to Buffalo from Fredonia in my early twenties, I couldn't afford a car, so I walked a lot. I found the buildings and the quality with which they were built and the lush greenery around them uplifting. I frequented estate sales and vintage stores and felt a sense of gratitude to people who came before me and who left such marvelous, well-loved marks of their lives for me to stumble upon and find inspiring. As an artist, it's essential to be in a place that touches you and feeds your thoughts. Buffalo has always done that for me and in a way, my years here have been a kind of romance.

I love Buffalo for its hidden beauty, but also for its generosity: it's given me a place to live where I can afford my rent without working all the time or without working in jobs unconnected to music. It's given me the time to create music and think about making music and devote to touring my music. When I moved here in the 1980s, the city had a bohemian, anything-goes attitude. I paid $110 a month for a two-bedroom apartment on the third floor of a house on Norwood I shared with a friend. Today, the rents are higher, but artists can still manage them or they can find an old house that's affordable to renovate.

I also love Buffalo for its stark seasons, which compel me to pay attention to time. My music and career, too, has had seasons. I've played classical, new wave, jazz, and sung standards and torch songs. I'm currently working on putting W.B. Yeats' poetry to music.

I've played in many of Buffalo's venues and went from subbing on viola in the Buffalo Philharmonic to a few years later, having the Philharmonic accompany 10,000 Maniacs as special guests. I went from sitting in the back of the viola section to standing at the front as lead singer. I've played small venues with a handful of listeners to a few stadiums of 50,000. I was invited to play at the Kennedy Center for President Bill Clinton's second inaugural ball. I've also collaborated with the Irish Classical Theater for pieces where I wrote, played, and sang music during plays.

Meeting John in 1988 changed my life.

John and I have opposite energy that creates a magnetism between us. He came out of the punk movement, but has an appreciation for British folk rock and reggae. John is a social person and likes to stay out late and he remembers names and dates. I'm a-stream-of-conscious thinker and writer and my background is in classical viola and folk music. I like to be in quiet peaceful places and I remember emotions and feelings. Melodies come to me easily and often I pull melodies from John's chordal structures. Our love of folk music and poetry brought us together and our music comes from our conversations.

As I have grown up as a musician, I've seen Buffalo grow up. The city went from being a misfit sort of place to being on the cusp of becoming a destination. Yet, it's still authentic. It's still exquisitely livable. It gives me wide berth for experimentation and collaboration, which is necessary because the rock-and-roll world has always been unregulated. There is recklessness in terms of business practices, but also in terms of lifestyle that can be tough. There is a sense of making it, of having a reputation, fans and success, but beneath it all, you always struggle. The arts are always about struggle because as you grow as an artist, you outgrow where you were before. Buffalo has always afforded me a soft landing.

When I was younger, I felt I had to leave Buffalo to explore other places and test myself with other people. In my thirties, after living happily in Buffalo for years, I moved as far west as possible—Santa Monica, California, right at the mouth of the roaring Pacific. I had a love affair with the land, but still felt the pull of Lake Erie and Buffalo.

Sometimes it takes a while before you can say you are home. Maybe that's also because you need to be at home with yourself first.

That's where I think I am now, in Buffalo, my hometown.


**John Lombardo** was an original member of 10,000 Maniacs, and has been performing with Mary Ramsey since 1989. He grew up in Jamestown and went to Southwestern High School, got a bachelor's degree from SUNY Geneseo and a master's degree from the University at Buffalo. He couldn't play any instruments until he was twenty. He lives in the Delaware Park district.

**Mary Ramsey** has been the lead singer/songwriter/violist for the alt/rock band 10,000 Maniacs since 1996. In 2006, she and John Lombardo formed the Buffalo-based band John & Mary and the Valkyries. In 1997, Mary sang lead on 10,000 Maniac's Top Forty hit "More Than This." Mary and 10,000 Maniacs have toured extensively throughout the U.S and globally and are actively touring now. Mary has worked and recorded with The Goo Goo Dolls, Billy Bragg, Alex Chilton, Jules Shear, Natalie Merchant and Ani DiFranco. She received a bachelor's of music from SUNY Fredonia. She lives on the West Side.

# Music is Art

## Robby Takac

The Music is Art Festival ... man, where do I start?

Well, I had a studio on Franklin and Allen Street in the late 1990s called Chameleonwest. We opened as a resource for bands and musicians in Buffalo to make music and help boost the Western New York music community's reach into professional recording.

Long before we had large audiences around the country we could be sure there would be an enthusiastic homecoming after every road trip. I think we had them all fleeced into thinking the crowds we had at home were the norm back then ... that was certainly not the case. Buffalo was always so good to us when The Goo Goo Dolls were starting out, playing late nights at The Continental, The Cabaret, The Pipe Dragon, and so many other local haunts, I felt a real connection to the scene and really wanted to try to make some sort of a contribution.

Studio manager Marc Hunt and I came up with dozens of late-night schemes to make this mission a reality. During one of these late night idea sessions (probably leaning on a bar on Allen Street) we commented on how our neighborhood bustled for a single June weekend a year as the prestigious Allentown Art Festival took over our neighborhood. We sensed an opportunity for our mission to be furthered through sheer proximity ... the wheels began to turn.

We decided the two-day Allentown Art Festival provided a chance to showcase Buffalo music, and we wanted to showcase a whole bunch of it. We reached out to some of our friends and the community loved the idea; we asked thirty-five bands to come and play that 2002 weekend, over the two days of the Allentown Festival on two stages, one in our studio and one on an outside stage next to the studio building. We also had a couple of DJs spinning from the second-floor windows.

Since it was an art-inspired crowd in our neighborhood that weekend, we thought it would be nice to invite some of our friends who weren't necessarily of the money-making "mainstream festival" persuasion to display some art that didn't have a place at the Allentown Festival.

Then the shit hit the fan.

The Allentown Festival folks got word of our event and it turned out there was a problem with doing events outside your business during the Allentown Festival. This made us confused, angry, and motivated to see it through ... don't mess with a gang of punk rockers trying to do something good .... We brought the three local television stations, the newspaper and an eager arts community to the fight ... and I guess that's where the story began.

Oh yeah ... and during this process we came up with a name for the festival ... Music IS Art!

Since the early days of the MiA Festival, we've moved a few times due to some issues I will be too classy to go into here, but despite the odds we've grown ... grown from two stages and about twenty artists to twelve stages and over 100 artists, including DJs, poets, painters, dancers, sculptors, fashionistas, musicians, technicians, and chefs and supporters of the arts all working hand in hand, through whatever Mother Nature chooses to deal out to us that day. This amazing group of people has been making this yearly event happen for fourteen years now ... mind blowing. For the last ten years we've been behind the Albright-Knox art gallery, growing throughout the park into the beautiful Marcy Casino, Shakespeare Hill, Lincoln Parkway all the way back to The Ivy Bridge ... a pretty amazing setting to experience a hearty portion of Western New York's creative culture.

Over the years we've hosted thousands of local artists and musicians such as The Incredible Lance Diamond, Cute Is What We Aim For, Willie Nile, Green Jello, and The Goo Goo Dolls, as well as national acts such as Lisa Loeb, Shonen Knife, Magician Rudy Cobe, Qrion, escape artist Jonathon Bryce, Pinky Doodle Poodle, and The Enigma from The Jim Rose Circus.

But something else happened, something I don't think any of those pissed off punk rockers had foreseen—the arts community stayed aligned behind the Music is Art concept and we became a NYS 501c3 Not For Profit and slowly and very organically began doing programming in Western New York schools, collecting and refurbishing instruments (to date we've put nearly $500,000 worth of musical instruments into the community). We run summer camps, a jazz series, high school battle of the bands, music business mentoring, and other various programming throughout the year. All of this is managed by an amazing board of directors, including board chair Phil Aguglia, several committees, and our Executive Director Tracy Shattuck who work tirelessly to make sure MiA stays on course and vital to the community.

This fourteen-year metamorphosis from conflict to asset is a great example of why I will always love being in Buffalo, and this is why I return home after tours and other adventures excited to see what the next chapter will bring. Because the arts community in Buffalo is continuously supportive, always exploding with creativity and as we all know ... Music is Art ....

**Robby Takac** is a member of four-time Grammy nominated, ten-time platinum-selling rock band The Goo Goo Dolls. He is also the owner of Good Charamel Records and GCR Audio Recording Studios in Buffalo as well as founder and president of Music is Art, a NYS 501c3 Not For Profit serving the arts community in Western New York. Robby attended West Seneca East Senior High School and graduated from Medaille College. He currently lives in downtown, with his wife Miyoko and daughter Hana.

Illustration of Kleinhans Music Hall by Mickey Harmon

# Kleinhans Music Hall, 4:30PM

## JoAnn Falletta

The musicians are gone,
the stage empty, the lights extinguished.
But Kleinhans is not silent
not at all.
As I sit alone in the dark
the hall hums around me
reverberant with thousands of acerbic oboe A's
sweetened into perfect fifths by strings that
tumble into an exuberant cataract
spilling over the stage and
flooding the hall with sound.

The fragrance of music has pervaded every inch
soaked through the wooden boards
permeated the tapestries
the very varnish crafted of ancient layers of music.

Elusive tendrils of Mozart and Brahms swirl at the fringe of my
        consciousness
the stage still rumbles with the opening of *Zarathustra*
the angel voices of Mahler live in the blackened balcony
the thundering chords of *Eroica* echo in the confused sonority
and Petrouchka's little ghost cackles from the rafters.

Remnants of thousands of concerts
the heady perfume of decades of passion
played out on that stage
vibrating forever in the belly of the hall.

**JoAnn Falletta** serves as Music Director of the Buffalo Philharmonic and Virginia Symphony, and has conducted over one hundred orchestras in North America and prominent orchestras throughout Europe, South America, Asia, and Africa. She has won many of the most prestigious conducting awards, served on the National Council for the Arts, and is a newly-elected member of the American Academy of Arts and Sciences. Her recordings have won two Grammy Awards and multiple Grammy nominations. When not on the podium, she enjoys writing, cycling, yoga, and is an avid reader. A native of New York City, JoAnn has lived in the Waterfront Village neighborhood of Buffalo since 1999.

# Home
# &
# Belonging

# A Hydraulics Boyhood

## Tom Dudzick

Feelings for my old neighborhood run like the mighty Niagara itself—strong and deep. The old saying is true, you can take the boy out of the Hydraulics, but you can't take the Hydraulics out of the boy. Much of Seneca Street wound up in *Over the Tavern*, my 1994 play about the Pazinski family living over Chet's Bar & Grill in 1959. You only need to substitute *Chet's* for *Big Joe's* and you'll find the Dudzick home. *Big Joe's* was my father's gin mill and we lived one flight up. Come to think of it, every one of my plays has some connection to the Hydraulics or at least to Buffalo. I can't help it, I'm infected.

In case you've never paid attention to Buffalo lore, the Hydraulics was the city's first manufacturing district, the birthplace of Buffalo industry. During the 1800s, tanneries, woolen mills, grist mills, breweries, and shoe factories filled the area. The Hydraulics got its name from the water system that turned all the wheels and powered all the factories. In 1900, Buffalo held the title as second largest soap manufacturing city in the world after Cincinnati. This was thanks to the Larkin Soap Company, established by John D. Larkin and his brother-in-law, writer and philosopher Elbert Hubbard. Larkin's Administration Building, plopped down in the epicenter of the Hydraulics, was built by some upstart named Frank Lloyd Wright.

As a 1950s kid I was not aware I was living amidst so much history. To me the Hydraulics was simply a wonderland with endless places to play: railroad tracks, train trestles, empty box cars, coal chutes, abandoned factories, grain silos, overgrown fields, and garbage dumpsters. Of course we also had the official school playground provided for us by the good sisters and priests of St. Patrick's, with clean pavement, swings, and a baseball diamond. But, I'm sorry, they just didn't have the same kind of grunge appeal as the boxcars and dumpsters.

Our stretch of Seneca Street was filled with small family-owned businesses: Frank's Hardware Store, T.L. Terry's Jewelry and Watch Repair Shop, Hydraulic Tobacco, O'Connell's Liquors, Benny Miller's Candy Store, Gladkowski's Bowling Alley, Winkler's Grocery Store...

Winkler's Grocery Store figures heavily in my plays. I couldn't leave it out as it was an absolutely one-of-a-kind establishment. Walking into F.X. Winkler's Sons was like stepping into the Way-Back Machine. It never changed

Dad's Tavern

F. X. Winkler's Sons

décor from the day it opened in 1857 until it closed its doors in 1968. It had dark wooden shelves and counters, grain bins, a coffee grinding machine that looked like something out of an H.G.Wells novel, glass displays of mammoth cheeses, bushels of fruits and vegetables lined up on the floor, string coming down from a spool on high so Mr. Winkler could tie up your meat in white paper. A display of baked goods on which sat Hostess Cupcakes with "Howdy Doody's picture right on the label," as Buffalo Bob Smith used to point out on his TV show. (*Bragging Point*: Buffalo Bob was born in Buffalo and went to Fosdick-Masten Park High School *with my father!*) We had a charge account at Winkler's, so every day when school let out for lunch I'd stop in, pick up a package of Hostess Cupcakes, and wave it in the air so Mr. Winkler could see and make note of it from his command center, a window-encased office.

My sister, *who was not supposed to be eating this junk*, gave me the inspiration for the scene in *Over the Tavern* where sixteen-year-old Annie catches holy hell for sneaking Twinkies into her room. All I did was write down the humiliating details exactly as they played out in real life. I was quite pleased with the way the scene turned out. My sister could have lived without it.

In Winkler's front windows—*peanuts!* The windows were about a foot deep in unshelled peanuts. It became Winkler's trademark. "Winkler's? Oh yeah, that store with the peanuts." I was recently told by a Winkler descendant that the front window was so loaded with peanuts because it was a way of celebrating that they were the first store in New York State that *sold* peanuts. No one believes this story, but why would the Winklers make it up?

Seneca Street had barbershops aplenty. And from one of these I borrowed an idea for my play *Miracle on South Division Street*. It seems that Joseph Battaglia's Barbershop came complete with a twenty-foot shrine to the Blessed Mother adjacent to the shop. Not the sort of thing you usually spot next to a barbershop, but barber Joseph Battaglia claimed that the

Blessed Virgin Mary appeared to him one night in 1950, with a message of peace and good will for the world. Why she picked a barbershop in Buffalo for delivery of this message, I cannot say. But to memorialize the visit, Mr. Battaglia commissioned a statue to be sculpted, giving a detailed description of Mary to the sculptor. The result is a Blessed Virgin Mary we are not used to seeing. That is, her legs are showing! Mary is wearing a dress that a teenage girl might wear to a prom. Not a full-length job, but cut to mid-calf. (Maybe a *junior* prom.) In any case, the beautiful life-size statue was then encased in a shrine the barber built himself. It still stands, is lovingly cared for, and has a mail slot where people leave notes, asking the Blessed Mother for miracles. They usually leave coins as well, to give their cause a little boost.

The shrine was a great curiosity to us kids. We'd stare at it and wonder, "Did it really happen? Did Mary make a guest appearance in our neighborhood?" Sometimes, being on Catholic autopilot, we would drop to our knees and say a prayer at Mary's feet. One day we bragged to Sister Cuthbert about what good little children we were to say prayers to the statue on Seneca Street. Sister promptly set us straight about this *ersatz* miracle. "Do not pray to her," she said. "There was no visitation. The barber is just a nice man who had a dream, that's all. Forget about it."

A block north of the miraculous barbershop was Seymour Street, which began the residential section, with the church and the school and my friends' houses. Past that were railroad tracks. "Don't go near them, they're dangerous!"—which meant we couldn't stay away from them. They were almost impossible to avoid, anyway. In the Hydraulics there were railroad tracks in every direction, on all sides of our six-block area.

Getting back to the historic Frank Lloyd Wright Larkin Building, it fills me with pride to think that my grandfather was a janitor there. Joe Dudzick, Sr. learned the art of wallpaper hanging at Larkin. John D. Larkin took a liking to him and made him a deal—"I'll rent you the ground floor of a house dirt-cheap if you'll be the exclusive paperhanger for all my houses on Seymour Street." Grandpa jumped at it and my father grew up there with his five sisters at No. 44.

Imagine my surprise when I learned that Seymour Street, our favorite street for rollerskating, used to be a canal. They filled in the canal after it started a cholera epidemic in 1850. Nearly 900 people died in that epidemic, almost 3 percent of Buffalo's population. But the Dudzicks were spared since we didn't appear on the scene until roughly 1900. As kids in the 1950s we didn't know anything about a canal or that the whole place was so damned historic. If we did, we probably would have dug a lot more holes. We were always digging holes, looking for treasure. Once while digging in a vacant lot between two houses, we unearthed a ceramic water pitcher. Part of one, anyway. The handle. Still, it might have been used to hold water for our early settlers! Pretty damned exciting for eight-year-olds. If we didn't find treasure we'd bury our own, usually a box containing something that had meaning to us at the time. Like "army guys," those little green plastic soldiers every boy played with in the '50s. And because I was the artist of the gang, I would draw the treasure map. We'd bury it, hide the map for future generations, and then, demonstrating the patience of eight-year-olds, the next day we would get out the map, follow it, and dig up the box.

Another reason we dug holes was for traps. Traps for people, not animals. We'd dig a hole about one-foot square, then cover it with sticks and leaves and dirt so it would blend in with the dirt path. Then we'd hide behind bushes and wait for some hapless soul to step in it and fall on his face. When he did we'd laugh ourselves sick.

Sister Clarissa   St. Patrick's School and Church (Convent in the Rear)

Photos courtesy of the author

*Over the Tavern's* protagonist, twelve-year-old Rudy Pazinski, has a nemesis named Sister Clarissa. The real life Sister Clarissa lived three blocks away in a convent tucked behind St. Patrick's school, along with a few other choice Franciscan ladies blessed with nasty tempers, of whom there seemed to be no shortage. Mean nuns did exist, they were not just the stuff of urban legend. I often wonder how many nuns taught because teaching was their true calling in life, and how many were simply told, "Hey, you. Yes, you. You're a teacher now. Here's your syllabus, your chalk, your ruler, your clicker. Like it or not, you're spending the rest of your life with third graders. Move it out!" It would certainly explain their sour dispositions.

In second grade I had my ear severely yanked by Sister Paschal Marie because I got the hands of the clock wrong in my drawing. A surprise slap across the back of the head was very common. So was being shaken violently by the shoulders and screamed at.

But the nun's assault of choice, trite as it sounds, was the legendary whack with the ruler. And an effective little disciplinary tool it was because it hurt like *hell*. On the palm of the hand. *WHACK!* Never on the knuckles, though. That could cause damage. The St. Pat's nuns must have held a meeting: "Don't do damage, just hurt them." I point that out because my friends who went to other schools swear their nuns hit them on the knuckles. And I don't want our nuns lumped in with those savages.

But don't get the idea that acts of nun-violence were senseless and random. *Au contraire*, we were hit for a reason. Talking. Fooling around. Talking. Getting clock hands wrong. Talking. And the results—some of the most well-behaved classrooms on Earth. So what if we feared authority figures for the rest of our lives? An orderly classroom was worth the price.

During my research for this story I was thrilled to discover that a prominent theatrical figure came out of the Hydraulics and not only went to my school, but lived on my street. She's all but forgotten now, but an old newspaper story reported that "Peggy O'Neill, who came out of St. Patrick's School, played four years straight in Chicago in *Peg O' My Heart*." She went to England and had London theatergoers at her feet for two years while she starred in *Paddy the Next Best Thing* at the Savoy. It was for this actress from my old neighborhood that the popular song *Sweet Peggy O'Neill* was written.

When I learned this I immediately went to my computer and there it was on YouTube, a 78 RPM record playing a charming ditty entitled *Sweet Peggy O'Neill*. (Unfortunately, the lyricist forgot to mention the Hydraulics.)

The Hydraulics is being revitalized now. It's quite stunning. Not only is it clean, friendly, and exciting, but for me it now has the additional *oomph* of having theatrical significance. After all, Peggy O'Neill was once a star of the first magnitude with all of London at her feet. And those feet once trod Hydraulic streets, perhaps transporting her to St. Patrick's where she was yelled at by a Hydraulics nun. And because of *Over the Tavern,* people all over the United States are now aware of Seneca Street, Chef's Restaurant, and Winkler's Grocery. By the way, Winkler's building is still standing. And as of this writing it's empty. By George, it would make a nifty theatre!

My wife spent her first twenty-five years in the same little neighborhood of Queens, New York. She had a happy childhood but, frankly, she couldn't give a rat's rear end if she never saw the place again. So when we are out in public it's no wonder she is puzzled when, at the mere utterance of the word "Buffalo," my ears perk up like a dog sensing a squirrel, my head spins around and I yap, "I'm from there! I'm from there!" When listening to our favorite New York classical music station she'll notice that I sit up a little taller when the announcer says, "That was the Buffalo Philharmonic

Orchestra under the direction of JoAnn Faletta." I think it's that way with most Buffalonians. For some inexplicable reason we care deeply about our first home. We believe that industry will be drawn back to Buffalo, the arts will continue to flourish, and the city will keep on reinventing itself. By God, we *do* give a rat's rear end.

**Tom Dudzick** is a playwright whose first play, *Greetings!*, opened at New York City's John Houseman Theatre in 1993 and starred Darren McGavin. His semi-autobiographical comedy *Over the Tavern* has had over 200 productions, breaking many box office records throughout the United States. The Irish adaptation, *Over the Pub*, broke the box office record at Cork Arts Theatre in Ireland. Tom has written eight plays to date, most published by Playscripts, Inc. A Buffalo native, he attended St. Patrick's Parochial School, Cardinal Dougherty High School (both now defunct) and SUNY Fredonia. He was recently honored with a memorial plaque embedded in front of his boyhood home on Seneca Street in Buffalo. An even greater honor—he was once a question on *Jeopardy!* He lives in Nyack, New York, with his wife, novelist Holly Caster.

# My Buffalo Roots

## Wolf Blitzer

Growing up in Buffalo never goes away. My early years there have always played a critical role in shaping my life. And for that, I will always love Buffalo.

It was there that I learned about the news. My parents always instilled in me a love of our newspapers—the *Buffalo News* and the *Courier-Express*. Even as a little boy, I would read the paper and I became fascinated by world events. I was always drawn to Page Two—where there was a good, solid review of the latest global news. And I was always drawn to watching our local news on TV. I still remember Irv Weinstein, Tom Jolls, and Rick Azar on Channel 7's WKBW-TV. Years later I realized that they helped inspire me to become a news junkie.

It was also in Buffalo where I clearly was blessed with an excellent education. It started at Public School 81 in North Buffalo and continued at Washington Elementary School in Kenmore and Kenmore Junior and Senior High School. Later, I spent four years at the State University of New York at Buffalo where I majored in history. I was blessed with world-class professors, including Milton Plesur, Selig Adler, and Clifton Yearley. It was Professor Yearley who advised me to get a master's degree in International Relations at the Johns Hopkins University School of Advanced International Studies in Washington, D.C.

It was very good advice. It was my introduction to the nation's capital.

I always loved sports in Buffalo—all sports. Like other kids growing up there, it was such a powerful part of our lives. Names like Cookie Gilchrist, Poncho Herrera, and Bobby Del Greco still remain with me all these years later. And I was blessed to spend some quality time with Jack Kemp long after he retired from the Bills. As a congressman or cabinet member, he was always keen on his Buffalo connection. Me, too.

But most important, it was my family's history in Buffalo that clearly shaped my life. My parents—both Holocaust survivors—came to Buffalo after World War II. President Truman had signed the Displaced Persons Act into law granting visas to 400,000 refugees. My parents were blessed to be among them.

They came to a very warm and welcoming community in Buffalo. They worked hard, played by the rules, and created wonderful lives for our family.

Buffalo gave them a second chance, and I will forever be grateful.

And it was in Buffalo where I met my wife, Lynn, and her wonderful family. For that and for so many other amazing Buffalo memories, I simply say: Thanks.

**Wolf Blitzer** is CNN's lead political anchor and the anchor of *The Situation Room with Wolf Blitzer*. He got a bachelor's degree at University at Buffalo and a master's degree at Johns Hopkins University School of Advanced International Studies. He grew up in North Buffalo.

# The Capital of My Heart

## Erik Brady

My world spins on a Buffalo axis. You'd think by now—after thirty-four years as a sports reporter at *USA Today*—I could see stories purely through a national lens. But I always see things first from a Buffalo point of view. Niagara River water runs through my veins.

I was born in Buffalo on the day Roger Bannister ran history's first sub-four-minute mile. This apparently destined me to my ink-stained, lucky life as a sports reporter.

Bannister ran his mythic mile at Oxford. The definitive sports experiences of my formative years came at a pair of less elegant locales: War Memorial Stadium, the Old Rockpile, watching Buffalo Bills football; and Memorial Auditorium, the Aud, rooting for Canisius College basketball.

The Bills and their rib-busting tacklers won American Football League championships in 1964 and 1965. When they lost the AFL title game a year later, one game shy of the first Super Bowl, twelve-year-old me just knew it was only a matter of time before they'd win the big one.

Alas, fifty years later, it is still a matter of time.

Canisius reached the National Invitation Tournament championship game in 1963. I just knew it was only a matter of time before the Golden Griffins would be golden again. Alas, more than fifty years later, they've been less often gilded than gelded.

The Rockpile radiated a phosphorescence of decay; *Sports Illustrated* suggested whatever war it was a memorial to seemed to have been fought within its confines. A cloud of cigarette smoke in the rafters lent atmosphere to the Aud; stomping an upside-down paper cup on its ascending series of ramps produced a pop that echoes through time.

Bulldozers took War Memorial in 1988, leaving only the façade, and the Aud in 2009. Still, their ethereal spirit of place remains as firm in my imagination as the steel girders that once blocked our Rockpile views.

As much as I cherished the Bills and Griffs of that era, I soon found I was even more taken with the columnists who chronicled their feats. Waggish wordsmith Steve Weller of the *Buffalo Evening News* and populist firebrand Phil Ranallo of the *Courier-Express* were daily marvels. By high school I knew I wanted to do what they did: Go to games for a living.

The first thing I covered for the *Citadel* at Canisius High School was a Manhattan Cup basketball game at Erie Community College. Guard Joe Mitchell beat Bishop Neumann with a seventy-foot buzzer-beater—and I was hooked. At Canisius College I wore the Griffin suit at the Aud, and then wrote about the games for the *Griffin*. (This fulfilled family destiny. My father was born in Buffalo on the day the Titanic sank and often said it determined his bent toward epic things, including his incandescent invention of the Griffin as mascot during his own student days. It flew through history from the prow of LaSalle's *Le Griffon*, built on the Niagara River in 1679.)

Luck beckoned, and before graduation I began work at the *Courier-Express*, roughly 100 years after Samuel Clemens, Mark Twain himself, had been editor of the *Buffalo Express*—and roughly 300 years after *Le Griffon* set sail on the Great Lakes, "those grand fresh-water seas of ours," as Melville styles them in *Moby-Dick*.

Eventually I moved from city-side to sports, where Ranallo offered generous counsel. One day I succeeded him as sports columnist, a childhood dream. Alas, a year-and-a-half later the dream was done.

The *C-X* closed when the guild voted to spurn Rupert Murdoch's offer to buy us. Ranallo, with his gift for distilling complexity into simple phrases, called it Jonestown.

Luck beckoned again: *USA Today* opened the same week the *Courier* closed. I've been there since, grown old watching grown men and women play children's games. I was, at twenty-six, the youngest lead sports columnist in Buffalo newspaper history. Today, in my sixties, I'm *USA Today*'s last founding member still toiling there. And I believe I've set the unofficial record for most Buffalo datelines at a national publication.

The Niagara Frontier has a way of pulling you back, always. My wife and I come back every summer for two weeks on the Canadian shore. (It isn't in Buffalo, but you can see it from there.) We met in the *Courier-Express* newsroom on the luckiest day of my life. She grew up in Northern Virginia, as did our kids, but they all love my beloved Buffalo, too—for the magic of living water that surrounds us and the surfeit of family it affords us.

I've lived since 1982 in Arlington, across the river from Washington, D.C.—as Fort Erie is to Buffalo. Forget Buffalo's infernal inferiority complex. Washington suffers a sort of superiority simplex, believing itself the most important city in the world.

Please. Twain knew better. He wrote an editorial for the *Express* in 1869 that offered a modest proposal: Make Buffalo the nation's capital. Lovely thought, but no need for that. Buffalo forever remains the capital of my heart, paradise with snowbanks.

**Erik Brady** is a reporter for *USA Today Sports*. He grew up in the Town of Tonawanda at the Kenmore line and attended Canisius High School and College. He and his wife, Carol Stevens, director of communications and media relations at the American Bar Association, have two children and one grandchild.

# Along Came Zeus: How My Dog Helped Me Find Home In Buffalo

## Jody K. Biehl

Photograph by Mary Gardella

I got a dog instead of having a third child.

We brought him home from Syracuse on a snowy Valentine's Day in 2012. He weighed twelve pounds and had an enormously wobbly head, inquisitive brown eyes, and a pink tongue that hung an inch out of his mouth. He rode home on my lap as a warm black-and-white mound, and our invisible bond was sealed.

I told people we got the dog for the kids—to teach them unconditional love and responsibility. Really, I got the dog for me, to ease myself into my forties and help me quash the lingering urge to swaddle.

My husband wanted neither a dog nor another baby. He thought our family was complete and used logic he knew would sway me.

*It will tie us down. We'll never live in a big city again.*

*Kids can cram into a tiny city apartment; a dog can't.*

A dog meant we were staying in Buffalo.

My desire for a dog came upon me suddenly. It was ironic, because I was (and still secretly am) a cat person.

I identify with cats' prickly independence, their insistence on privacy and on setting their own rhythm of affection. But our son has a severe cat allergy, and when he was four, and we lived in a three-room apartment in Berlin, the allergist told us we had a choice: our two cats—the ones who had snuggled against my belly while he was in it and who had flown from Berkeley to Germany with us—or his lungs.

Even if we got a dog, the allergist warned, our son would become asthmatic. The only pets he recommended for our family were turtles, fish, and snakes.

But in 2012, our son was turning ten, our daughter six, and he hadn't wheezed in six years. We'd been in Buffalo four of those years, and our pie-shaped lot and Colonial house had more space than we'd ever imagined owning or could possibly use. And we had a front yard that needed an excuse for why we didn't keep up the flowerbeds. Buffalonians are serious about flowerbeds.

A shelter dog was not an option, so I scoured the internet for breeds that are hypoallergenic. We settled on a Portuguese water dog, like the Obamas, except ours doesn't particularly like water or have a Kennedy-compound pedigree.

My husband remained skeptical, even as we drove the sleeping puppy home. We were wanderers, he kept saying. We had lived in Berkeley, Washington D.C., New York City, Paris, Berlin, and Cambridge, England. I was a journalist who had reported from around the world and now was trying to jump-start the journalism program at the University at Buffalo. He was an archaeologist, chair of UB's anthropology department. Our families were on opposite sides of the world—mine in Los Angeles, his in Germany.

We'd never stayed in one place longer than five years. Buffalo was a stopping ground for us. It would never be home.

The kids named our boisterous, large-pawed pup Zeus because he was the biggest in his litter. Today, he weighs sixty-seven pounds and still has those deeply human eyes, with eyelashes to envy. My son hasn't wheezed once.

Zeus is a bouncy, shaggy playmate who prances when he runs, and who, I believe, has an emotional range that surpasses that of some people. He's also more obedient than my children.

Buffalo, I quickly learned, is a dog-lover's city.

Strangers started talking to me because of my puppy. Now people recognize me on the street because of my dog. He was included in a 2015 Buffalo dog calendar, the July pin-up.

Having a dog has allowed me to quietly observe Buffalo from the end of a leash—or sometimes, when he runs free—with both hands behind my back. It's caused me to gaze at the city's magnificent and abused waterways and parkways and to meditate on Lake Erie, which has an oceanic presence. Zeus has sniffed the bushes of a house designed by Frank Lloyd Wright and has roamed the South Buffalo forests and creeks that inspired artist Charles Birchfield. We've frolicked under the spooky twin towers of the 140-year-old H.H. Richardson complex, crossed the Peace Bridge to the Canadian beaches, romped Ellicott Creek's dog island, shared an ice cream at Canalside, and watched flocks of Canada geese holding court in LaSalle Park.

My dog hasn't imprisoned me in Buffalo. He's grounded me here.

Zeus has connected me to this hulking, beautiful-boned city with its unrepentant seasons and irrepressible natives.

Walking my dog, I watch people.

At Delaware Park, my standard walk, there are dog-walking cycles. The steadfast 8:00 a.m. dog people are year-round walkers like me. They come with their treats and plastic bags and earnestness. Some have heated gloves and ice-gripping shoes for winter. One woman cross-country skis alongside her golden retriever.

The dog walkers include couples and singles, married people and divorcees. They huddle in a circle near Rumsey Field as their leashless dogs wrestle, run, and roll across the soccer pitch with a joy that we humans are too afraid to exhibit in public.

I smile and wave hello to the other walkers, but only sometimes join them. Zeus, for all his wondrousness, is socially awkward. He is intimidated by groups and hangs on the outskirts, a canine wallflower. He's also not a hunter; I think he is afraid of squirrels.

They say people look like their dogs. But I also think dogs act like their owners. The giddy poodle belongs to the couple who run every morning. The squirrel-chasing hound's owner shouts loudly and throws balls farther than I can see.

Like Zeus, I'm shy. I don't always know what to say to other dog people. And I often wonder if I will ever make it into this generations-thick Buffalo society, whose people know one another because their grandparents were friends in grade school or their brother once dated a second cousin or because their uncle had the only generator during the blizzard of '77. I hover on the outskirts of these Buffalo tales, an awed and awkward interloper.

The dog walkers are proud of their pets. They smile when their dogs are popular enough to be chased or show good manners by not jumping.

One man always tries to impress me with how obedient his boxer mix is by loudly shouting for him to "sit," "stay," "shake," or "roll."

Yet these same people are also marvelously accepting of their dogs' foibles. When a dog doesn't want to play or misses a ball or muddies the owner's clothes or slams into someone's knees, dog people shrug it off. *Que sera, sera.*

Some dog owners are so connected to their pets that they make an imaginative leap; they begin to see the world as their dogs see it. "She just jumped on you because she's excited to be out," one explains, or, "We chased balls for hours yesterday, so today he's bored with them."

Some are making excuses. But a few are having an out-of-body moment of empathy. I want to love people like that—inside out, with understanding and humor and without expectation.

If a dog is ugly or maimed, dog people love it even more fiercely.

That's how Buffalonians love Buffalo—fiercely and possessively, despite its flaws or what others say about it. I've started to feel that way, too.

My friend Mitch calls Buffalo the civic equivalent of a beloved ugly dog. The less attractive it seems—the worse its weather, its sports teams, its politicians, its developers or its school boards' actions—the more loyally people defend it.

There is rhythm in repetition. My daily dog walk has imprinted Buffalo's seasons and moods onto me.

In winter I trudge through the early-morning snow and acquiesce in the season's insistence on introspection. There are no colors or bird interactions to distract me. The dog-walking ranks are thin; walks are short and conversation stilted. When spring awakes, in April and May, with its barrage of daffodils, tulips, and apple and cherry blossoms, it is like a daily miracle. I revel in the simple happiness of bare arms, warm toes, and sidewalk-café laughter.

I watch the baby geese floating in family clusters in the polluted water of the Scajaquada Creek and Hoyt Lake. I marvel at nature's resistance to human ineptitude and wonder about the decades of chemical and sewage waste beneath those baby feathers.

Summer brings fairs and concerts and all-day porch sitting. The park comes alive, practically euphoric with picnickers, runners, cyclists, soccer players, squirrels, and Shakespeare in the Park actors and audiences.

People become chatty. They kiss on blankets and in hammocks slung between trees. New immigrants toss fishing lines into the lake and ignore my pleas not to eat their contaminated catch.

Zeus and I have to be careful. The park no longer belongs to us.

Fall arrives, feisty and inebriating and smelling of possibility.

I have never felt such awe at the seasons as I do in Buffalo. Kinder, gentler seasons stir up fewer emotions. I've come to count on the extremes.

I know some people scoff at the idea of animals having feelings or complex reasoning capacity, but my dog—like many dogs I've come to know in Buffalo—definitely does.

Zeus is the polar opposite of a human child. He senses when I need space and when I'm needy.

He doesn't care if my daughter can't divide by four, if my son didn't get picked for the team, or if we'll be able to afford to send our kids to college. We're never inadequate to him. His wagging tail and pink belly offer ancient healing. He communicates in ways I'll never be smart enough to understand or mimic.

He lives in the present tense and reminds me of the value of such minimalism.

Buffalo is my family's present tense. It has been for nine years.

Our roots here may be shallow, but they've become expansive. My son came here in kindergarten and he's about to start high school. My daughter doesn't remember any home but here. They know which sort of gloves keep the cold out best, not to plant before Mother's Day, and that borders are easy to cross—except on summer weekends and holidays. For them the smell of Cheerios will always mean home.

They're resilient, humble; they lack the swagger of big-city kids. They're the opposite of smug. They're Buffalonian.

I still don't know if we'll be here forever, but the thought no longer vexes me like it did years ago.

When I do start to worry, I grab my leash and head for the park.


**Jody Kleinberg Biehl** is a faculty member in the English Department at the University at Buffalo and directs the department's journalism program. She also serves as adviser for the university's award-winning student newspaper, the *Spectrum*. She is a former editor at *Der Spiegel International* in Berlin and a former foreign correspondent for the *San Francisco Chronicle*. Her work has appeared in *USA Today*, *Newsday*, the *Boston Globe* and the *Economist*. She lives on the border between Elmwood Village and the West Side.

# January in a Jar

## Noah Falck

We cross our legs as if sharing a bench
with someone from the future.

Let the city lights inside us go dim
to a near nothingness.

Our first ideas become snow,
become a sky punched inside out.

We say water
and let our minds go under,

let them freeze and glass
the land into a reservoir of stillness.

This place where no one belongs
where the wind throws fist

after fist of scarred breath,
where we never feel more at home.

**Noah Falck** is the author of the full-length collection *Snowmen Losing Weight* (BatCat Press, 2012), and several chapbooks including *Celebrity Dream Poems* (Poor Claudia, 2013) and *Measuring Tape for the Midwest* (Pavement Saw, 2008). His work has appeared in *Boston Review, Columbia Poetry Review, Denver Quarterly, Kenyon Review*, and *Poets.org*. Originally from Dayton, Ohio, he now lives on Buffalo's West Side. He works as education director at Just Buffalo Literary Center and curates the Silo City Reading Series in an abandoned grain silo along the Buffalo River.

# Tom Toles's Final Cartoon for the *Courier-Express* September 1982

**Tom Toles** is a Pulitzer Prize-winning political cartoonist. A Hamburg native, he drew for the *Buffalo Courier-Express* from 1973-82 and *Buffalo News* the following twenty years, winning the Pulitzer in 1990, before joining the *Washington Post* in 2002. His cartoons appear in more than 200 newspapers. Toles is the recipient of the Herblock Award, the National Headliners Award, the Overseas Press Club's Thomas Nast Award, the John Fischetti Award, and the H.L Mencken Free Press Award. He also has been honored as Cartoonist of the Year by *Editor & Publisher* magazine, The National Cartoonists Society, and the *Week* magazine. Toles, a 1973 graduate of the University at Buffalo, spends his summers in Hamburg.

# First Home, Last Home

## Lynette D'Amico

*Between 1900 and 1920 Buffalo's Italian-born population increased almost three-fold from 6,000 to 16,000.*
> —*Family and Community: Italian Immigrants in Buffalo, 1880-1930*, Virginia Yans-McLaughlin

*The voice said cry. What shall I cry? All flesh is grass, our days are like grass.*
—Isaiah 40:6

Growing up in six houses in as many cities in three states, I heard a refrain, a constant trickle of sound, through all the years of my childhood: *I want to go home*. My mother recited this litany from the time I was five years old and we left our first home in Buffalo in 1960 and moved to the West Coast. No matter where we were living, Buffalo was always home; where blood, hot peppers, red wine, and hard-crusted bread were familiar; where everybody lived on a bus line.

My mother never wavered in her conviction.

Wherever she was living, her home was always Buffalo. After I moved away from my family in my early twenties, leaving St. Louis, Missouri, my mother and I had the same conversation every time we talked. "Grandma told me my place was with my husband, so I left Buffalo. Now every day I have regret. To live with regret is a terrible thing. It bends your head, clouds your eyes. Food turns to shit in your mouth. You spit and spit but the taste is with you always. My dreams are filled with flapping black wings. All my days are like grass. That was my marriage. I'll say to you what Grandma never said to me. *Come home, come home.*"

This is the story of my family: we left our home in Buffalo, and could not find our way back.

Growing up listening to my mother, I learned that home was never the place where we lived. Home was 3,000 or 800 miles away, or it was that place across the ocean we had come from but had never been. I was raised with nostalgia for a city, a culture, a family that I learned about second-hand, on hearsay. Buffalo was our home, our sense of history and connection, our Old Country.

I didn't understand my mother's grieving for Buffalo—for a people, a place, a landscape of bars and bowling alleys, clam stands along Niagara

Street—but I felt her loss as a palpable sadness that infected my life, that judged anywhere other than Buffalo as inadequate.

We returned to Buffalo twice a year every year when I was growing up in San Diego and then in St. Louis. The point of our long distance pilgrimages was to enforce our sense of extended family affiliation—to know and be known. I grew up believing that ethnicity was dependent upon place, not only where you or your parents were born, but where you lived. I can't remember when I didn't know what I was. I was Italian, my grandparents were born in Italy. My parents were born in Buffalo. I was born in Buffalo. In Buffalo we were Italian, among our people, in our place, where the grass was high, the air sweet. The rest of the country was a vast, white, flat-faced Protestant wasteland.

## Italians Live Here

*During the course of the holidays Mrs. Bridge would drive the children around to see how other houses were decorated, and on one of these trips they came to a stucco bungalow with a life-size cutout of Santa Claus on the roof, six reindeer in the front yard, candles in every window, and by the front door an enormous cardboard birthday cake with one candle. On the cake was this message: Happy Birthday, Dear Jesus.*

*"My word, how extreme," said Mrs. Bridge thoughtfully. "Italians must live there."*

—*Mrs. Bridge*, Evan Connell

In 2008, I had traveled to Buffalo to meet my parents who were there visiting family. We were sitting on the stamped concrete patio in Uncle Vinny—my dad's youngest brother—and his wife Gloria's backyard. It was a beautiful late spring day; I was sipping a glass of white wine, and Vinny had just turned on the backyard fountains: the bare-breasted nymph pouring water from an urn at her waist, the three-tiered Tuscan fountain, the lion's head wall hanging spouting a stream from his pursed lips, the angel pouring water into the pitcher held by a cherub, the Blessed Virgin Mary grotto and pond. The sound of water splashing and bubbling almost drowned out the sound of Vinny with his gas-powered blower, blowing grass clippings into the street. Vinny's yard was impeccable and pristine. The hydrangeas, hostas, and calla lilies were planted in tidy borders. There were herbs and box hedges in pots on the patio, a gas grill as big as the 1991 gold Cadillac Vinny kept parked in his impeccable and pristine garage.

Vinny and Gloria's white and gold living room has maintained the same look since the fall of Rome or at least since the 1970s, which is as long as they have lived in the house. The marble top hallway table, the white, wrought iron stair railing, the gold and crystal chandelier, the white carpet, the gold couch, the antique gold Roman column plant stand, the artificial trailing ivy, the Renaissance tapestry wall hanging. The house and its furnishings are so timeless and static there are no verbs, no action words.

In fall 2015, Vinny and Gloria left Buffalo and moved to San Diego to be closer to a daughter and her family. The daughter promised they could transplant their life in Buffalo to the West Coast. Forty years ago, in my mother's experience, that was not possible: "Living without winter is not healthy. Look at California: Palm trees! Hippies! Drug addicts! How could I raise my children in such a place? But I was afraid to leave your father. I had children. What kind of life could I provide for you without a husband?"

In Buffalo, there was no downsizing, no sorting, no discarding. Vinny and Gloria moved everything: the second refrigerator that was in the basement, the chest freezer that was in the garage, the framed jigsaw puzzles of scenes from Italy, the console stereo, and *50 Guitars Go Italiano*. The backyard fountains were crated; the Cadillac, garden hoses, and riding lawn mower, shipped. "Will you have a lawn?" we ask. "Isn't there a drought in California? When the time comes, where will you be buried?" we ask over and over. "Where will your funeral be? Even if you die in California how will you ever rest there?"

## Home Again, Home Again

*Prepare to follow*

—Headstone inscription

Nobody comes to the funeral of "Mr. Nobody from Nowhere," as the bull of a bully Tom Buchanan refers to Jay Gatsby, the Great American imposter in *The Great Gatsby*, the story of the true love of money, the fate of pedigree, and the American dream of the conversion of raw materials to consumables. It's raining at the cemetery when Gatsby goes into the ground. His father buries him "back east," Gatsby's "new world, material without being real," a world of lavish parties and beautiful shirts and secret money, rather than bringing him back to poor, plain North Dakota.

After living more than forty years away from her own "back east," my mother returned to Buffalo in death. All the people she had known and talked to in life, that she carried on conversations with—alive or dead—were at Holy Sepulcher, the Italian cemetery in Cheektowaga. There are signs posted on the cemetery grounds that say "No digging allowed" and "No inground plantings" and "No shepherd's hooks, crosses, vials of blood, relics, or unsightly flags." But when my mother visited the cemetery annually, she packed gardening gloves and a hand trowel, potting soil, a watering can, a flat of seasonal flowers—usually geraniums or impatiens. She dug and planted with good cheer at the graves of friends and family.

"This one hated red; we'll plant the pink."

"She made the cuccidati—not as good as mine."

"He wants a drink not flowers. May he and his thirst be at peace."

"I like this view," she had told me, referring to the stained glass window of some saint in a mausoleum named after another saint. Her dead brother Leonard was a neighbor, her brother-in-law Carmen another; around the corner lay sister Jennie, Grandma and Grandpa, Cassie from Busti Avenue, the Guginos, Lombardos, Aronicas, LiPomis, and Mancusos. All dead, all laid to rest—the cemetery was an essentialized version of the old West Side neighborhood, a thick, basil-seasoned cliché of nostalgia, that other American dream.

*Between nostalgia and anticipation* there is what? Regret? More days of grass? Whitman's *beautiful uncut hair of graves*.

The first time I visit Buffalo after my mother's death, before Uncle Vinny and Aunt Gloria go west, I'm walking along the Ellicott Creek Trailway. My mother had died in April, *when lilacs last in the dooryard bloom'd*. It's August now. Hot. Here are the trees and the grass. So many newly-planted trees with memorial markers to loved ones, "Forever in our hearts," "They can no longer die, for they are like angels," "In Memory of." The earth gives a little with each step. *Mercy*, I think. I am at the mercy of the elements, the whiplash grass.

Lynette D'Amico's work has appeared in the *Gettysburg Review*, the *Ocean State Review* and at *Brevity* and *Slag Glass City*. Her novella *Road Trip*, published by Twelve Winters Press in 2015, was short-listed for the Paris Literary Prize, and was the first runner-up of the 2014 *Quarterly West* Novella Contest. She holds an MFA from the Program for Writers at Warren Wilson College and lives in Boston, Massachusetts. Her family is from Buffalo's West Side.

# God is Dead: How about Laughlin's?

## Pat Green Obermeier

In the mid 1960s, the ladies bathroom in the Allentown bar, Laughlin's, was gag-inducing disgusting. You needed a buzz on to gather the courage to enter. Dim lighting. Wet floors. Vomit. Overflowing sanitary bins, useless empty toilet paper holders, and cruddy sinks that trickled cold water. I half expected to find men in there. The stalls, however, had stop-and-read memorable graffiti. Amidst the usual phone numbers offering sex with women like Rhonda and Candy was felt-tipped scrawled poetry. Some I remember to this day: "*No need to stand on the seat. The crabs in here jump 50 feet,*" complete with illustration; and this existentialist scribble:

God is dead.

—Nietzsche

Nietzsche is dead.

—God.

That was Laughlin's. A mix of weird and wonderful. The sweet smell of pot on the sidewalk. The jukebox repetitively playing "If I Had the Wings of a Dove." A police cruiser habitually parked out front. It cemented the notion that there was a world beyond Buffalo. I felt at home amidst a signature blend of hippies, artists, musicians, cosmopolitan folks, and yes, druggies, in Buffalo's answer to Greenwich Village. No one gave a damn who you were. Go in one night in ripped jeans and the next night in a gown and get the same reaction. Blasé to the point of cool. A place to remake yourself —recognized by those who floated between the reality of graduating from a private Catholic high school and wanting to break free of the constraints that privilege bestowed. Trying to describe the atmosphere at Laughlin's is the definition of "You had to be there."

I've recently returned to Buffalo after working close to twenty years in New York City in the world of network TV. Home to focus on my writing. I could talk about the renaissance that is happening downtown today: the medical corridor, the thriving waterfront—all indications that Buffalo is on the upswing. Skirts swishing, face scrubbed, ready to go. The carnival barker shouts, "Loft living! Arts on the waterfront. Professional sports. Elmwood Village!"

But all I can say is, "Buffalo. I've come home. Ya got anything like Laughlin's happening? God, I hope so."

**Pat Green Obermeier** is a four-time Emmy-winning creative writer and producer who worked in the world of TV in New York City for close to twenty years for networks from CNBC to Studios USA and NY1. Her political satire, *The President Factor*, came out in 2015. A graduate of Holy Angels Academy and Buffalo State College, her work has appeared in the *Buffalo News*, the *Flash Fiction Press* and *No Extra Words*. She lives in downtown Buffalo.

# Who Would Move to Buffalo?

## Kay Patterson

I didn't expect to be charmed by Buffalo when I arrived for a job interview late in 1980. I had a new master's degree and a desire to be closer to my family across Lake Erie in Toledo, Ohio. With chauvinism honed by my ten years living in New England, I thought "Buffalo will be a test run in choosing a new place to live."

Then I walked into Delaware Park, sat down, and gazed in wonder. Frederick Law Olmsted's gorgeous, gentle meadow surprised me into an attitude adjustment.

When I announced the decision to my comrades-in-arms in New Hampshire, they were stunned.

"Buffalo?"

"Buffalo."

They sputtered. They shook their heads.

"But they just had a big blizzard there a couple of years ago."

"So did we."

"And, and, that twenty-two-caliber killer is running around shooting people."

"I know."

We'd spent the previous ten years launching our adulthoods together. That meant catching the second wave of feminism and surfing to its crest.

Healthcare was our particular focus; we took on the medical establishment and won. The evidence stood right there on Main Street. Concord Feminist Health Center was successful beyond our wildest imaginings.

And now I was moving to Buffalo. It was so uncool.

About a month after my shocking announcement, I was sitting at the reception desk at the center when Judy rushed up with a look that said: I figured it out.

"You grew up in Toledo, didn't you? That must have prepared you for Buffalo."

Now I was the one sputtering.

In retrospect, maybe that perception had some merit. Buffalo has always felt like Toledo to me. Much more Midwest than Northeast. Rust everywhere.

But the job sounded good. After ten years in a small New Hampshire city, Buffalo's array of people, cultural offerings, and feminist activity was an alluring smorgasbord. Restaurants everywhere, most even open on Sunday!

This seemed promising.

Buffalo and Western New York welcomed me, sometimes with a warm embrace, sometimes with a knowing wink and a smile.

My job interview was thirty miles south in Colden. It's a bucolic little place at the foot of some rolling hills. The town center is a church, a grocery store, and a hardware. That's about it, except for the building that housed the mental health program where I'd be working. It's a pretty town that could as easily have been located in New England. Familiar. There's the warm embrace.

During the interview people said casually, "This is the Snowbelt, you know." It seemed curious to me. I knew I was moving to Buffalo, after all.

My job started January 2. Every day for the first two weeks, I'd head south through light snowflakes and hit a furious blast when I got to Route 219. On day eight, when the blood drained from my lips as I went into yet another slide on the road I could no longer see, I knew I was getting the Western New York wink. "This is the Snowbelt, you know."

I lived in New Hampshire for ten years, but Western New York taught me to turn my wheels into the slide like a pro.

My feminist allies in New Hampshire gave me contacts at the Women's Studies Program at the University at Buffalo. When I was here for my job interview, I sat in on a class and a student said: "My girlfriend and I are renting a room, if you actually move to Buffalo."

Really? I'm going to call somebody I met once in a class and say "Let me be your roommate?"

But I did. I had this overwhelming sense that this was okay. And it was. In fact, it led to another big change I didn't know I was ready to make right at that moment.

A few weeks after I joined Meg and Ellen in their apartment just a short walk from Delaware Park, Meg sat me down and said, "So, are you a lesbian?"

"Yes."

This was the question I'd been tripping over for years and, in that moment, the answer was clear. Yes.

Buffalo was a cool place to come out: People everywhere ready to welcome me into "the tribe." Monthly women's dances at the Unitarian Church on West Ferry. The Lavender Door bar on Tonawanda Street. A whole course on lesbian history at the university. And so many organizations. Whatever your interest, you could find a group heading in that direction.

I've met many LGBT people who moved here from bigger cities. They grouse about my city, calling it provincial. "The community" is so small, they say.

Not for me. Small is Concord, New Hampshire. It's a wonderful place that is friendly to LGBT people. In fact, New Hampshire legalized marriage equality before New York did. But "the community" is tiny. Buffalo was the big time for me.

So, love and marriage. Let's talk.

Soon after setting my feet down in Buffalo, I joined Common Ground, a news journal collective whose mission was to let women's voices be heard. The collective process requires endless meetings.

One time when I was exasperated, having the heretical thought that too many women's voices were being heard, I cracked wise. Across the room, a bright, funny, and talented woman snickered behind her hand as her eyes danced. That was Susan and it was the beginning of something grand.

Romance took a while to unfold, since we were, after all, adults with complicated lives. But once those complications were dispersed, it was magic and we were in it for the long haul.

That was 1984. New York State had no interest in enacting marriage equality, which was ok, since we never considered it would be an option. I had some conflicting thoughts about marriage anyway.

In my feminist circles in the 70s, marriage was out. Patriarchal institution that oppressed women. And we were very intense about it. My best friend took me on a walk one day, saying in hushed tones, "I need to tell you something." I thought, "She's pregnant!" I knew she wanted to be. No. She had to confess that she and her long-term boyfriend got married.

Flash forward to 2011 and the world is a changed place. Sitting in the living room of our home in Buffalo's struggling University Heights neighborhood, Susan and I watched as the New York Senate passed marriage equality into law. Our own senator was one of two Republicans taking an enormous political risk to give the bill its winning edge. Hooray!

But then we were stunned in silence. We'd been happy together for twenty-seven years and now we could be happily married. It was a lot to take in.

On a sunny April day the next year, we did get married and Buffalo cheered us.

The event planner at Woodlawn Beach State Park in Hamburg, the caterer at Romanella's, and Zilly the baker weren't just open and accepting. They were thrilled for us.

We sent out invitations, expecting the usual number of Regrets, but there were few. In fact, three people lobbied to be the "plus one," not wanting to miss the chance to see us step into the circle of married people. When we walked down the aisle to the jaunty strains of "Life is a Celebration With You on My Arm," they burst into applause.

Those who had always had the privilege of marriage seemed the happiest, as if they were saying, "Welcome. We've been waiting for you."

People ask if it's made a difference. Yes, it has. Not in how we are with each other, but in some deep internal place that continues to want—and be amazed to get—that sanction.

So who would move to Buffalo? She who thinks it's a cool place to be, getting cooler every day. Buffalo has been my rusty smorgasbord for thirty-five years and I have no plans to move away.

**Kay Patterson** started writing for her high school newspaper, later earning a bachelor's degree in journalism from Michigan State University and reporting for newspapers when print was the only way to read them. Her essays, profiles and travel pieces have been published in the *Buffalo News*, *Forever Young*, and *After 50*, among others. A retired licensed mental health counselor, she is married to Kenmore native Susan Clements, another widely-published writer. She lives in University Heights.

# Notes from the Expatriate Underground

## Margaret Sullivan

We were so tired of those people—the ones who had moved away from Buffalo, but still wanted to lay claim to it. The ones who gathered at Buffalo taverns in various cities to cheer (or grieve) the Bills, but didn't have to think about the rusting steel mills along Route 5, or the problems of the second poorest city in the United States, or the constant infighting on the School Board.

Although we true Buffalo people—the ones who actually lived in the Queen City—welcomed them back, with wan smiles, on the Wednesday nights before Thanksgiving, on Elmwood or Chippewa, we didn't think for a minute that they were really Buffalo People.

No, they were poseurs, in their "City of No Illusions" t-shirts, swigging Genny Cream Ale and debating the virtues of wings at Duff's vs. Anchor Bar. Because after the holiday, or the wedding, or whatever had brought them back for a few days, they were gone, and we were here.

Still here.

I tolerated them for years, for decades. Now, I'm one of them: a Buffalo expatriate. And now, finally, I get it: the constant craving for the hometown, the need to talk about it all the time, the nostalgia for what was left behind.

I left for New York City in 2012, after most of a lifetime in Buffalo, including thirteen years as chief editor of the *Buffalo News*, a place I had come as a summer intern after college in Washington and graduate school in Chicago. Three decades, somehow, went by. Parents died, children were born and raised. Then a job at the *New York Times* beckoned.

Now, after four years in Manhattan, I live in Washington, D.C. These cities have their wonders, no doubt—glamour, spectacle, a sense of importance and being at the center of the world.

But so far, I haven't found anything as real as the First Friday fish fry at St. Mark's parish in North Buffalo. Or the Turkey Trot as a crucial calorie-burner before the big meal of the year. Or the first warm day of the spring when Delaware Park is alive with runners, tennis players, would-be hoop stars, and toddlers in strollers.

And that sense of place—that authenticity—is why we expatriates hold on so tight.

It's why we gather together in other places—for example, in a Buffalo bar in Sarasota, Florida, to watch the Bills get crushed on their overseas road game in London. Or why we gravitate to other Buffalo people who have made the same move. When I moved to New York City, I found a group of literary women with Western New York ties; we called ourselves the Buffalo Gals, and met monthly for dinners to speculate on such matters as whether the Peace Bridge had been lit purple for Prince's death or for Queen Elizabeth's birthday, and to talk about the accumulated snowfall in the Southern Tier.

It's also why Tim Russert, who grew up in South Buffalo, never stopped mentioning Buffalo sports teams when he was the host of NBC's *Meet the Press*. It's why Lauren Belfer, the novelist who wrote the Buffalo-based *City of Light*, comes to her hometown so often to speak to groups as varied as the working-class patrons of the Tonawanda Public Library and the white-gloved ladies of the Twentieth Century Club and the hipsters of Larkin Square. And it's why I've been so happy to write book reviews for the *Buffalo News*, and to come around every summer to delight, from a kayak, as the late-afternoon sunlight sparkles upon beautiful Lake Erie.

In short, we want the connection. We need the connection.

And while we know that this yearning may seem, to you who shovel the snow and pay the real estate taxes, like the passing interest of a mere dilettante—you may even feel it has a whiff of condescension—we must beg your indulgence.

Allow us expatriates to lay claim to the Buffalo that forged us and that sustains us. Because we frankly aren't sure who we would be without it. Without those roots grounding us and feeding us, we might wither away altogether.

So when we come around for the Wednesday night before Thanksgiving, or for the Fourth of July family reunion, or for our best friend's wedding reception at the Historical Society, we'll be listening for the words we want to hear.

Even if you deliver the phrase with an invisible roll of your eyes, please say it: "Welcome home."

**Margaret Sullivan** was born and raised in Lackawanna, graduated from Our Lady of Victory grade school and Nardin Academy, and was a longtime resident of the Parkside neighborhood and Elmwood Village. A journalist, she spent most of her career at the *Buffalo News*, including thirteen years as chief editor, before becoming the public editor of the *New York Times* and, now, a columnist for the *Washington Post*.

View of Lake Erie from Front Park by Julian Montague

# Acknowledgements

Hearty thanks to Luke Hammill, Mitch Gerber, and Lenore Myka who helped me edit this book and who kept me motivated when the project felt overwhelming. Julian Montague's graphics and lovely photos enliven and enrich these pages; his invisible fingerprints are everywhere. I could not have asked for a more talented team nor could I have created this book without them. I am grateful to call each a friend.

Thanks also to Leslie Zemsky and Jonathon Welch for outreach efforts and to Gridlock Lacquer and Lisa Menchetti for early support of the anthology and to Michael Jauchen for proofreading.

I burned several meals and missed numerous family weekends editing these pieces, but my husband and kids never complained. I am lucky to have them and am grateful for their love and encouragement.

All of the contributors devoted hours of time and thought and several endured numerous edits. For their tenacity, attention to detail, patience, and raw love of this city, I offer thanks.

Finally, thanks to Anne Trubek, Nicole Boose, and Martha Bayne at Belt Publishing for initiating this project and entrusting it to me.

—Jody K. Biehl